Violence
and Hope

in a U.S.–Mexico Border Town

Violence and Hope

in a U.S.–Mexico Border Town

Jody Glittenberg

WAVELAND
PRESS, INC.
Long Grove, Illinois

For information about this book, contact:
Waveland Press, Inc.
4180 IL Route 83, Suite 101
Long Grove, IL 60047-9580
(847) 634-0081
info@waveland.com
www.waveland.com

This book is dedicated to those individuals worldwide
who live with tenacity and courage
when others cower in fear or complacency,
and to those who work toward solutions
while others avoid the truth and live with myths and rumors.
This work is dedicated to all those
who live with hope—esperanza—
of becoming part of a less violent world.

Contents

Acknowledgments   xi

Introduction   1
Organization of the Book   3

1   A Violent U.S. Border Town   5
Beginning Fieldwork   6
Focusing on Fieldwork   14
Summary   23

2   A Profile of Esperanza   25
The Beginnings of a Hispanic Town   25
Weed and Seed: The Bootstraps for Hope   32
Habits of the Heart   33
Social Institutions   39
Views of Ordinary People   50
Community Rituals   52
Summary   52

3   The Culture of Alcohol and Drug Use and Abuse   55
Background Information on Alcohol and Drugs   55
Drinking and Drugs in Esperanza   57
The Drugs Most Commonly Used in Esperanza   62

Narratives of Alcohol and Drug Users   64
Cultural Patterns   70
Summary   73

4   Prostitutes and Gangs   75
Sexual Behavior as Culture   75
Problems of Prostitution in Esperanza   77
The High Cost of Prosecuting Prostitutes   79
A Covert Menace: Gangs   80
Perceptions and Opinions about Gangs   86
Summary   88

5   Drug and Human Trafficking   91
Conspiracy and Illegality   91
The Network of Drugs and Dealing   94
The Business of Drug Trafficking   96
Controlling Drug Trafficking in Esperanza   98
Human Trafficking: A Long-Standing Problem   100
Summary   103

6   The Structure of Violence   105
The Criminal Mind and the Violent Family   106
Murder Statistics   107
Homicide Survivors' Support Group   108
Rape and Sexual Assault:
    Violent Acts Feared in Esperanza   110
Violence as Perceived by People in Esperanza   111
Zero Tolerance for Domestic Violence   118
Mi Voz Vale (My Voice Counts):
    A Community Effort to Empower Women   120
Funerals as a Community Integration of Violence   121
Summary   123

7   The Culture of the Shunned   125
The Homeless   126
HUD Apartment Dwellers   134
Monolingual Spanish Speakers   140
Summary   143

8   A Shift in the Paradigm   145
    Causes of Violence   146
    Doing Something about Structural and Personal Violence   150
    A New Paradigm for Transformation   154
    Reflections   158

    Appendix A: Questions Posed to Focus Groups   161
    Appendix B: Questionnaire Used in Esperanza
        (a shortened sample)   163
    References   167

Acknowledgments

No research can be done without special support from many people. First and foremost are the citizens of Esperanza who allowed us to live with them and to become part of these findings. Members of the community advisory board were essential for the directions they gave us and for feedback on the validity of our findings. Thank you, all.

I gratefully acknowledge the financial support given by the National Institute on Drug Abuse (NIDA) and especially to the Program Manager Arnold Mills for his wise counsel and gentle encouragement. I thank also Dr. Susan Martin, from the National Institute on Alcoholism and Alcohol Abuse (NIAAA), for she first encouraged submission of a natural study proposal of this risky research. Special thanks go to Dr. Paul Sypherd, former Provost at the University of Arizona, whose grant award enabled us to complete the household survey. For his insight, unending loyalty, and critical fieldwork, Charlie Anderson was a key to the success of this research. To the superb research team: Mary Lou Chacon, the late Roberto Corona, and Belinda Acosta, many thanks for your work. Thanks to the many students (especially Maureen Campesino and Vincent Stuart) and friends who were part of this decade-long inquiry that began in 1991 with pilot fieldwork with students from the University of Arizona, including Lucy Colbert, Earl Sher, John Schwarz, and Anne Woodtli. I thank three awesome anthropologists who critiqued the NIDA research report: the late Agnes Aamodt, Beverly Hackenberg, and Margarita Kay. Thanks also goes to friends with fresh eyes for help in the final writing, Joel H. Hinrichs and Donah Grassman. Thanks, Jeni Ogilvie, your careful editing skills made this a better read. Tom Curtin, without you, nothing would have come of this work. Your honesty, frankness, and positive attitude are priceless. You are the best! Thanks.

Introduction

The Summer of Violence—1993—spread fear across the nation. Newly elected President Bill Clinton was concerned about the rampage of violence in the streets and homes throughout the country. The First Gulf War had ended, and the atmosphere should have been quiet and peaceful, but it wasn't. Levels of homicide reached new heights; gang warfare, drive-by shootings, and the deadly rampages of adolescents were regular features on the nightly news. Debates were hot between opponents of gun control and those who advocated stiffer restrictions on handgun sales. The underpinnings of violence needed to be understood. "If only we could find someone who would actually live in a violent community to uncover what causes violence and how people living there cope," challenged Wendy Baldwin, Associate Director of the National Institutes of Health (NIH), in 1994. "I can do that," I responded.

Funded by the National Institute on Drug Abuse (NIDA), I, as principal investigator, along with a team of four fellow researchers and residents of Esperanza, a one-mile square town just 45 miles from the Mexican border, began a four-year natural study to discover the roots of violence in this community. Our study is called a natural inquiry; it examines the activities of daily living in a community without injecting our or others points' of view and describes what naturally occurs on a daily basis. The work is also called an ethnography because it studies the town from the perspective of the people themselves and uses their voices to tell about different aspects of the town. The first step in our natural inquiry of Esperanza is to get inside the town.

Living 24/7 in Esperanza, my colleagues and I listened to the voices of 5,600 residents, the total population, of whom 84 percent identified themselves as Mexican American and over one-third were monolingual, Spanish-speaking recent immigrants. The voices are cacophonic—reflecting diverse and sometimes conflicting points of view. From all angles—360 degrees—we looked at violence within the boundaries of this town and discovered that the causes of violence extend far beyond it.

1

All names used in the ethnography are pseudonyms unless they have appeared in public print (except for a former mayor as his name is linked directly with the actual name of the town). Data collected from participant observation, focus groups, individual interviews, life histories, and a random household survey are encapsulated within summaries and stories. All stories are voiced authentically, and the stories of two people have been combined, retaining the essence of both.

The University of Arizona researchers are myself, a cultural anthropologist, and Charles (Charlie) Anderson, a legal anthropologist. From Esperanza, we were joined by Mary Lou Chacon, an administrative assistant, Roberto Corona, a drug counselor, and Belinda Acosta, a nurse practitioner. A 12-member community advisory board guided the credibility of the ethnography, while over 40 students from three universities had various field experiences in the town. Two PhD dissertations and three master's theses were written from these data.

Approach reading this natural study as if you were solving a puzzle or discovering a way to answer these questions:

- Why are some communities more violent than others?
- What is being done to eradicate violence in Esperanza?

We believe this study can expose myths and inaccurate perceptions, and also give direction to reducing violence and building hope throughout the country and even internationally.

Alcoholism, drug addiction, homelessness, discrimination, poverty, and fears are human problems that play a central role in violence. Teenagers, mothers, fathers, the elderly, teachers, clergy, police, town leaders, and plain citizens in a small U.S. border town share their stories of drug trafficking, gang wars, and prostitution, as well as of efforts to make their town a Hispanic place of courage, resilience, and *hope*. To honor these people, we have named their town *Esperanza*, a pseudonym that means *hope* in Spanish.

This monograph tells the *whole* story. It contains rich descriptions of how all groups of people interact, compete, and survive as one community. It is a local story that takes place within the global context of historical and sociopolitical strife and power along the border of two nations—Mexico and the U.S. It is an area dominated by inequality of opportunity, illegal immigration, gangs, prostitution, and drug and human trafficking. The change from a town of fear and disconnections when we first encountered the town in 1991 to one of *esperanza* in 2001 is a powerful testimony of how humans can adopt new beliefs, behavior, and roles in order to survive. As tensions play out, the story unfolds. Catalyzed by a violent event, a grieving town is transformed to one in which hope begins to emerge.

Organization of the Book

Chapter 1 sets the stage for this natural study, describing the sights and sounds of a small border town where two-thirds of the population are migrating continually and very likely living in the U.S. illegally. The physical structure of a dilapidated town tells a story of poverty and loss of hope. The setting is ripe for violence, and so it happens when a drive-by shooting kills an innocent 11-year-old boy and the town becomes enraged and mobilized. After presenting a glimpse of Esperanza, and the research team's initial reactions to the town, we share our research methods, how we were able to elicit the perspectives of the people.

Chapter 2 explores the lives of individuals who have worked toward building a strong, resilient community and the social institutions that carry out their will. When outside sources provide finances (the bootstraps for change), the appearance of the town improves and support for social programs and police protection increases. Chapter 3 reveals the realities of violence connected with alcohol and drug use. This chapter uncovers cultural norms that encourage or control such behavior. Chapter 4 relates how a culture reflects the tensions between citizens and gangs and prostitutes. It uncovers how blinders for self-protection become complicity. Reliance on social institutions such as the police, the courts, and churches complements personal involvement. Chapter 5 focuses on the illegal world of drug and human trafficking and what costs these have on individuals, the community, and society. How can one small border town resist a powerful, lucrative drug network? How can law enforcement and judicial systems provide safety for the citizens as well as protect human rights with limited resources?

Chapter 6 examines violence as a cultural construct, uncovering patterns on all levels of society. Cycles of violence seem mysterious, but are they? Chapter 7 discovers the lives of shunned people: the homeless, the HUD families, and the monolingual Spanish speakers within the boundaries of a stigmatized town. Chapter 8 summarizes the wholeness of the study, pointing not only to individual strengths but also to institutional and global contexts of inequalities and barriers. In conclusion, two leaders share their views of changes that are still needed to propel, uphold, and embrace an era of transformation.

Chapter 1

A Violent U.S. Border Town

> I am the masses of my people and I refuse to be absorbed—I shall endure.
> —Corky Gonzales, *I am Joaquín*

OSCAR, AN INNOCENT BYSTANDER

"They've killed me, momma" were Oscar's last words as he lay dying, another victim of a stray bullet from a gang-related, drive-by shooting. Moments earlier, he, his mother, and his three older sisters had been celebrating his eleventh birthday. It was a beautiful evening in October 1996, and the family had gone outside to enjoy soft drinks on the front porch when two cars, filled with rival gang members, came barreling down the street; rapid gunfire spurted in all directions. One bullet struck Oscar. He died moments later in the arms of his hysterical mother.

Sorrow enveloped Esperanza, long held hostage by the ever-increasing street violence. The townspeople were incensed at losing one of its most promising youngsters. Local news media unfolded the story of Oscar, a model student in a town of poverty-stricken, recent immigrants. The media pounded on the fact that gang-related violence was not the only form of civil disorder in the town, where prostitutes and drug dealers openly conducted their trade and local residents were fearful to leave their homes after dark. The townspeople and leaders were dismayed and in conflict about how to change this destructive path. Oscar's parents and sisters, friends, teachers, clergy, and thousands of others marched down the town's main street to generate collective action as a way of changing the trajectory of violent crime.

The mayor asks, "Are we really more violent than other towns?" "Yes, crime statistics show that Esperanza is about five times as violent as other

5

towns of similar size," I respond. "Then help us find out why, and what we can do to change it." So begins our hard look at the facts.

Oscar becomes the symbolic martyr of the town. Churches fill with concerned citizens, and emotional issues are debated hotly. People shout, "*Nunca mas!*" (No more). Other murders follow, but the town changes after Oscar's death and slowly begins to transform from a town of violence to a town of hope.

With this mobilizing event, we begin our formal fieldwork in April 1997. We are not going to be studying something safe and beautiful—like how to weave baskets—we are going to be studying hard facts about crime—like murder and drug dealing. We are going to be walking the streets with the prostitutes and drug dealers. We are going to be sleeping and eating with all of the people living in this diverse community. No one is surprised by us as we make our presence known publicly.

Beginning Fieldwork

Michael Agar (1999) describes ethnographic fieldwork as a process that is "like studying snow in the middle of an avalanche." In the beginning everything is a whiteout—we are in the middle of an avalanche. How do we decipher patterns? How do we know if a pattern lasts more than a moment in time? We have to get *into* the community and become a part of it; we cannot study violence from the outside looking in. Somewhere, in the streets and alleys, the bars and churches, the schools and courtrooms, the homes, we are to discover why the town is violent.

"We've got to live here!" we say. "Let's rent a HUD apartment so that we can be right in the middle of all the drug dealing and see violence firsthand." We need an invitation from the mayor to rent a HUD apartment, and we get it.

The mayor says, "Living here, we expect you to do something for our town." I reply, "We'll tell the truth of what we find." Thus, an informal contract begins in August 1997, and the fieldwork team partners with the townspeople to tell their story of how violence is shaped in a border town. We call the study the Community Empowerment Partnership Project (CEPP).

To launch CEPP we hold an open house on a summer evening in our HUD apartment for neighbors, town leaders, and faculty from the University of Arizona. Friends, colleagues, and town leaders show up, but no neighbors. Our plentiful supply of cold drinks and cookies sits, barely touched. Mary Lou, one of our research team members, has a great idea: "Let's invite all the kids who are milling around and looking at us to come in. Let's give them cookies to take home to their families." It's a brilliant idea and one that works well—in a few minutes all the cookies are gone, and the word spreads rapidly that we are okay. The townspeople are curious about who we are, so we tell them—over and over again. Building trust is a first step in fieldwork, and it involves being open and honest, answering many questions, and asking as many in return. It helps that the CEPP gets media coverage in both English and Spanish newspapers and on television and radio.

As you read this monograph you will discover, as we did, that among the 8,000+ data points we collected, patterns emerge and form a picture. Data points are facts, such as information obtained from conversations, from reading newspaper articles or government documents, or from direct observations. Each fact is recorded on computer files. More is described later in the chapter about the research process of this study. Some of the patterns that emerge reveal beliefs and behavior that keep the community cohesive, while others illuminate those that are destructive, such as homicide, domestic violence, and poverty, and create fear and distrust. We call these patterns a *cultural consensus profile* that symbolizes and summarizes various explanations derived from diverse viewpoints. All of the viewpoints come from the people themselves. These insider views are called *emic* views.

First Impressions of Esperanza, 1997

Fieldwork for a natural study is diachronic, meaning it spans a specific time period. As you read about Esperanza you will see that change evolves over the four-year period. Some problems at the beginning are resolved before the study ends in 2001. Settling into our two-bedroom HUD apartment, we ask: "Could this town really be called *Esperanza*?" Stores and public buildings are marked with graffiti; every night we see streetwalkers plying their trade and hundreds of homeless people living under bridges and in gutters or wandering in the park. These people are not violent. What is going on in this town? Once again, we search for more answers on the streets and in the alleys.

We read news reports that describe competing, gun-toting, vengeful gangs and aggressive drug dealers who tempt buyers in the alleys and openly on street corners. The town is filled with rotting crack houses. Townspeople are afraid to leave their homes. After a few weeks we ask, "Where are the police, the fearless fighters of the drug war?" They are here, but they are too few and too often hampered and crippled by old, dilapidated squad cars with dead batteries. Their wages are insufficient to keep the bravest and the best on the force. The despondent police chief even leaves for a better-paying job on the East Coast.

Where are the church leaders charged with upholding the morals and values that arm citizens against crime and corruption? Many of the church leaders keep silent (oh, not all of them!) as they do not want to risk their reputations in wrestling with alcohol abuse, drug trafficking, gangs, and violence. Women, largely monolingual Spanish speakers, seem to keep silent; their husbands, struggling hard to make a living, often target them with domination and sometimes violence. Children, as well, often are victims of physical, mental, and sexual abuse.

Where are the business and school leaders? Businesses don't last long—there is little profit to be made from customers who are undocumented immigrants with meager paychecks. Local Mexican restaurants, to make customers who go there from other towns feel safe, hire armed guards to stand outside their doors. Grocery stores in Esperanza charge higher prices than markets farther away for lesser-quality foods (we monitored this for several weeks). People without transportation are unable to shop at competitive stores outside of Esperanza and have no choice but to buy from the more-expensive local stores.

School leaders fight a losing battle; school attendance is spotty because parents migrate from town to town, job to job. Many children live in crowded, extended-family homes where only Spanish is spoken. Not knowing how to speak, read, or write English hampers their ability to assimilate into U.S. culture. Many youngsters find the rigors of schoolwork too difficult, and they give up, drop out of school, and become pawns in the hands of drug dealers. Female dropouts often become mothers while they are still children themselves. Will the children of Esperanza ever be able to move above the poverty line?

Are these signs of suffering found in all populations plagued with poverty, or is there something or someone else to be blamed in Esperanza? What changes can be made? Who will instigate these changes? Can the people do it themselves, or do they need outside help? Elected officials blame outsiders and discrimination against Hispanics for these problems. Are these accusations true? Are outsiders causing poverty, crime, and family violence? Are there other reasons such as unemployment or unequal opportunities?

A Fragile, Diverse Town

The nearly futile situation has existed for over 40 years in this island surrounded by the large prosperous city of Tucson. Many legal battles have been fought as Tucson has tried to annex the small town three times. The town stands stubbornly in all its poverty, resisting annexation. Why? Because there is *hope*. Esperanza, with a population of over 84 percent Mexican immigrants and Mexican American citizens, is striving to become a distinct symbol of the proud Spanish conquistadors and uprooted Mexicans (Glittenberg 2001). The resilient townspeople desperately want Esperanza to be a haven of all that is good in Hispanic culture—the food, the *fiestas*, and the *familia*.

To simplify the multidimensionality of our research we compiled a cultural consensus profile as three concentric circles: the individual, the family, and social institutions. For example, at the individual level we see people who are abusive as well as those who are positive role models such as the chief of police and a nun who directs a social service agency. At the family level we discover dysfunctional families in which multiple murders have been committed alongside families that encourage their children to contribute positively to society. At the social institutional level are numerous agencies that succumb to pressure to misuse resources and destroy human lives and others that serve as a resilient force against violence and chaos.

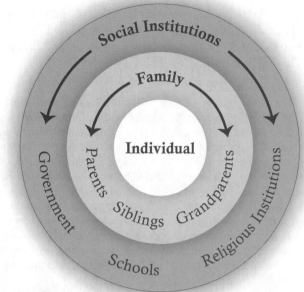

Cultural Consensus Profile

The town is simply not one monolithic tribe, bur rather it is composed of diverse people. The lives of three people illustrate the points of diversity in Esperanza: Jorge, a drug dealer who has the wrong name, is in the wrong place, and is there at the wrong time; Maria, an abused woman, drug user, and longtime resident; and Angela, a former resident faced with overwhelming losses who brings a message of faith and hope.

JORGE, A DRUG DEALER: FIELD NOTES, AUGUST 1999

Jorge, a desperate drug dealer, attempting to escape vengeful rivals, finds himself surrounded by gunfire, so he tries to crawl underneath his car. Bullets tear through the bottoms of his feet and more than 75 bullets rip through his body as it jerks and twists with each strike. The two shooters continue pumping bullets into his lifeless body and then turn their guns on his house, spraying it with more bullets.

This account was given by one of the shooters during their trial for murder. Jorge has a common Hispanic surname. After murdering him, the shooters discover they killed the wrong Jorge.

The network of drug dealers is a covert force throughout the area, and violence is a common way to resolve conflicts. The possibility of violent eruptions for the sake of revenge creates an environment of fear, distrust, and suspicion—especially knowing one can be a victim as a result of mistaken identity.

MARIA, A DEALER AND USER

Maria grew up in Esperanza, uses drugs, and is a small-time dealer. Her friends are drug-using "homies" (loyal friends from the neighborhood). She is married to a local gang leader (now in prison), and they have a small daughter. This is Maria's story told in her own words.

Early Life on the Street

I'm 24 'n I've served a couple jail times for drug possession, dealing, 'n stuff like that. I really never got hooked, no matter if it was weed or powered cocaine. A lot of homeboys [neighborhood best friends or buddies] who are dealers, would say, "Come on, get fucked up with me"— I never really paid for drugs—that's why I didn't get hooked. I have more mind control, but not my husband—when he does drugs, he can't control it; he needs more 'n more. He would do anythin' to get 'em, that meant jackin' somebody—fuck'n somebody up—trying to take their shit. He went to jail for it—drugs just took over totally his body.

It's easy, so easy to get drugs in prison. One time I wen'ta visit him, the dog alerted on me, 'cause I smoked a joint on the way. I was in a hurry so I forgot to put perfume on. They searched me 'n didn't find any, then they searched my car 'n found a seed of marijuana. I got my visits taken away forever! You can get anythin' in there.

We never used needles—not that shit, but I'm not afraid of AIDS. When I got pregnant I gotta AIDS test, 'n I was okay. I'm no ho [whore]; I heard a lot of shit about my husband—like—"I saw your man goin' in with this person or that person" you know, that kinda shit. It doesn't scare me 'cause I'm monogamist—that's the right word, right? I'm pretty sure he is, too. The only reason why he leaves is to do drugs. When he's not on drugs, he's totally faithful.

When I first met him, all we'd do is drive around all day. I'd be gettin' high, drinkin' a little bit, but he'd be smokin' crack. We was always together 24/7 at hotel rooms every day, dealin' every fuck'n day. In the house that is all boarded up, that's where I was for a year, every day, every night. The woman who lived there, her husband—my husband would lock me indoors with her—to be safe 'cause people were drivin' by shootin'.

Rules and Perception of Cycles of Violence

Basically violence happens at the house—it's mostly like the homeboys 'gainst homeboys. Somethin' happens and somebody is goin' to get beat down, but for outsiders, violence is pretty much in the streets. Violence is okay, dependin' on what is goin' on. When my husband's on crack, he thinks that everybody's out to get him—even me. So I just get away from him and just shut up—I won't hit him back 'cause I might get beat down too bad. The people who don't get violent are the dealers who make a lot of money, 'cause they don't smoke the shit.

Staying with Abuser and the Fear

A lot of people ask me, "Why do you stay with him?" most the time I'm with him, he's sober—he doesn't talk down to me; he doesn't lay a hand on me. It's just the drugs—I think it fucks up their brain. Like when they're on alcohol, on drugs, they don't trust nobody—one minute they would be lookin' at you in one way—the next, they can't find their dope, so they're sayin', "You took my dope." So right there, they're hittin' you 'n sayin', "Let's fight!"

The first time he hit me it was just on my arm—I was like "fuck this!" We were only together like two months, 'n I said, "It ain't gonna work." The first time he hit me in the face, he did it in front of all his friends. He knocked me out. He was lookin' at some bitch, 'n I told him, "You know, what the fuck are you doin'? I'm right here, you don't be lookin' at no bitch"—'n he said, "You shut up." He knocked me out then threw me in the car 'n his friends were all watchin'. He went down the street—after I came to, he just startin' cryin'.

No one would help me; they're all his friends 'n all too scared of him to do anythin'. One of his friends told me, "If I ever see him hit you, I'll do somethin'." About a month later we were in the backseat 'n my husband just backhanded me. He hit me in my face, 'n the guy didn't say shit. I started yellin' "You're such a pussy, you were tellin' me that you were goin' to back me up 'n this 'n that." Both of the guys ended up gettin' out of the car laughin', laughin' 'cause they think it's all good. Nobody does nothin', no. Actually the one person who did was my homegirl, who said, "What the fuck is wrong with you? Why you hittin' a girl? You know, she's your lady." But guys, no! His friends would tell me, "You better leave in case he beats your ass 'cause we ain't gonna stop him."

I think he could end up killin' me. Like the last time, I knew for sure I was gonna die—you know that you're gonna die 'n you're so scared. He saw a guy get out of my car. He said, "Give me a ride" and I said, "Okay," knowin' that you're goin' to die 'n you're so scared. He said, "I told you if you fucked up on me, I would kill you, Bitch, I'm gonna kill you." I said, "What the fuck" [slapping sounds]. Boom he hit me at least 30 times. Like I have scars on my lip—my face, it's not really the same, one side's different 'cause he smashed it right here. I needed stitches. He puts the gun to my stomach 'n told me, "I'm gonna fuckin' shoot you." I moved the gun 'n then he just started hittin' me again with the gun—he knew he was 'bout to kill me. The cops stopped the car 'n booked him. This is his third goin' back to prison 'n it's his last chance. I'm gonna give another chance—he has such a bad rap sheet—drug use, gang leader, abuse, everythin'.

Drug Dealing in Esperanza

We was always runnin' from the cops, like every day we would run from a cop—get a chase off. We got caught once or twice. There's everythin' right here in Esperanza—got the drug dealers, drugs, the clucker. A clucker is somebody who comes and they basically cluck—they'll give up anythin' for crack. They'll tell you, "Here's a camcorder—take it." Anythin' for the drugs. That's where I got all my jewelry, all my gold—a 20-inch piece of gold. "Gimme this, gimme that."

No one wants to get involved, 'cause they just want to keep the peace, just kissin' ass. When my husband and me would be driv'n down the street—all the neighbors, old men with canes, ev'ry body knows the way my boyfriend is so they'd say, "What's up?" saying "Hi" to my boyfriend—he used to run the neighborhood—he caused a lot of trouble—so they was nice to him—they was pretty scared of him.

Most of the houses look good, but they're all drug dealers. They keep it under profile; maybe they don't have drugs in the house, but they're all drug dealers. No one protect anyone, not the neighbors. Hell no, you're on your own.

Maria is the wife of a drug dealer and user. Her life is entrenched in her husband's activities, although she does not view herself as an addict. She was not born into a violent family, but began a dysfunctional life in her teen years with drug-abusing friends—her "homies." With a drug-dealing gang leader as her husband and with whom she has a daughter, she is in a "drug-user" family. The subgroup Maria associates with can be considered a "drug user community" (Singer 2006b:73). They have norms of inclusion, rules to obey, and support in surviving. In trying to find support, the drug users develop an inner group, a "community" with "family values" of protection, affection, and loyalty. She lives in an abusive, controlling relationship with few social supports other than the drug community.

Maria has a pattern of denial and self-centeredness with no future plans. She represents a group of drug-using people in Esperanza who are connected through their mutual illegal economic activities—drug dealing, burglary, and theft. She is not connected with legal support systems such as mental health agencies, churches, or social service groups that could help her change her patterns of living.

ANGELA, A RESILIENT MEXICAN WOMAN

I am Angela; I am Mexican. My struggles and successes in many ways epitomize the resilient side of Esperanza. My experiences allowed me to serve as a role model for many young and older Mexican women. Born in Nogales, Mexico, almost 50 years ago into a family with nine children, I was blessed with a mother and father who sacrificed all for us. My brother, Raul, was killed on a hill near our home when he was working for the FBI as a narcotics investigator. We do not talk about his death in our family, and that is how I've learned to live my life, not to dwell on negative things that happened but to persevere—don't look back but move onward without complaint.

Despite personal trials and prejudice, I moved to the U.S. about 30 years ago. I went to live in California with my sister and took care of her kids. I could not speak English, but worked hard on it. I made many new friends and even made it as a finalist in a beauty contest in a large city in California. Never for a moment do I waiver about my proud identity as a Mexican.

I met a Mexican man named Omar; we dated, ultimately married, and moved to Esperanza. We lived in a house on the west side where soon I noticed strange people in the neighborhood, coming in and out all hours, fights, and police were called. It was a center of prostitution and drug trafficking. My husband never let me walk anywhere in town alone. We began to prosper and saved money to build house and have children. I worked, listened, observed, and learned. I saw great misery and how drugs were challenging residents.

I knew that if we women would work together with unified front to local politicians and businesses, we could change things. Men worked long hours and often many miles from Esperanza; but nothing happened. I knew I could not make any changes by myself.

We moved to a better neighborhood in Tucson, and my husband's work was successful. But he became ill, diagnosed with Hodgkin's disease; he grew progressively worse and I cared for him at home, still raising our children and working long hours every day. Omar lost weight—from 230 pounds to less than 100. I had to be nurse, mother, and function in a world where I still had not mastered the language. My average day was 20 hours and sometimes I had only

2–3 hours of sleep a night. Finally Omar's suffering ended and he died; I had to pull myself together and move on. The Catholic Church ostracized me because it constantly reminded me that my role was to be with the children, but as a single mother I had to work. So I joined the Baptist church and became active in it.

I went to school to provide a better life for my children. I worked 60 hours a week and attended community college in the evening, but I also made certain the children were involved in school activities. My average week was 100 hours. I persevered and I succeeded! I had no choice. It seems I became a role model to many Mexican women—my story was told over and over again. Women came to my house after I got back from classes to hear my story. I like to think that I became a source of hope for them. I would never let myself forget my roots and that I am proud to be a Mexican. My children were brought up with the same pride. I was discriminated against at every turn, but I succeeded.

I really thought my life was going to be better when I married a well-known college professor, but after the honeymoon I realized my new husband was an alcoholic. His drinking got worse and he became verbally abusive. Although I never lost my love or respect for him, I separated from him for two years. We had a trial reunion, and he worked hard to turn himself around. He attends Alcoholics Anonymous, and we go to meetings together. During this time I also had trouble with my youngest son, who was grieving for his father, Omar. He used meth, cocaine, and heroin. He became violent during the time I was separated from my new husband. When my husband came back, we dealt with these problems together. It was so hard for me to see my son led into the courtroom in handcuffs and worse when I had to testify in front of everyone about his behavior. I knew he thought I was betraying him, but I just wanted to see him well. My husband was there and his presence provided me with strength. The situation ended and my son moved out of state where he is doing well, as long as he adheres to his medication regimen.

There was a lull in the suffering, as I worked hard and received recognition twice as the employee of the year. I learned to speak three new languages: Portuguese, Italian, and French. Life seemed good, when I was hit with the ultimate test. I was not feeling well so my husband took me for tests at the hospital. The tests showed that I had ovarian cancer.[1] I was confused and angry. Again, I found myself asking how could this happen to me? But I said to my husband and family, "I'm going to beat it—because God is going to heal me." God will work a miracle in me. My faith is stronger every day. After six chemotherapies and 7.5 hours of surgery my C125 count is decreasing. There are days when I'm so sick I wonder if it is worth it. I feel awful but still work, as the medical expenses are mounting, and my husband tries the best he can. I have a new life-threatening experience, which can add power to help others who reach for hope.

From humble beginnings, I have persevered over life's tribulations. I hope my experiences provide others with lessons they can use to fight their problems. Some of us seem to be chosen for this type of life. There is a higher power behind us that decides that some of us are to experience these things for a reason. Maybe that reason is to share. I do know Esperanza is full of other stories of courageous people.

People must live on. Faith breeds faith; strength breeds strength; love breeds love; and hope breeds hope. This is my life's story—my spirit will not die but lives on in Hope.

In contrast to Jorge and Maria, Angela, a strong-minded woman who identifies herself as Mexican, has overcome many adversities with individual energy and optimism; she has succeeded through using social resources and her inner strength. Angela carries out the role of a loyal wife and mother: caring for a dying husband, staying with an alcoholic second husband, defending a drug-using son, and identifying with parents "who sacrificed for the children." Angela contradicts the myth of *marianismo*. Marianismo is a word often used to describe a passive Hispanic female. It will be discussed in chapter 2. Angela is not a passive woman: she leaves her abusive second husband, and even watches her son being taken away in shackles for committing a crime, knowing that being incarcerated will force him to get the appropriate medical treatment. In her battle against ovarian cancer, Angela remains hopeful and, as a warrior woman, she speaks to crowds of Hispanic women about being strong and brave.

Summary of Three Narratives

These narratives represent the diversity of residents living in Esperanza. Jorge and Maria represent adult Mexican Americans who become part of a disconnected group through their lifestyle and choices. Jorge was known in the dangerous, deadly network of drug dealing but was accidentally mistaken for another and murdered. Maria's story is a clear illustration of the norms and rules for violence. Maria represents a group of drug-using people in Esperanza who are connected through networks of mutual illegal economic activities (e.g. drug dealing, burglary and theft). This drug culture is at odds with support systems such as churches, social agencies, schools, and mental health professionals. Angela represents the resilient people in Esperanza who have the strength to make a difference.

Focusing on Fieldwork

Some natural inquiries begin with a clean slate, with no preconceived ideas or prior information. We did not approach our research with a clean slate, but rather we read widely about the town, the surrounding city, and the region. Little has been written about the area, so we relied on a mimeographed document created by a former town employee and some newspaper articles that cover a 25-year history. We gathered vital statistics from the county health department. Although sparse, this information gave us a base upon which to compare factual changes in the town. The perspective we gained from this strategy increased our awareness of the struggles people had.

Now into our sixth month of fieldwork we still seem to be in the middle of the avalanche. Thus far, we cannot see specific patterns. Our two-bedroom apartment is on the end of the building, next to the street known for drug trafficking, gang activity, and prostitution. "This is a great place as we can see

HUD team apartment

and hear it all." Charlie and Roberto, my colleagues, occupy the apartment during the week, and I stay there on the weekends. This arrangement is a big mistake; neighbors ask, "Who really lives there? Sometimes we see two guys and then this older woman with a dog. What is going on?" Our random comings and goings create confusion and distrust.

"We need a full-time occupant—but who?"

"What about you, Mary Lou, you want to give it a try?" I ask.

"Absolutely, without paying rent [the NIDA grant paid the rent] it would give me a chance to save money to buy my own place. I already know all the neighbors. A great idea!" she replies enthusiastically. Mary Lou is the ideal person. As a Hispanic single mother of a teenage daughter and as surrogate mother to a four-year-old grandnephew, she lives with considerable family and financial concerns, as do most of the single women in the HUD apartments. Mary Lou, the key to our growing acceptance in Esperanza, is on the HUD Advisory Board, publishes a monthly newsletter (*The Corazon* [The Heart]) about the HUD happenings, organizes the women through all types of activities, and holds weekly get-togethers with the neighbors. Mary Lou's observations and connections throughout the apartment complex are invaluable, and leaders in the town trust her.

The apartment field site becomes a busy place for focus group meetings (focus groups are meetings in which group interviews are conducted and will be described in detail in chapter 2), many interviews of key participants, and parties for the research team and neighbors. After two years in the HUD apartment, we needed to broaden our involvement even further, so in 1999, we moved the field site (more will be told about this move in chapter 7) to a storefront office across from Bar Macho—a bar with a reputation of persistent drug trafficking and violence. Townspeople know where we are and what we are studying. Many drop in just to chat at both the HUD apartment and later in our storefront office. We continue to partner with the community to understand the cause and scope of violence.

Collecting, analyzing, and interpreting data is an ongoing process with the overall goal of accurately transcribing how the *townspeople* explain violence, its causes, and possible solutions. In addition to focus group meetings and interviewing key participants, we conduct participant observation, that is, participating in activities, events, and circumstances along with the townspeople, such as attending a local church service; collect the life histories of 10 people; analyze events to discover trends, patterns, or consistencies; and conduct a random household survey. To obtain a credible cultural consensus profile, we made sure that participants involved in the study have equal voices, equal power, and equal meaning in the responses they give to our questioning. For example, viewpoints of both male and female teenagers, middle-aged household heads, and undocumented immigrants are equally valued. This approach is known as *horizontal validity*. From the vast amount of data, from the various stories and viewpoints, we need to discern how all the facts fit together and organize them into a cohesive story. This process is called *vertical validity*. Throughout our fieldwork, we check and recheck our sources, making sure that at least three data sources are in agreement on one point in question to assure that the patterns that emerge are consistent and not random. This process is known as *triangulation*.

Cultural Geography of a Research Site

Knowing the cultural geography of a research site is critical. Mapping is a common way of knowing spatial relationships that help in interpreting some kinds of behavior, like stress from overcrowding, or learning how long it takes an individual to walk from one part of town to a bus stop under certain variables, such as after dark. This information gives the researcher a better perspective on dangers in the community and ways in which people cope with them. Charlie and Roberto do a community inventory and update the city map. They walk each street and alley, noting specific landmarks and neighborhoods of Esperanza. They know where every business is located and the people who work in each place.

We divide responsibilities for data collection based on how our individual areas of expertise match up with different aspects of the town. For instance, Charlie, a legal anthropologist, collects data related to the police department, the judicial system, businesses, city hall, and politics. Roberto, a drug counselor, focuses on drug users and dealers, prostitutes, and gang members. I collect data on family dynamics, health issues, schools, churches, and religion.

Typical shopping area

Mary Lou collects data on the lives of women and leaders in town. Belinda, a nurse practitioner at a local clinic, works with older, monolingual women. Using each team member's strengths, we complement each other.

Participant Observation

Participant observation is the foundation of ethnographic work; walking the walk with the people being studied leads to understanding, which then leads to questions that need answers. Being good neighbors is one way of conducting participant observation. We incorporate such a strategy from the first day of the study to the last. Agar (1983) describes this role as "professional stranger," or the professional role of participating as a stranger in the research site. Our roles are more specific, more involved, so we call our roles "professional informants." For instance, we help clean up the neighborhood, participate in fiestas and civil activities (such as peace marches), attend ceremonies (such as dedication of the new fire engine) and many events, teach classes on parenting and social skills for dropout kids, do individual counseling for gang members and at-risk youth, manage health clinics and do physical examinations for elementary children and the elderly, wrap gifts for Christmas parties, adopt families for the holidays, and participate in parties for the HUD neighbors and in fund raisers for social services agencies. We help write grants, and we work with community groups in a zero domestic violence program. Being professional informants gives us in-depth experiences as if we are actually Esperanzans.

We are present for whatever is happening in town, but our observations are focused on the police department, courtrooms, businesses, bars, social agencies, churches, schools, parks, hospitals, and mental health treatment centers. I, for example, participate in church services throughout the town—sometimes attending three services each Sunday and attending services at least three times in each church. Charlie rides along with the police when they respond to a call, which gives him quick access to violent events. The police keep us informed, but also respect the fact that we will not reveal any illegal activity we encounter unless someone is being abused or injured. The ethics involved in doing ethnographic work mandate an objective neutrality to the daily lives that we observe.

Charlie and Roberto focus more on dangerous events. Their night interviews and observations give us a better understanding of the policies, dangers, and importance of controlling illegal activity and protecting the public at large while still preserving individual legal rights. Charlie and Roberto routinely alter their participant observation throughout the day, evening, and night—so we can know the variation in patterns for a whole 24-hour period.

During our weekly team meetings we share data and insights, and on newsprint, we diagram networks of power, alcohol use, drug trafficking, and violent events. Any gaps we identify in the webs of meaning and cultural explanations tell us we need to gather more data—to go out and walk the walk. This type of inductive research sets anthropologic research apart from deductive research where facts are validated. Inductive research is a discovery *process*—always evolving, as is illustrated in the following street work field notes.

Street Work, January 29, 1998 9:00 AM

Roberto and I decide it is time to go back on the streets for a day and just observe what is going on. We do this, on a schedule, about every two weeks in addition to other times during evenings, nights, and early morning hours. Something is always going on. We literally walk the entire one-square mile, including alleys. At about noon we stop and have a soda and maybe a burrito. We take our stuff outside and sit and talk with anyone who cares to chat with us. We can tell that now no one pays much attention to us as being out of the ordinary. They don't think we're cops.

The illegal activity from our place of observation is unbelievably diverse with at least ten drug transactions observed in just a few hours. The ethnic mix is as diverse as one can find anywhere. They're talking, dealing, using just as if we are not there. People talk to us about a variety of things. The alley is teeming with several African American males, extremely young Native American males and females, Hispanics of both genders and all ages, and middle-aged Anglo men.

Many of the drug deals happen by people just standing on the side of 28th and waiting for a car to drive by. The drivers of these cars know they are copping drugs. Little hand or vocal signals are all that is necessary for a drug transaction. A young Hispanic male even asks Roberto and me on two occasions if we want anything. Of course, we say no. Several individuals that Roberto counseled in the drug rehabilitation center, known as Peaceful House, walk by and greet him. They are living on the streets and using drugs and alcohol as they were before entering treatment.

Henri, an old African American longtime user and small-time dealer, comes and sits by us, conversing for a while. Two young girls along with several males of several ethnic groups come up from the south from an alley. Henri asks us for some change to get a beer. I give him 50 cents. He looks at it and says, "I need about 50 cents more to get a quart." By this time the two girls yell at him again, "Hey you want to go with us to cop some drugs?" He replies, "Nah, don't bother me now." And he keeps on talking. One of the girls comes over and bums a cigarette from Roberto and asks me, "Do you have any money on yah?" "No," I respond. Soon Henri gets up and joins the growing group and walks back with them into the alley.

One really young African American male comes staggering along and sits down between us on the store steps. He just looks back and forth at Roberto and me for a while. The male reeks of booze, and Roberto and I just look at one another because we both (as we conversed later) feel that he might pick a fight with us. Finally he slurs, "Aren't you guys afraid hangin' out in Esperanza?" We answer, "No, why should we be?" He responds, "'Cause you both are white." Roberto says, "I'm not white!" When the guy persists, Roberto holds out his hands and asks, "Look at my hands. Do these look white to you?" The young male then turns his attention to me and asks, "How's come you're not afraid hangin' out in Esperanza?"

I told him there is no need to be afraid and ask him if he is afraid. He responds, "Sometimes," and then tells us he'd just gotten into a fight. This is what made Roberto and me nervous even before he began talking to us, as we can see that both of his hands have cut knuckles. Roberto then told the guy, "I am 6'7" and weigh 250 pounds, and have a black belt in Karate." He appears impressed, but soon bores of our company and begins staggering off, walking north and crossing 6th Avenue. He calls back to us, "I'm not from here—I'm from South Park [a very poor section of Tucson]."

During the last 6–7 months we have been seeing more activity in some alleys on the west part of town. What does this mean? What is so striking about all of this activity is that it is so blatantly overt. Several families can be seen walking by us, even mothers with children, apparently paying no attention to all the drug dealing. The kids just keep walking, and it is clear that this is a common sight to them. Across the street are bunches of children dressed in school uniforms playing in full view of the illegal activity only about 25 yards from their school playgrounds. And there are no police in sight—anywhere. There seems to be a "blindness" that keeps the activity from awareness, perhaps for protection or, is it the high cost of prosecuting small drug dealing?

Money generated from street-level dealing, as well as from outside dealing, sometimes goes to legitimate enterprises in town. For instance, some experienced dealers covertly give to churches and other worthy causes. During church services I saw well-dressed men occasionally drop large-denomination bills into the donation plates. According to one participant at a youth agency, many of the more successful local drug dealers give to local families in need. These donations become incentives for not doing anything about stopping drug dealing. Such complicit incentives are part of the larger picture of the informal economic distribution that complicates curbing illegal trade and disclosing neighborhood activities. Is it, therefore, culturally acceptable to only "talk" about the drug problem without seeking a way out of the long-standing dilemma of what to do about illegal drug dealing? (Drug trafficking will be discussed in chapter 5.)

Selecting Representatives

Carefully selecting representative members of the town who could provide us with information by participating in focus groups, by giving interviews, and by providing life histories began after we were in the field for nine months. The selection is complicated because the population is not one monolithic group but rather consists of roughly three subgroups: the marginalized, migrating people (almost two-thirds of the population); the resilient, longtime homeowners (almost one-third of the population); and a covert group that participates in illegal activities (an unknown size) that can overlap with the other groups.

Migrating people are often undocumented immigrants, and keeping on the move prevents their detection, arrest, and deportation. These immigrants tend to be an honest, hardworking group, often living in crowded conditions with relatives or others in the same situation. Their goal is to become established enough to send money home to relatives in Mexico. Immigrants also spend their money in town, though their buying power is limited because of low wages. Local businesspeople welcome their buying power and their episodic employment. Our greatest challenge is to get accurate representation from the migrating group as it moves within the town and between the U.S.–Mexico border.

The second subgroup is an easier group to know because it consists of longtime residents who, for the most part, own their homes, attend church, and have graduated from the local schools. Although this group is not on the move, not all of its members work in Esperanza. They, therefore, can be somewhat disconnected from certain activities in town, and lack knowledge about local commerce, because they tend to shop near where they work.

The third population group—drug and human traffickers and prostitutes—engages in an illegal economy that affects many aspects of life in Esperanza, such as the police, who are consumed with making arrests and presenting evidence in courts, and other departments that provide public services. The cost to control crime in the town is so high that other public services, such as maintaining streets, suffer.

All three subgroups participate in a strong informal economy that seems adaptive to the lives of very poor people. For example, an exchange of labor (such as babysitting for one another) or an exchange of skills (such as auto repair or electrical house repairs), are inventive ways of procuring a service without spending money. Some women cook and serve lunch in their homes for regular, paying customers, profiting like an informal restaurant. A long list of such exchanges shows a creative, mutually beneficial system of cash and labor exchange.

Although these informal activities are legal, such activities may overlap with the illegal economy. Even longtime, stable residents may engage occasionally in illegal acts. It can be difficult to separate legal and illegal operations. The blending of informal and illegal actions increases fear and lack of trust among the citizens as they may be confused about the boundaries between the two actions.

As our understanding of the parameters of the subgroups grows, we are able to select a representative sample from each group for focus groups, key participant interviews, life histories, and event analyses.

Focus Groups

Eight focus groups, with eight members each, meet for two-hour sessions, and six of the eight groups are repeated a week later. The groups are divided by categories: older monolingual females, older monolingual males, former male gang members, former female gang members, young adult females, young adult males, social agency representatives, and HUD apartment dwellers. Group members respond to a standard set of questions. The purpose of conducting focus groups is to gain consensus on a specific topic by interviewing members of each group. Interviews are conducted in Spanish to facilitate individuals in giving their opinions. The interplay of focus group members allows for in-depth responses, establishing the social context, and the display of emotion, which enriches the meanings that are uncovered. When there are differences of opinion, the reasons for the differences are explored and an essence of diversity and universality is gained. The sessions are tape recorded, transcribed, and analyzed before the next focus group meeting so that unclear explanations can be clarified during the follow-up session (see appendix A).

Key Participant Interviews

Over 50 people, representing a wide range of individuals living in Esperanza, are selected for key participant interviews. As our engagement in the town deepens, we are either able to recruit participants on our own or on the recommendations of key leaders. We record participants' viewpoints on violence, alcohol abuse, drug trafficking, gangs, and prostitution, as well as their perceptions of what changes would improve the town. Although predominately a Mexican American town, our sample includes Anglo-Americans, Native Americans, and African Americans. About half of the participants are women and half are men. No magical number is used for an ethnographic sample size. We consider a question fully answered once we achieve at least three points of agreement on a single issue or topic. This is called "saturating the data."

Life Histories

The life histories or case studies of 10 participants inform us about a specific topic or validate hypotheses that have been raised by the focus groups or individual interviews. We learn more about the process of using drugs or engaging in violent acts, as well as the opposite—resisting violence, alcohol abuse, drug use, or drug trafficking. We capture the essence of how subgroups differ and what kinds of interventions can be conducted by social action programs or implemented by social policy or judicial reforms to combat problems of at-risk youth.

Event Analysis

The day-to-day life in Esperanza results in fear or, in contrast, hope, in the town. Key events like copping drugs on a street corner, or the large-scale and longitudinal drug dealing engaged in by our HUD next-door neighbors, tell us that people deal with daily challenges.

Through participant observation of courtroom events, we can ascertain the effectiveness of law enforcement and the judicial system in maintaining control and security. The attorneys and judges now expect our usual appearance in court on Tuesdays, and at least once a week, one team member attends the court hearings where all types of cases are prosecuted. The following event illustrates the control of drug trafficking, at the local level, using few resources.

A DAY IN THE COURTROOM, JANUARY 20, 1998: CHARLIE AND ROBERTO'S FIELD NOTES

One of several African American males is called up. This individual had been arrested seven times in December and January to date—including a zone violation. A $2,500 bond is placed on him. A zone violation restriction from between 4th and 7th Avenues is placed on him because of his drug dealing. This means that if he is seen in that zone restriction area he can be arrested without cause. We hadn't seen many of these restrictions enforced, but had heard of them from police officers. It seems the only way to protect the public as well as the offender is to have posted zone restrictions. A Hispanic male is called next. Apparently he had been arrested numerous times before and failed to show up for the dispensation of his case. This young man is classified as a heavy drug dealer, so the judge orders a citywide zone restriction against him. This is a first in our experience to hear of a citywide restriction and it shows the seriousness of the crime. If this guy so much as puts his toes over the city boundary, and he is caught, he will be arrested.

Random Household Survey

What is the overall prevalence of violent behaviors, drinking, and drug trafficking in Esperanza? Is it different from the national norms? Do behaviors vary from centuries or even decades ago? Who do the citizens view as their protectors and role models? To find answers to these questions, we do a random household sample the second year into the study.[2]

Charlie and Roberto recheck the map they completed two years before to see if little shacks or hidden trailers have been constructed during that time period—adding house numbers where there had been none. A questionnaire is developed—a sample of questions asked is found in Appendix B—pilot tested, and modifications are made. The town is physically divided (based on our perceptions) into three subsections: the west side (more settled), the east side (less organized), and the HUD apartments for those in economic need. Using a random table of numbers we select 200 household addresses. Flyers written in Spanish and English are placed in public places, announcing that the Community Empowerment Partnership Project will be conducting a survey. The flyers describe that the purpose of the survey is about alcohol and drug use, violence, and ways of controlling problems in Esperanza. A payment of $10 for participating in the survey will be made. We explain that we will be knocking on a random number of neighborhood doors in the evenings and on the weekends to conduct the survey.

Summary

Perceiving patterns within the avalanche of snow is the way we describe our beginnings in a partnership known as Community Empowerment Partnership Project. The project involved knowing the community and living in the town. Several examples were given to illustrate the diversity of townspeople and the systematic way of gaining multilevel, multivocal patterns. As a picture of the town emerges, the story continues to unfold.

Notes

[1] Ovarian cancer is difficult to diagnose as it has few symptoms in early stages, hence it often spreads, making its treatment less successful.

[2] An almost 10% sample is reached, yielding a 95% level of confidence of the findings for the overall sample as well as for the subsamples. The data are analyzed using SPSS format and the findings are interspersed in appropriate places throughout this book. SPSS, statistical software designed for social science research, is used to calculate and analyze survey data, such as the household survey in Esperanza.

Chapter 2

A Profile of Esperanza

> The distribution of sadness . . . by this I mean the overrepresentation of Mexican-origin populations in the bilges of poverty, and among the undereducated, underemployed, and underrepresented who suffer from poor mental and physical health and lack protection. They are also over-represented in penal institutions and as war casualties.
> —Carlos G. Vélez-Ibáñez, "Regions of Refuge in the U.S."

The Beginnings of a Hispanic Town

How did Esperanza come into being? What kinds of leaders shaped the culture, politics, and economics of the area? What kept this town together and separated it from the big city that surrounds it? Why is it violent? By examining the historical roots of the town we learn how it was shaped. We learn about survival from studying the history of settlers, immigrants, wars, family culture, and social institutions that were shaped within this town. A very brief description of the historical settlement of this border region will illuminate some of the cultural patterns.

Background to Settling the Land

The undocumented migrant problem of today has its roots in the long history of settling the land around Esperanza. The harsh environment now found around this region was severe even around 300 BC when indigenous people known as Hohokam lived in the area. Long-lasting droughts prevailed in the region, and over time the population was diminished to only 10 percent of its original size (Vélez-Ibáñez 1996). Such a decimated population had to adapt or become extinct, and the Hohokam adapted. They intermingled with other tribes eventually becoming known as the Aztecs. Even today some Esperanzans identify themselves as Aztecans.

25

Meanwhile, in what is now Mexico and the Yucatan, tribal fighting was occurring. So the disorganized native people offered little resistance to Cortez when he and his conquistadors, with their devastating, highly advanced weaponry and horses, quickly overpowered the indigenous people. So that his soldiers could not return to Spain, Cortez burned the ships in the fleet. With no means out of the new land and without the presence of women from their homeland, the Spanish soldiers married native females, blending the two cultures. Their offspring were designated *mestizo* (mixed blood). Populations in Mexico and many parts of the Southwest retain that mixed blood heritage.

The conquistadors migrated northward, in search of gold rumored to be buried in parts of the region, where indigenous tribes such as the Aztecs lived and that would eventually become Arizona. At about the same time, an Italian Jesuit missionary named Fray Eusebio Francisco Kino established agriculture, schools, and churches on the land near Esperanza, further spurring immigration into the area. The blending of Aztec and Catholic beliefs is one of the most unifying forces within the Mexican culture (Isasi-Díaz 1993:159). The close relationship between the Aztec religious system during the time of the Conquest and today's practices in the Catholic Church illustrate a syncretism, a blending of religious beliefs. An example of this syncretism is the legend of Our Lady of Guadalupe. A miracle is said to have occurred in 1531 when the Virgin Mary appeared to a Náhuatl-speaking Indian young man named Juan Diego. He saw a brown-skinned Náhuatl-speaking Virgin Mary (who is part of the Catholic belief system) at the spot where the Aztec earth goddess Tonantzin (known as Our Mother to the Aztec people) had been venerated for centuries (León Portillo 2000). Since Juan Diego's discovery, Our Lady of Guadalupe has become the patron saint for all of Mexico. (More will be described in later chapters of the influence of this patron saint.)

War and Land Disputes

The historical context of the conflict between indigenous people and the Spanish has relevance to the eventual settling of Esperanza. After Mexico won its independence from Spain in 1821 after a decade of fierce fighting, it was nearly bankrupt and the government was in disarray. As a way of stabilizing itself, Mexico awarded large areas of land, now the state of Arizona, to worthy Mexicans (Hayes-Bautista 2004; Sheridan 1995). However, the Republic of Texas also laid claim to this same land, so frequent disputes erupted over its ownership. The disputes finally erupted into the Mexican–American War (1846–1848), which ended with the bloody Battle of the Alamo and the signing of the Treaty of Guadalupe Hidalgo in 1848. The U.S. paid Mexico $15 million; in return, Mexico forfeited half of its territory that today includes parts of Arizona, California, Colorado, New Mexico, Nevada, and Wyoming.

Subsequent to the Mexican–American War, the U.S. purchased land that is now southern Arizona and New Mexico under the terms of the Gadsden Purchase. A sovereign border line was drawn between Mexico and the U.S.

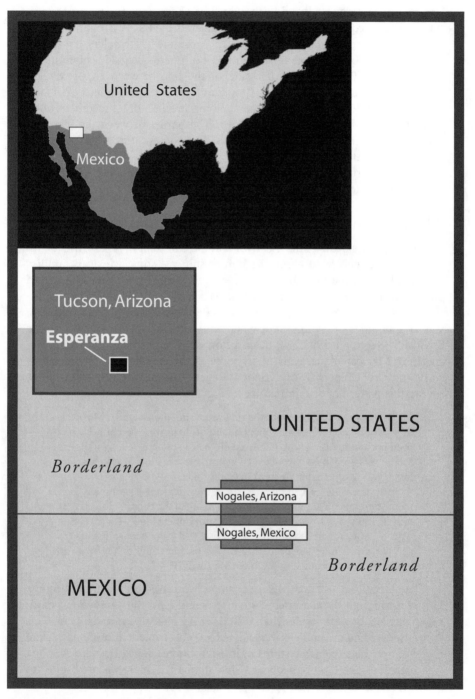

Diagram showing location of Esperanza

The routine crossing back and forth, which had been done for centuries without legal consequences, now became regulated by the two countries. No longer were those who crossed into the U.S. welcomed as travelers, but rather, they were now looked upon as immigrants—or often—illegal immigrants.

The land 50 miles on either side of the line between two sovereign nations is called a borderland. Throughout the world, borders exist and change as political forces shape them. Some are friendly and others hotly contested; others are fragile or defended. The border between the U.S. and Mexico has been hotly contested for nearly two centuries. Esperanza lies within that contested borderland, and problems involving distrust, illegal trade, and poverty are concentrated in this one-mile-square town. Such problems have been long-standing.

The Shifting Identities and Discrimination

After the Mexican–American War and the Gadsden Purchase, the identities of people who lived along the border shifted—some Mexican families that had been in the U.S. for six to seven generations were now considered aliens. "Confusion would reign because Mexican residents could not be distinguished from Mexican immigrants. . . . Being born and raised in the U.S. was no guarantee of civil liberties when your skin was brown and you spoke Spanish" (Sheridan 1995:284). Confusion still exists today: Are Spanish-speaking Mexican Americans really citizens, or are they illegal aliens? A story told by University of Arizona Regents' Professor Oscar Martinez reveals this pattern of discrimination:

> My mother has told me about the thousands and thousands of Mexicans they deported on trains and buses, many of them were people who had been born in the U.S., who had lived all their lives here. All my mother's family was sent to Mexico even though they were all U.S. citizens. Her father was Mexican, but he lived in California since the 1890s. They sent them to the state of Chihuahua where the Mexican government gave them some land. They could not make a living in the countryside, so they moved to the city. My mother relates the story of the family's repatriation with a great deal of resentment because it was a big change for her . . . she felt her family had been thrown out as something which was no longer needed or wanted in the U.S. (Martinez 1994:231–232)

The U.S. promised that Mexican people who lived on what had become U.S. land through the Gadsden Purchase would have the "enjoyment of all the rights of citizens" (Menchaca 2001:215). This did not happen. This "promise" had no meaning as the U.S. federal government allowed each state to determine the citizenship status of its Mexican residents. Because Arizona was a territory and did not become a state until 1912, there was no "state" to grant residents any citizenship.

Another problem faced by Mexicans living in the U.S. was that they were given the status of "Indian"; thus they fell under the laws that governed Indians. As "Indians," they were ineligible to own property, testify in court, or become citizens (Hayes-Bautista 2004:26), resulting in additional injustices. As part of The Homestead Act of 1848 that allowed U.S. citizens to stake claims on land in the West, only a white citizen could claim a homestead. Mexicans could not apply because they were not considered U.S. citizens (Hayes-Bautista 2004:27). Thus, Mexicans overnight lost their land, forfeited their citizenship, could not homestead, and were labeled aliens (Arzaladua 1987). The landless Mexicans living in the Arizona Territory were without political power. They had to work for less wages and more episodically than did Anglo workers (Vélez-Ibáñez 1996). We learn from history that, faced with multiple layers of discrimination, the early settlers of Esperanza still retained their courage and resilience.

The Mexicans living in the borderlands faced problems similar to those of Mexican immigrant workers who were used for the economic welfare of the U.S. due to labor shortages during World War II. At that time, a guest-worker program called the Bracero Program provided emergency labor for designated employers in the U.S., whose employees left to fight in World War II. Guest workers were given no rights; they could not rent or buy property, bring their families to live with them, or marry. After the war, when the labor crisis ended, Mexican laborers went back home, but then they were invited to come back—this time with their families—again to work, because there was another labor shortage. The immigrants came slowly, not trusting the fickle system. Distrust remains today, and many conflicts that surface in Esperanza can be traced to distrust of *la migra* (the immigration). Uncertain, fluctuating labor needs have created conflicts with a mixed "welcome" and "go home" immigration climate.

La Familia Mexicana

Understanding the Mexican family acknowledges the difference in how the countries of Mexico and the U.S. were first settled. Mexico was a country invaded by soldiers who came to conquer, and they came without families. They brought their own faith, the Catholic Church. In contrast, pilgrims and pioneers of the U.S. came as families, not to conquer but to settle and develop a new nation (Spicer 1962). These pioneer families also came with religion in the form of many denominations and a belief in freedom of religion. From the beginning, Mexico became a land of mestizos when Spanish soldiers had children with native women. The Spanish Crown and the Catholic Church blessed these unions since they increased Spain's subjects and added newly baptized members to the Church.

The search for the gold that was rumored to be in the new land motivated the speedy conquest of Mexico. In contrast, the pioneers in the U.S. moved more slowly to achieve their goal. Pioneers came as families in need of establishing agriculture, townships with schools, churches, and industry. The pioneers displaced native populations along the way, seldom intermarrying as they pushed ever westward. The meeting of the mestizos and the pioneers happened in the area now known as the Southwest (New Mexico, Texas, Arizona). Here, the mingling of these two groups created new patterns of family structure, such as those found today in Esperanza.

Fighting to Keep the Town

Presently, little is known about the beginning of an incorporated Esperanza. The only source of history comes from a mimeographed paper written by Charles Johnson, an employee of the town, published in 1986. He wrote that the town was first incorporated in 1939 when there were 1,034 property owners. In 1948, soon after World War II, property ownership grew to 10,000 owners who were all living within a space of one square mile (Johnson 1986). By that time the town was showing its ethnic roots, as many elected leaders were Hispanic. Anglos began to move out of Esperanza to Tucson, and this exodus was seen as a sign of Esperanza's deterioration. Esperanza became the "wrong side of the tracks." City leaders assumed that when the Anglos moved out, the little town would simply crumble into a slum. How wrong they were!

The city planners from Tucson tried three times to incorporate the one-square mile town into Tucson, but failed. Baffled planners asked, "Why would anyone want to live in such a blighted area?" These Tucson leaders "failed to acknowledge the degree of continuity within neighborhoods . . . and [the] possibility of working-class Hispanic neighborhoods maintaining a sense of community and solidarity" (Johnson 1986:5).

In 1973, a man of strength and character began his assent in politics. Ernesto Hanson (a pseudonym), known as the "boy" mayor, took the reins to govern the town of Esperanza at age 26. "Born to a Mexican mother and a Norwegian father, he gained awareness of both the Mexican and Anglo worlds. A political fighter . . ." the *Tucson Weekly* (2001) called him. The newspaper noted that in 1982 Hanson built his home in Esperanza to demonstrate his faith in the community in which he was born. His legacy as a leader in Esperanza comes from the tenacious belief he still retains and fights toward making the city habitable (*Tucson Weekly* 2001)—and so he has.

The young mayor's reputation grew as he saved the town from bankruptcy. In 1984, a lawsuit against Esperanza, brought by a Tucson police officer paralyzed from injuries he sustained during a joint police operation, was settled for $4.5 million (including interest). Hanson, through negotiations, was able to pay off the debt, but it still left the town in a dire economic state. Instead of folding, the young mayor focused on securing federal and state grants to face-lift the town with new streets, new lighting, a library, some new businesses, and a very attractive city hall. This first face-lift occurred 15 years before the second one in 1998.

The mayor led the town's survival tactics by himself and through his thick kinship system—cousins, siblings, children, and *compadres*. A kinship system in any society is an important cultural institution to study. Patterns of relationships, if by blood or by marriage, are maps for defining behaviors such as honor, respect, or avoidance and distancing between roles (e.g. father, mother, in-laws, etc.). Fictive relatives are also important. These are "pseudo" relatives, acknowledged as such by their role or status in the culture. One important fictive relative in the Hispanic culture is the *compadre*—or "coparent"—a role gained through the baptism of a child. This fictive role comes with many obligations and honor. Compadres are a very important part of the kinship system in Esperanza; they may also be part of a kinship drug-dealing network.

The Hispanic kinship system is describe as being "thick," meaning that many people with many relationships are involved in the society. This is in contrast to a "thin" kinship system that includes fewer relatives with fewer obligations and less reciprocity among the members. There is no "right" or "wrong" system, just differences that affect behavior in many ways. Examples of the Hispanic kinship system will be described throughout the book, and you can identify aspects of behavior that are influenced by the kinship system. Hanson used this thick kinship system to protect the town. Hanson became known locally as a "guard dog," because he protected the community and fought for an improved image of the town. As summed up by one town leader, "Without his leadership . . . Esperanza would have become a slum."

Esperanza of the 1970s was a mixed population. "There were all types of people: blacks, Asians, Anglos, and Mexicans then, but now it is all Mexican," remarked a 60-year-old female who was returning "home" again (Field Notes, August 1999). A 75-year-old male, monolingual Spanish-speaking resident said, "These are my streets; this is where I grew up, speaking my lan-

A popular Hispanic restaurant

guage, eating Mexican food; some of my kids live here, this is family." Lupita, a 40-year-old, describes herself:

> You come into my house and you know the minute you walk in you're walking into a chicana household, because of the way I cook, because of the way I greet you, because of my garden, and the meals I prepare. The dishes I serve them on, the way I decorate, and everything about me is very, very closely tied to my Mexican roots.

Although the physical appearance of the town improved, drug trafficking became an international epidemic in the 1980s. The large-scale drug problem could not be overcome or even controlled by the mayor or other leaders, as drug use and dealing led to the violent environment found there in the 1990s.

Weed and Seed: The Bootstraps for Hope

Throughout the U.S., violence reached a peak around 1993—the Summer of Violence (see the Introduction). Civic leaders sought the federal government's help in addressing violence and fear. Several new directions were tried at the national level. For example, community policing became popular as a federally funded program, and it was strongly supported by the Clinton administration with a goal to curb violence across the nation. The goal of community policing is to place officers at the level of the people living in a community or neighborhood. For instance, an officer walking the beat, riding a bicycle, or riding a horse in the neighborhood is more personally involved with residents than is one or two officers riding in a patrol car—distanced from the people themselves. As the study will show, the people endorse community policing.

Other national efforts to do something about violence included the Brady Gun Law, enacted to control handgun sales and tougher laws in dealing with drug traffickers. Local changes took place simultaneously with national ones. Willingness for Esperanza's town leaders to enact changes ushered in the CEPP. Esperanza received federal grant money through a Weed and Seed program. This National Institute of Justice program targets communities at risk—those with poverty and drug problems—and "weeds out the bad and seeds in the good" by making physical improvements and by building connections between committed townspeople. In Esperanza, Hanson and a former mayor became The Weed and Seed project's coleaders. The $250,000 grant was matched with numerous other grants, reaching a total of $13 million in just two years.

An advisory council was organized that included the chief of police, the fire chief, a couple of police officers, and directors of social service agencies. Project proposals by grassroots organizations were presented to the council who would award Weed and Seed money on a competitive basis. Dozens of outstanding local projects were funded during this period. This outside money was important—it was the bootstraps. Without bootstraps, perhaps, hope would be only an illusion.

It was the structure and process of the town's organization, however, that empowered the people. A network of interested, instrumental people from Esperanza and the outside gathered at informal monthly Weed and Seed meetings. Usually about 100 people came for a Mexican meal and a face-to-face exchange with well-intentioned leaders of the town. The lively meetings, buoyed by optimistic success stories, expanded on the motto of the 4Fs: Family, Fun, Food, and Follow Through. Change was directed at raising awareness, pride, and participation from the grassroots to the top leadership. It began with a desperate need to engage in action, to reduce fear and violence, and to have hope.

Habits of the Heart

In spite of pressure to assimilate into U.S. culture, the Mexican immigrants survive and thrive within their own culture. Why? What cultural beliefs and behaviors contribute to the survival of the landless people? Survival has been the result of retaining Hispanic customs, a stock of knowledge that builds resilience (Berger and Luckmann 1966:41). These customs are also called "habits of the heart" (Hayes-Bautista 2004:181).

Familism and the Mexican Kinship System

Familism (also spelled *famialism*)—family—is a core value among Hispanics, and family bonds persist irrespective of socioeconomic status or acculturation (Hurtado 1995; Marin & Marin 1991). In a Mexican culture, the family, or kinship system, instills traditional values that are so resilient they have withstood erosion and have fortified families from being assimilated fully into the dominant culture of the U.S. Family formation fascinates anthropologists, for the nuclear family (father, mother, and offspring) is the smallest unit in a society that has multiple, multilevel social roles and obligations.

Families are an essential fabric of the town. For example, in addition to being called a town, Esperanza can also be called a *barrio*—a neighborhood. Hispanic people like living in clusters with other Hispanic people, "Like birds flocking together" (Schelling 1971, quoted in Agar 2004:413). Historically, the barrio has been a positive resource and an important cultural referent for Mexican families. Kinship systems found in barrios are reinforced through the values of reciprocity and sharing among extended relatives.

Enduring Mexican roots as identified by the long-standing values retained by families hold the people of Esperanza together. In spite of centuries of marginalization and discrimination, they still survive. Connections that are spiritual, intangible, and ethereal, going back to the blending of the indigenous and Spanish blood and beliefs, cannot be broken (Berger and

Luckmann 1966:41). For over 500 years these spiritual intangibles have been passed on from generation to generation—they are resilient. As one respondent explained, "We are Americans, but as Mexicans."

This adaptive strategy uses the extended family as a corporation, establishing informal economic methods and combining households (Vélez-Ibáñez 2004:13). An example of how power can be accumulated through kinship systems is the political power of the Ernesto Hanson family.

The Hanson family is similar to those found throughout Mexico today in many traditional small communities and villages. The head of the family, at the top of the hierarchy, is the patron who rules with power and respect. Those who retain their social obligations to him are given rewards, and those who do not are shunned or marginalized.

The Hanson family is an exemplar of a cultural ideal in Esperanza. The Esperanza town hall is named in honor of Ernesto, the boy mayor who still retains complete political power through his extended family linkages, both consanguine (blood) and affine (by marriage) relations. After living in the town for six months, the team realized that most of the members of the town council were part of the extended family of Ernesto. Replacing him as mayor when he resigned after almost 30 years in power was his cousin, and today's new mayor is his daughter. A long line of relatives keeps a close hand on shaping and retaining its power in the town. It is this informal network that also works in the network of drug dealing, retaining power and secrecy.

The patron cannot sit idly by as others do his bidding; he must continue to reciprocate like in giving gifts and political recognition and appointments. An example of such reciprocity is the "potlatch" gift giving at Christmas. This is an abundant giving—an emptying of the Christmas stocking. Thousands of donated presents are publicly wrapped by a crowd of Ernesto's friends and family and ceremoniously given to about 1,500 children in the town. The cheers and applause given to Ernesto are part of the reciprocity tuned to retaining the power and respect for him—the patron. Whereas the Hanson family has extensive political influence on Esperanza, the same principle of reciprocity also extends to the networks of drug trafficking to be discussed in chapter 6. Such tactics for survival are very prevalent in Esperanza.

We found these intangible family connections in all of our data collections. Esperanzans often describe how their sadness, fears, and struggles were countered by family support. Responding in the survey to the question: who protects you from drugs, alcohol, and violence, 57.6 percent said grandparents and parents do. Focus groups and interviews also revealed this connectedness. "My grandparents were always there for me" (65-year-old social worker). "The first persons I go to when I need help are my mom or dad" (17-year-old male). The chief of police described his deep respect for Mexican family values. He explained: "Family—it is the most important thing in my life." These connections extend also to fictive kin. The system, called *compadrazgo* (coparenting), is achieved through baptism of children. This enduring spiritual network of reciprocal relationships provides strong support and protects against loss and sorrow. The kinship network includes relatives and compadres on both sides of the border and is continually strengthened through recurrent migration, such as periodic visits for personal and employment connections. Understanding differences between the deeply connected Mexican families and the highly independent ideal U.S. family system is essential when studying borderland relationships.

Machismo and Marianismo in Traditional Mexican Families

Gender roles in Mexican families are distinct and follow traditional Catholic teachings that say the male has an authoritarian role as provider and controller, while the female has a submissive role as sustainer of the physical, emotional, and spiritual needs of the family. The saying is often heard, *el hombre en la calle; la mujer en la casa* (the man in the streets; the woman in the house). In many cultures women, especially mothers, are the keepers of the culture. Through them knowledge of the rules and contingencies of life are passed on to the next generation. Such a sustaining role is clearly a major contribution women make to the Mexican family. Rodriguez points out that women are strong, enduring figures, hardly the passive weak beings as some describe them (1994:86). In Esperanza, mothers are called the *alma de la casa* (soul of the home)—or *ama de la casa* (love of the home)—both are powerful symbols.

Machismo, a term heard frequently among the participants in interviews and focus groups, expresses the emic meaning of "violent, drinking, bravado, jealous, physical, demanding, womanizing, unfaithful." Oscar Lewis, in *Children of Sanchez*, quotes a male, "In a fight I would never give up or say, 'Enough' even though the other was killing me. I would try to go to my death smiling. This is what we mean by being 'macho,' by being manly" (1961:38). A man in Mexico City said, "We cheat on our wives because we're men and because we want to be macho" (Gutmann 1996:231). Machismo is characterized as an "exaggerated aggressiveness and intransigence in male-to-male relations and arrogance and sexual aggression in male-to-female relationships" (Stevens 1973:90). The death of Hispanic males between the ages of 15 and 45 is blamed on violence stemming from machismo (Kutsche 1984:6–7). Homicides are related to saving face, revenge, or "dissing" (being disrespectful) (Field Notes 1998).

To counterbalance aggressive males the traditional cultural ideal for women is known as *marianismo*. This term describes an ideal female who is "self-sacrificing, weak, timid, passive, fearful, voiceless, abused, rejected" (Rodriguez 1994:85). Hispanic homes are *matrifocal*—males are absent and the female dominates (Rodriguez 1994:80). In such matrifocal households women are *not* timid and passive. Single-headed female households are common in Esperanza, especially in the HUD dwellings, and as we learned, such women are for the most part resilient and resourceful. However, as we also learned, monolingual Spanish-speaking women are often abused and some are voiceless, fearful, and controlled because of circumstances, such as poverty. More will be described about the fearful monolingual women in chapter 7.

Childrearing is a source of power as well as a burden and is the primary role of women whose needs are secondary to those of the children. Raising children is especially a burden for females who seek to develop a career or have an education. It is rare for women to break out of this traditional child-raising model, however, and in a very traditional town as Esperanza such an escape is not easy but can be done, as we learned in Angela's story in chapter 1. Angela finished college, spoke five languages, was a beauty queen, and kicked an alcoholic husband out of their home. She is not passive. Younger generations of females are less likely to follow a traditional marianismo, self-sacrificing model.

Several hypotheses have been raised about the origin of machismo and marianismo. For instance, Ramos (1962) links machismo to a feeling of inferiority as being a conquered people. Machismo, or acting brave and threatening, compensates for these feelings. Kutsche (1984) looks to the effects that the Roman Catholic Church has on male–female sexual relationships. Church dogma states that proper marital sexual relations are for procreation only. So the ideal good wife would submit to sexual relationships only with her husband, as a sacred duty, and only for procreation. She is not actually to enjoy sex, as she is pure. This rule shapes the male's response as one protective of his wife's sacredness. Thus, he is permitted to seek sexual affairs to protect his wife's pure image. One 20-year-old male, a gang member, said, "Macho to me . . . is drinking and fighting and screwing around; it's the Mexican way; it's having *huevos* [balls] it's being *muy hombre* [very manly]. But you keep your wife pure like a virgin." The public behavior and the private behavior merge and result in the sexual prowess of the Hispanic male and the passive submission of the Hispanic female (Kutsche 1984:6–7).

Machismo begins in the folklore of the Aztec woman Malinche, who became the concubine of Cortez. She is also called *La Chingada*, or "the fucked one"—symbolic of the indigenous women who were raped by the Spanish soldiers while the native men were unable to save them. Such an inability to save the women has been viewed as a reason why contemporary males overcompensate to cover their sense of inferiority (Mirande 1997). To Ramos, machismo originates in a prototype of the Mexican male national character known as *pelado*. This word literally means "stripped, naked, plucked" and connotes a nobody. The naked nobody finds compensation in his male genitals, in particular his testicles—his balls. Ramos notes that someone who has little economic power can strut around "holding his genitals saying '*Tengo muchos huevos!*' (I have a lot of balls!)" (1962:60).

Gutmann points to the tension machismo creates in the home and to the resistance to empowering women in a culture that prefers the silent, suffering, perfect mother (1996:165). La chingada is a degrading slang term used only occasionally in Esperanza for a woman who is not behaving honorably, one who does not abide by the code of being an honorable, pure, submissive woman. As one 18-year-old male participant said, "Yeah, you can hit a woman if she's talkin' spank [speaking disrespectfully; confrontational talk]—dissin.' Women are supposed to be pure like the Madonna." In one of the group meetings on domestic violence, a woman said, "I felt I deserved to be hit—that's how my dad treated my mom when she wasn't takin' care of him." In contemporary exchanges between males and females in Mexican households there is still tension between being a passive, ideal wife and an emancipated woman. Some of these exchanges will have deadly consequences, as described in subsequent chapters.

The issue of machismo/marianismo in Esperanza is an important one in its relationship to violence. A few quotes by focus group members give a flavor of the complexity of the issue:

> Mexican men are pure machismo, meaning fighting. And when there is drinking the machismo comes out and there is fighting. I think it is evil, all this fighting, I never saw a man do nothing in the house, but sit and wait for his food or for whatever, king of the casa and then the drinking, the hitting and punching. I know it's in their blood. (56-year-old female)

Another quote links machismo to poverty and immigration.

> I think it is the money, one gets mad because you don't have the money, when a man sees he doesn't bring home enough he feels bad, and he can't work in this country legally so he is macho—he beats his wife. (55-year-old female)

Passing the cultural norm of machismo from one generation to another is expressed by an older female.

> My uncle says to my cousin, "See what I have to do to your mom because she acts bad. You hit her, too, hit your mom when she's bad." So you see the little boy is expected to be macho too, a bruiser. (68-year-old female)

As with all cultural rules, they change over time, and so it is so in Esperanza.

> Machismo . . . that's a thing of the past I think. Divorce, sure, I'm for it and the young priest says to me "get out of that marriage," so we have to stand on our own feet and not let it happen anymore. I have my own job and my self-respect. (28-year-old female)

> More than that, we are warriors, we women. In the Mexican War we fought side by side with the men, with guns and everything. I think we have to be warriors again; we're strong and brave and strong men don't want some weak woman. (17-year-old female)

> Machismo, I'm not for that at all. . . . I think fighting and drinking it's just stupid. You got to get an education and do things in the world, not just sit around and boss women; they are our equals. (16-year-old male)

We found diverse views of male and female roles—some fit the emic viewpoints of passive females and aggressive males, and others do not. An example of nonmarianismo is the female mayor of the town (the last two mayors have been female), and she is not "passive" but is bright, articulate, and assertive. Contrary to expectations, many men of Esperanza are gentle and caring people in their family lives as well as in the public.

THE CHIEF OF POLICE, RESILIENT AND COURAGEOUS

The following life history of a male, illustrates a nonmacho person. He is the chief of police, who gave permission for his story to be told. He grew up with family support and positive role models. The story is simple, but also shows he made decisions and choices based upon a vision of making the town safer.

Family and Social Support

Our family lived in a little farming community; there were about 500–600 people, and I lived there until I was about 5 years old. We lived like a lot of Hispanic families; when my mom and dad got married they built a house right next door to my grandma and grandpa, so I had the benefit of an extended family—I had my mom and dad, my grandmother and grandfather next door plus two aunts and two uncles, and they all had brothers and sisters. I got married when I was almost 30; I followed my dad's advice and waited.

My grandparents were very, very affectionate. My dad lived every day of his life as if it was his last day and my mom was a traditional Mexican mother who was there every day—there was always food. She was a real good cook and had a lot of love and affection. My folks were very, very proud when I became a police officer—there were a lot of other kids my age going to prison, using drugs.

Family Values and Beliefs

My wife has been very influential in helping me. I find satisfaction and an inner peace in spending time with my kids and trying to impart some of the wisdom I received from my parents and others on to them. My wife keeps me centered in being a person, a husband, a father, away from the chief's role. I believe in God, in fact probably more now than I did 10 years ago.

Job History and Influential People and Events in His Life

I began as a police dispatcher when I was 20. Every day was different. I liked the hot pursuits—a lot of adrenaline rushes—it was really neat. I worked as a police officer for the City of Tucson for 25 years. I worked with people I really admired, for instance, one had very simple values. He said "You need to step on somebody's shoes without ruining the shine." That really stuck with me as when you're dealing with people, you have to know when to back off sometimes, you're hitting the wrong buttons, or you're just not communicating because the chemistry isn't right. I'm trained to size up people. You know how to evaluate and to size up body language and get a feeling if these people are sincere or fake or do they want something.

Goals in Role of Chief of Police

I'd like to bring the city crime rate to more normal levels, and tomorrow we will announce a 50 percent reduction in 2 years. When I came, I came with a mission, not because I was looking for a job. It seemed that crime had been out of control for decades. Old people and kids would suffer.

You don't see many crack houses operating any more. When they do, we close them down immediately. I think we got the upper hand on crime now, rather than the criminal having the upper hand. Crime will always exist, but if we whittle it down a bit to the lowest levels, then I'll think we've done it. Also we want to help people feel more comfortable about living and consequently staying here. I believe about 50 percent of the people live in rental properties—the number of new homes that were built last year surpasses the numbers of any other year, by far. We're trying to create a safe environment, particularly in the schools where kids don't have to fear gang members and don't fear walking to school. We showed that we were able to reduce crime, and one person didn't do any of these things alone; it takes a lot of people.

Social Institutions

In order to grasp the wholeness of the community (the individual family and social institutions) we will describe key institutions that are protective entities in the town. The police, courts, churches, schools, safe havens, and services for the addicted and the homeless are all social institutions that operate as positive forces that control violence.

The Police

The twenty-seven-member police force is fairly stable. It has one female officer who has been the assistant chief for several years. The department has a small two-cell jail and a two-person dispatcher system. In the police station are video monitors for viewing the action from cameras placed in hot spots such as main roads, bars, and businesses around town. Watching these key areas structures a 24/7 surveillance of the community. A popular bike patrol also keeps watch on everyday activities on streets and alleys, and the patrollers answer citizens' questions. It is common to see an officer surrounded by kids, simply talking with them. The police force includes a detective division, a domestic violence specialist, and SWAT and GITEM (Gang Intelligence Team Enforcement Mission) teams that collaborate with Tucson and state police forces. The police building sits next to the court building and backs up to the fire department. All of these departments are part of a city hall building. The Sam Lena Library is also housed here, so these municipal buildings, on the main street, set an attractive stage for Esperanza.

At one point, the Chief brought a police officer (who had been a SWAT team supervisor and dog handler) into custody on drug charges. He was arrested for receiving $200,000 for an airport pickup and an additional $9,000 for transporting what was believed to be cocaine. After his trial and conviction, the former officer went to prison. The Chief had received a tip that "You've got a crooked cop." He hated to hear that as such a crime can destroy a department, but he faced the issue with courage and as a role model for all; he arrested the bad cop.

The Chief set into play a plan of "cleaning up" the town. His success, some said, is due to sharing a similar background with many of the townspeople, such as being Hispanic and a graduate of the local high school. The Chief also has personality traits that make him an effective leader. He is an excellent speaker with high energy and an open, sharing attitude. His forceful, honorable way of handling some difficult policing events has earned him admiration from townspeople and others in the state.

Courts

Charlie, a legal anthropologist, investigated the courts. He found that Spanish-speaking attorneys are the norm. The chief judge is a Hispanic male who resolves disputes in a way that is respectful to all involved. The chief judge grew up on the border and lived in poverty as a "homeboy" and understands the life challenges of the poor.

The chief judge has a culturally appropriate role in condoning certain types of behavior and lecturing violators of the law on a personal level. His attitude of respect is important, as he gives the Hispanic (and other) defendants the opportunity to speak out on personal issues regarding their cases. The chief judge can be scathingly negative about domestic violence, and he chastises Hispanic males for acting dishonorably to women. It seems that his lectures are a more severe punishment than any sentence. Hispanic people traditionally have respect (*respecto*) for figures of authority, and this works in favor of the judge's admonitions about domestic violence.

Some cultural norms distinguish Esperanza's court system from that of other U.S. cities and towns. The rules of evidence often become more lax in their interpretation as these relate to established Mexican cultural norms in the town. From a power perspective, the Esperanza judge puts himself in the place of a citizen or an extended family leader, at a level more comfortable for the Mexican defendants and plaintiffs. The judge attempts to understand how a reasonable man or woman would resolve a particular situation within the town's prevailing cultural standards.

Another positive direction taken by the courts is the establishment of a Community Justice Board as a part of the Community Outreach Program. This program means that young people who break the law for the first time with misdemeanors deal with a Justice Board composed of parents, grandparents, and people who have family backgrounds in handling such problems. The young offenders become part of the community by listening to the victims who were hurt by his offense. The punishment for these lawbreakers is doing community service in their neighborhood, with the hope that such youthful offenders will be less likely to repeat the crime and to hurt people they know and care about.

Churches

Santa Cruz Catholic Church

The dominant religion in Esperanza is Catholicism, although views and alliances are changing, as the evangelical movement in Hispanic populations becomes more prominent. The main Catholic Church, the Santa Cruz Cathe-

Santa Cruz Catholic Church

dral, sits on the periphery of Esperanza, but it has great influence on the social and spiritual life of the community. It is the oldest church on the south side. With two daily and four Sunday masses, plus a parochial school, the parishioners have a very active religious life. In the Catholic services, attendance is about 1:8 males to females, and children are a part of the service attendance. The priests are not Hispanic but rather from Italy or Ireland, and they live on the premises. Seven nuns associated with the church live in a nearby private house. A parish nurse program works in the community with other social programs, such as teenage pregnancy counseling. Weekly attendance in combined masses averages 2,000, but only about one-third of the attendees is from Esperanza. Children who attend the parochial school and their parents are expected to attend church services at Santa Cruz. The cathedral has been the center for numerous peace marches and meetings about controlling violence. It is known that gang members come here to confess their sins, and they are said to always cross their chests as they pass by the cathedral.

Capillas

Two smaller neighborhood Catholic churches, or *capillas* (San Antonio and de Guadalupe) have special religious roles in the town, especially for more traditional townspeople. Daily, in the heat of summer or coolness of winter, you see the *señoras* [women], heads covered with black shawls, walking slowly to the Capilla de Guadalupe in the middle of Esperanza. They come to pray, to witness the statue of Our Lady shed tears; they know that miracles are happening. The older women do what their mothers and grandmothers always did—they depend upon the patron saint of all Mexico.

The less-acculturated women (mostly monolingual Spanish-speaking) rely upon Our Lady of Guadalupe as well as other saints for comfort and caring. They identify with Our Lady who "weeps with them and . . . has suffered injustice and the violent death of her son. She stands among them to reflect on who they are as mother, woman, *morena* (brown-skinned), mestiza (mixed blood), and gives them a place in a world that negates them" (Isasi-Díaz 1993:145). "I wait for her answer in my heart, I really feel that she hears me and understands, peace of mind, gentle caring, loving, comfort; she brings me happiness" (Isasi-Díaz 1993:163). Our Lady of Guadalupe is the Mexican Virgin Mary. She is the national symbol of resistance to assimilation and is viewed as essential for Mexican cultural survival. Our Lady represents the qualities of love, comfort, and an ever-present mother (Rodriguez 1994). Esperanzan women of all ages, even of Protestant faith, express dependence on the Virgin.

San Nicholas Indian Center (Blessed Kateria Tekakwitha)

The Center, a hub of many activities for the local Tohono O'odham tribal members who are Catholic, includes a weekly worship service. The altar depicts the image of Kateria Tekakwitha, known as the Lily of the Mohawk, a Catholic nun who has been nominated for canonization as the first Native American saint. The Center has a feeding program, health care facility, and provides support for those living a new urban lifestyle away from their reservation.

Protestant Churches

Beginning in the 1970s, sweeping across South America was a movement to educate the poor. Paulo (also spelled Pablo or Pavlo) Freire, one of the movement's leaders, believed literacy was a way toward liberation from poverty (Freire 1986). The sweeping reform was accompanied by a new liberation theology that advocates for the poor, the dispossessed, and powerless in society (Glittenberg 1994). As part of the overall liberation, many Hispanics began defecting from the Catholic church to Protestant denominations. It is estimated that each year 60,000 leave (Hughes 1992). Andrew Greeley, a priest, states, "the loss of almost one out of ten members of its largest ethnic group is an ecclesiastical failure of unprecedented proportions" (1988:62).

Approximately 11 Protestant churches offer services within the boundaries of Esperanza. Some have memberships of less than 100, and fewer than 50 people may attend services on a Sunday morning. The average collection is about $100 a week. Most of the clergy have other employment, so they are part-time preachers. In the larger Protestant churches, the attendance is an equal number of males and females, and in several of these churches, children attend separate services or are cared for in a nursery. In all of the churches, including the Catholic except the capillas, most attendees live out of town, and in the African American churches, they come from as far away as Phoenix. None of the Protestant clergy lives in Esperanza, except an African American couple who live in the basement of their church.

A new evangelical church opened in 1999 in a large warehouse, attracting hundreds of worshipers. Each Sunday the warehouse is packed with standing-room only. Men are dressed in dark suits, white shirts, and colorful ties; the women are elegantly dressed and wear high heels. Children, who also are well-dressed, attend with their parents. Informants say about 60 percent of the Hispanic population is shifting from Catholicism to becoming evangelical, but observations do not substantiate that perception. Still, the movement is very obvious. Perhaps it is because of the influx of divorced women who are not allowed to take communion in the Catholic church, so they leave the church as did Angela when her first husband died.

Two predominantly African American churches are active in the town. One evangelical church, Victory Outreach, is especially focused on reaching people with drinking and/or drug problems. A storefront church called Church on the Street opened next to the CEPP office on the main street for those with substance abuse problems, but it closed its door in 2005. About three churches a year move in or out of Esperanza, leaving a balance of around 13 churches in the town.

Does becoming Protestant change or influence the Mexican family? The perception of one employer is a common theme. When asked about employing people of different faiths, he says, "Give me an evangelical any day. The Catholics are always off to some funeral or some fiesta, but the evangelical will work any day, and he doesn't drink or chase women." Females who joined Protestant churches said, "I feel free now," and "I'm now a member where the preachers are married, too."

Pastor Thomas, Protestant Pastor and Member of the CEPP Advisory Board

My wife and I came to Esperanza because we wanted to come to a place that needed the Gospel. So many people walked in our lives that seemed to have lost a purpose for living. They were into drugs and alcohol and lots of depression. We looked around and thought Esperanza might be a place to serve, as there are not many African American pastors in Tucson. We moved four years ago, and live here in the church basement. This way we're always here.

Violence, yes, we've faced several very tense situations. Sometimes it has been just a homeless person wandering by and tries to come in, but there have been attempts to rob us, too. Afraid, but not terrified. Most of them are on drugs, and they don't know what they're doing. For my part, I believe most of violence comes from drugs.

Drugs are evil. They take good sense away—and of course selling to the poor. Why people think selling drugs is a way of life, I can't figure. The money isn't honest, it's against the law, and whenever you have groups of illegal people, you have trouble. They are always looking out for the next take, and you can't trust anyone. The only solution I believe is faith—building on the love of Christ.

Women who are victims of domestic violence, I find most of their men are alcoholics—seems the two go together. We just simply love them all and try to show there is forgiveness and a different way of life. Some days we do get discouraged, as the problems are so big. Most of all I worry about the children; they don't have good role models—some don't have a home, a steady home, and many, no fathers. Whom do they trust? On Sundays we offer an alternative, come to trust Jesus. We have all shades of people in our congregation . . . and they come and sing and [experience] fellowship. We have a big lunch every Sunday and we hug and love one another—no one is left out.

My wish is to get some sort of good jobs for the people, mostly the men who have lost hope. If we could have good training programs to help teach them skills and ways to feel good about themselves, that would be my wish. Unemployment just takes security away, just makes you doubt yourself. Then they look for help in the bottle or a drug. There has to be a better way.

Schools

Educational institutions in Esperanza are: two elementary schools, a parochial school, two middle "feeder" schools, and one "feeder" high school. The two elementary schools, Mission View Elementary and Ochoa Elementary, are different. Mission View draws children from the "marginalized, migrating population." The children attending are often the "couch kids"—they don't have regular beds to sleep in and may sleep on a different couch every night as their family finds shelter—and sometimes arrive at school without shoes and coats. Ochoa Elementary enrolls children from the more stable population. Feeder schools are those outside the town's limits, where children are bussed in and out. A magnet school, Borton's, is just outside the town's borders, but 51 percent of the students are required to be from the "neighborhood," that is, from Esperanza. There is a Head Start school and another private child-care facility. Schools are important cultural resources for extending the rules of the home and society.

Bilingual Education: A Cultural Value

Bilingual education has been debated in many venues, but in Esperanza teachers' preferred approach to learning English is through total immersion; classes should be taught in English only, as one teacher says:

> Children from Esperanza do not have a language bank, that is, they have not achieved mastery in their first language [Spanish] by the time they get to school. Spanish-speaking children sometimes identify objects by function, not by name. [For example, a child may ask, "Will you give me something to drink with?" rather than saying, "May I have a cup?"]

She attributes this lack of language skills

> to cultural child-rearing techniques that de-emphasize teaching children the names of objects and teaches, rather, only their function. If the child starts to school in a Spanish-only language classroom and continues in one throughout high school—these children have a deficit throughout life, as they never build that language bank.

To many, learning and speaking English is symbolic of caving in to the powerful Anglo culture and denial of one's cultural roots. At homes, Spanish

School with community art

is viewed as the language of the soul. Learning to speak and read English is necessary for success in school or work outside the home. Tension exists in the community where retaining Mexican roots clashes with escaping from poverty. To be upwardly mobile, the ability to speak, read, and write English is essential.

In spite of opinions about the importance of learning English, mothers of monolingual Spanish-speaking students oppose bilingual education, saying, "This keeps my child from advancing—and maybe forces them to drop out." Spanish-speaking students who attend a bilingual high school find they can learn to speak English, but only about half can read or write it. Such a finding underscores what is known about high dropout rates when students are basically illiterate in English.

BELLA, A PRINCIPAL AND MEMBER OF THE CEPP ADVISORY BOARD

I've been the principal of this school for nine years and it's something I always wanted to do—to help make a difference. This school is Hispanic in its culture. All the artwork, the music, the food is Hispanic. I know this makes the children feel valued—like they count. So many come who speak only Spanish, and they feel so ignorant and unwanted. But this is a place for feeling good . . . and for learning.

I have open hours for all parents who want to come and talk with me. All the staff speaks Spanish, and they know some of the problems the parents have . . . like working two jobs and wanting their kids to be successful. We have a school nurse, too, who works with families on health care. We care for the whole family.

Violence

PeaceBuilders is an international peace process, building from a curriculum for teaching elementary school children ways of self-esteem, empowerment to resist violent reactions to confrontations. The grades 1–6 and culture of the whole school were targeted for change. Dennis Embry, professor of psychology, University of Arizona, was the project director of PeaceBuilders in Ochoa Elementary School, funded by CDC in 1994. Many positive outcomes have been published on this program.

Yes, I believe it starts in the home, with all the frustrations and poverty. But I think it can be unlearned. We have a responsibility to teach new ways of dealing with frustrations. The PeaceBuilder program is making a difference. We teach children ways to handle frustration. Let me show you some of the posters the children have made. [These pieces of art were placed all over the walls, alive with color and symbols of life, such as piñatas, flowers, trees, and happy faces.] They take these PeaceBuilder lessons home with them, too. It's a wholesome way of facing the facts. And we talk about drugs and why not to use them, right from the first grade. It's so easy to lose track of these little ones. No, we're not perfect and we still grieve that Oscar, one of our star students, was killed in the gang shoot-out. But we are doing something positive in his memory. Come and see the Peace Garden (about a half block in dimension) that will be here for generations in memory of Oscar.

We spend 30 minutes walking through the Garden and reading inscriptions on the walls about peace, nonviolent goals, and love written by the children. Here is an oasis in the middle of the desert, as students and families have planted beautiful flowers and shrubs like a labyrinth for solo meditation. Colorful benches are placed around the garden for a pleasant pause.

Including Parents in Education

We include the parents in lots of ways. They come to the bilingual classes that help them teach their children new ways of communicating. So many are undocumented people who are illiterate themselves. It's a constant worry as they migrate around so quickly. Sometimes we have a child in class only two weeks, and they are gone—perhaps as migrant workers. If they could just stay one solid year, it would make a difference. In the other elementary school they have some young girls who are mothers—so they have parenting classes in the elementary school, and child care. Somehow we need to reach them earlier so their choices are more powerful. We try to work on self-esteem and self-responsibility, but our work is so interrupted.

Wish List?

I just wish we could help them out of poverty and ignorance. I can't help on that first part, but I can make a difference on the second, the ignorance. Architectural students at the university have designed the new grounds for the school. The design is to have it look like an oasis, too, and to be a place for lifelong learning, not just for the children but also for the families. It has received money through the Weed and Seed projects and is a sign of hope. I never lose hope or the vision; that's always on my wish list, as some days the problems seem overwhelming, but there is always tomorrow—a new day.

Las Artes

Las Artes is an alternative school for dropout kids and for townspeople. Pato is an art teacher at the school, and his brother is on the CEPP Advisory Board.

PATO'S MISSION AT LAS ARTES

Years ago we had little but spirit then, now we have received funding from the
Weed and Seed project. Now we can start more projects. These kids are all
dropouts, they really didn't have choices as I see it. Here it's to feel good about
themselves. Most have been abused somewhere along their lives. Most have
been in trouble with the law more than once. Just see 'em as kids who need a
chance. Here we give them guidance but they are on their own to make something that is not just about them but for the community, too. We do practical
projects—like the sidewalk benches, have you seen them? [Yes and they are very
colorful.] Yeah, we try to keep the designs Mexican—the colors of Mexico.
Once the kids get a feeling for the art, they can't be stopped—like a horse out of
the barn—they don't want to stop. Some of them never had a good word said
about them. Now they see what they do is really good—we don't make up the
compliments—we keep it to the real . . . no garbage here—that wouldn't work.

Problems? Yeah, we have 'em; sometimes kids try you out, to see how far
they can go—just to see—if you really care about THEM. We have had some
real successes . . . like the poem I want to show you. Okay? It's from this guy—
guess he's 15—I tell you it made me cry, I just couldn't hold it back. He says this
art has given him a chance again—he really wanted to kill himself. His dad and
brothers beat him, guess they all picked on him like a wounded chicken. He
was really shy when he came. Sometimes I helped him and we didn't talk, just
did the art together. Slowly he came around and said how much he liked art.

I asked him about his plans when he left here. He didn't have any—then we
started to talk about life—just ideas of about being honest and hard working
and going to school. He couldn't read when he started but then he did and
passed his GED. You see he's going to college—to major in art. He has real talent. [Pato teared.]

Come here, you've gotta see this. [We walk to a large mural on a wall.] This
is the mural that the old señoras are doing. See, they're putting in their own tile
squares about their own history and how they got to Esperanza. It is really a ter-
rific chance for them to put it out in the public . . . all they went through to get
here. Most can't read or write, but they can make the mural and get credit for

Social service agency building

their brave lives. I just gave them the idea one day and here they are—about 30 of them. It is going to be a wall we put next to the Library. Can you believe it?

It is a wall about 20 feet by 30 feet, very colorful with individual tiles, each depicting the life of an immigrant woman. Las Artes continues to bring hope to all types of people in need of advocates, respect, and new opportunities.

Safe Havens for At-Risk Youth

There are four safe havens for at-risk youth in the town, now funded through donations and Weed and Seed grants. The organizations, House of Neighborly Services, John Valenzuela Center, Project Y.E.S. (Youth Enrichment Support), and *Voz en el Desierto* (Voice in the Desert), are all almost equal in size and mission. Their programs include many activities for kids, such as swimming, movies, arts and crafts, cooking classes, fitness and weight training, Girl Scouts, bike repair, and karate. Skill-building and self-esteem educational programs are offered. Free lunches supplied by the school district are served to children ages 2 to 18. Keeping the kids in school is a high priority. After-school activities include classes on using computers and sports for older youth—basketball, baseball, and weight-lifting. Baile Folklórico, a Mexican folk-dance program for grades 4 through 12, is also well received. Students study the history of the various dances and the regions of Mexico where they originated, learn the dances, and make their own dance costumes. The young people perform in many places around Tucson and the region.

GED classes are part of the program and a charter school has begun. One haven includes counseling for families of murdered children (will be described in Chapter 6) as well as self-esteem and social-skills programs for gang members. The project offers several parenting classes both in English and in Spanish, and there are classes for grandparents who are raising their grandchildren.

Centro del Sur is part of a larger county health clinic that also has a boxing ring that has been here for over 22 years. It is also supported by Weed and Seed grant, and it is viewed as an alternative to gang activities and as a source for social skill building.

Sam Lena Library, the local library built in 1986, is a beautiful, well-run, culturally rich repository of Mexican history, handling over 6,200 checkouts per month, with 75 percent of these pieces being in the Spanish language. The library holds over 25,000 titles and has the largest holding of Spanish titles in books and videos in the region. During the many times we visited the library, it always had a feeling of activity, with at least 20 people of various ages and ethnic identities present. Volunteers offer health programs, such as ones that teach women breast self-examination. Through Weed and Seed funds, the library is being doubled in size and continues as a strong, positive influence within the community.

Social Services and Treatment Centers

The services for substance abusers and the homeless are abundant. Casa María, a soup kitchen, has food supplied from over 200 churches in the city with rotating responsibility for providing the soup and sandwiches given daily for approximately 1,000 meals. (See chapter 7 for more information about this social institution.)

There are three treatment centers for people with addictive problems, La Frontera Center, The Salvation Army and The Gospel Rescue Mission, and a large VA Hospital. La Frontera Center, a state mental health center especially for Hispanic people, offers multiple psychotherapy programs but no in-patient services. Programs meet a wide range of mental health needs including: alcohol abuse, child abuse, domestic violence, post traumatic stress disorders, and crisis management. The satellite program at the Tohono O'Odham reservation deals with alcoholism and drug abuse. It is a hub for cooperation with other agencies. La Frontera partnered with Esperanza police in the Domestic Violence Zero Tolerance Program (will be described in Chapter 6). Esperanza leaders were very influential in getting this center started in 1984, and they maintain a strong voice in its programs.

The Salvation Army treatment and residential settlement is three-story center on the main street and employs 60 people, including professional staff. A resale store sits next door; it is bright, clean, and busy with many customers for the used merchandise, attractively displayed and reasonably priced. Profit from the resale store plus donations support treatment that is primarily a 12-step program. Residents, if working, pay a portion

Belinda Acosta, nurse practitioner and interviewer

of their room and board and there are no restrictions or expectations for profession of faith.

The Gospel Rescue Mission is home for many transients as an emergency shelter for men. As a drug and alcohol rehabilitation center two programs are offered: one is 90 days and the other is 180 days. Managed by Christian people there is a strong spiritual emphasis in the treatment program. Residents receive three meals a day, chapel service, a change of clothing, a shower, a shave, a shared room, advice on employment, self-help counsel, and the opportunity to stay up to three days. Women are housed in a separate unit called Bethany House, and they may have children with them.

Views of Ordinary People

What do ordinary people—the neighbors, the resilient people who have lived in Esperanza longer than five years—think about living in Esperanza? What do they think about violence and how to cope with it? Eighty-nine percent of the people who took part in the household survey believe the police are protecting the community from violence, and 33 percent feel the courts and 29 percent feel the churches are protective. When asked which people help the most, the response is: parents/grandparents, 58 percent; neighbors, 50 percent; and teachers, 48 percent.

In regard to their personal responsibilities for maintaining a safe community, participants' viewpoints are similar. The expressed beliefs come mostly from older women, the keepers of the culture. A few examples illustrate how important personal responsibility can be.

> The worst thing is that we stay quiet. It would help if we knew the laws. No one helps, no one talks to nobody, we need to be involved. (57-year-old female)

> We should clean up the place. If we live in a dirty place, full of bottles and syringes and the houses not painted, we've got to clean it up. (52-year-old female)

> Because you live in low income doesn't mean you have to live messy—I take pride. The community itself has to help itself. We pamper our children too much. We need to set limits. We need to be there for each other. My neighbor watches out and you gotta have someone to confide in and actually trust. (25-year-old female)

Comments about the representatives of social institutions that offer support illustrate that people are respectful of the institutions and rely on them.

> The Chief, he knows the area, you can't fool him; he really looks out for us. (67-year-old male)

> A young priest told me, "You cannot continue together—you need to separate, there's too much violence." (55-year-old female)

Yes, the younger priests seem to know more, times are changing. (23-year-old female)

A life story illustrates the importance of both strong social institutions and personal responsibility.

SEÑORA MARTÍNEZ, AN ORDINARY WOMAN

Señora Martínez is a member of the monolingual women focus group. She has lived in Esperanza for about 50 years and is now 78 years old. Señora lives in the HUD elder apartments, a three-story, well-maintained building with an elevator and balconies. An iron fence surrounds a garden shared by all the residents. Señora's one-bedroom apartment is filled with green plants and is nicely furnished. Señora is active on the HUD board and is a member of the Capilla de Guadalupe. She has been a widow for over 15 years, and before moving to the apartments five years ago, she lived in a small house on the west side of town. Her oldest son and daughter visit her daily, and her other five children see her on most weekends.

> I'm safe and have good neighbors. We do a lot of social things together, and I go to the Capilla almost every day. My social security check covers my expenses; that's all I need. Esperanza has changed from a *muy tranquila lugar* [quiet place] in the '50s when we first moved here to now a lot of drugs and shootings. I worry about my grandkids—too many temptations for them. They aren't satisfied any more with some simple things in life, like going to church and singing; they want to watch TV all the time and drive in their cars. One is planning to go to the university and one to the community college.
>
> I keep up with things in Esperanza and I watch you across the street. I think you're doing a good job, just trying to help us to be safer and find ways for women not to be such victims. I'm glad I was in your focus group as I wanted to tell you that some men are good men, not all are machos. My Tony was a good man; he respected his mother . . . always respected me. He never wanted to live in the streets—you know what I mean—to chase after other women. He would say, "Why go in the streets lookin' for love . . . I have my love right here." He was respectful of our daughters, too, always wanting them to go to school, too. Neither of us went to high school, but we kept up on the news. He was a hard worker all of his life.
>
> Violence—too many guns and too much drinking. I see it all the time just watching the families across the street. That's one thing we didn't have in our family. My dad didn't drink but once in a while a beer, and my mom didn't even drink beer. I have never liked the taste so that's no problem. Our kids don't drink either, I think it runs in families 'cause I never preached against it. And drugs, no we didn't allow any of that in the house. It's a waste of money, I think that's why there's so much violence. I've seen the worst across the street. I hear drugs are being sold right here in [HUD housing] but I don't pay any attention to it. I hear people in the hallways at night and early morning sometimes, but I just mind my own business.
>
> When we lived in our house on 9th Avenue there were problems. There were gangs there and lots of times I was really afraid. We didn't have enough police

then and some of the gangs ruled the neighborhood. I stayed out of any trouble with them—just didn't look their way. After Tony died I moved into the senior apartments 'cause I was scared most of the time alone. Esperanza is better now. Streetwalkers are gone, and the place looks clean—not so much trash. There's good shopping right here in the town now with the supermarket. The crack houses are gone—they were such a mess. And our police are good people, they come when you call. The Chief is one of us, you know he went to school right here. He's a good man. It's a good place to live.

Community Rituals

Groups of people reinforce their ties, cultural rules, and norms through community rituals, patterns of behavior that demonstrate high esteem for the values of the culture. Two of the most common community rituals are parades and fiestas. Parades place in public view those in high status who represent values that reinforce the rules of the group (the town). In Esperanza, parades are frequent—about every three months—and include patriotic parades, kids' parades, parades against drugs, and so forth. People from all ranks and statuses, as well as both genders and all ages, participate either in the parades or as observers. Parades reconfirm and celebrate the town's people.

The fiestas in Mexican culture usually have a theme, celebrating a date (like Cinco de Mayo) or a geography (like Norteña—for northern Mexico). Most of the people present are Hispanic but other groups are welcomed, too. Fiestas also occur frequently and have the same pattern of restating the Hispanic way of celebrating uniqueness. Music is typically played with a bass fiddle, fiddles (violins), trumpets, and drums. The dance is a type of Texas two-step with everyone joining in—all ages. Males typically wear their white cowboy hats throughout the dance, and most wear cowboy boots. Children join as early as they can walk and are carried or danced with on the dance floor. Yes, there is plenty of liquor—mostly beer. The purpose is to have fun as a group, a Mexican family, and celebrate long into the night.

Another gathering that reinforces Hispanic cultural norms is a funeral, which will be described in chapter 6 on violence, when funerals for gang victims are described.

Summary

Centuries of discrimination, broken promises, and harsh environmental conditions shape the resilient people that today live in Esperanza. Wars and land disputes left early settlers of the town landless. But families survived because of cultural connections. More recently social institutions, such as the police, courts, churches, schools, and helping agencies are sensitive and responsive to the needs of the community, including those based on ethnicity. This support solidifies and maximizes Hispanic connections. This chapter traced events that led to a transformation through civil movements and the influx of outside, federal grant money that enhanced the physical appearance of the town. But it is individuals from Esperanza who framed and promoted the changes. The leaders we interviewed, all seem to have a sense of mission or a calling that through their work they can reduce violence and bring back hope. The structure of resilience includes the whole civil society from personal commitments, missions, and dreams to societal responsibilities. From individuals and groups we also gather a sense of hope.

Chapter 3

The Culture of Alcohol and Drug Use and Abuse

> Latinos . . . we're celebrating a lot—everything, it's our way, you know, and drinking, too. Yeah, it's okay with the family, at a party, at a wedding. It's okay to be drunk. But not be by yourself; that's not good, not okay.
> —18-year-old male in a focus group

The people of Esperanza explain violence as linked with alcohol and drug use and abuse. Is this true? What patterns support such beliefs? What are the tensions between conforming to cultural rules and exhibiting violence? Have patterns of alcohol use changed from the past? If so, how and why? Before turning to selected narratives of some of the people living in Esperanza to help us answer these questions, we offer some foundational information about alcohol and drugs.

Background Information on Alcohol and Drugs

Alcohol and drugs are *psychoactive substances*—they act on the central nervous system and alter the physical structure and functioning of the brain. Psychoactive drugs are not just the illegal drugs or prescription medications. They include easily obtainable substances like caffeine and nicotine. Psychoactive drugs can be depressants (alcohol, marijuana, morphine, heroin, barbiturates, and volatile inhalants), stimulants (caffeine, methamphetamine, crack, cocaine, nicotine, phencyclidine [PCP]), or hallucinogens (mescaline, LSD, and Ecstasy), which have both adaptive and maladaptive outcomes. The adaptive outcomes may be a feeling of well-being, inclusion, relaxation, or stimulation. The maladaptive effects may be anger, depression, anxiety, or suspicion. Cognition, the controller of emotions and behavior, may be clouded or confused. Suicide and/or homicide or other types of violent behavior may be the outcome of psychoactive drug use.

Alcohol, or liquor, a legal substance for people over 21 years old, can be made from almost any fermented fruit and other plants with sugar content. People drink liquor to celebrate, to mourn, to integrate, to socialize, to reciprocate, to forget, and to deal with stress. Drugs (some legal and others illegal) can be made from plants, animals, and inorganic chemicals easily found throughout the world. Reasons for using drugs usually fit within one of two categories: remedial, to deal with psychological or physical illness; and symbolic, to associate oneself with a group or with society as a whole. For instance in a drug community, sharing paraphernalia and drugs symbolizes being in the network (Singer 2006a). Or at events like funerals, drugs may be used symbolically for connecting with the deceased.

Drug (including alcohol) addiction is characterized by a craving for and compulsive use of one or more substances. Why some people become addicted to drugs (all types including caffeine, alcohol, nicotine, etc.) is debated. There are two schools of thought: one is that addictions are genetically predisposed and the other is that addictions are learned behavior. Now that the human genome is completely mapped, many genetic studies are being done but have not yet reached a conclusion. Some researchers believe, however, that the genetic influence on alcoholism is exaggerated, that although genetics is an important ingredient in human behavior, other factors are involved that outweigh being able to statistically calculate cause and effect. For example, the diversity and malleability of cultural environments defy simple explanations of human behavior (Peele & DeGrandpre 2004).

In studying causes of alcohol abuse, "Drinking at an Early Age Leads to Alcohol Abuse," a report from the National Institute on Alcohol Abuse and Alcoholism (NIAAA) found that drinking at an early age leads to alcohol abuse. This conclusion is based on a national sample of 43,000 adults showing that if a person begins drinking before the age of 15 he or she is four times more likely to develop alcohol dependence than those who begin drinking at age 21. Another study published in 2001 found that the early onset of drinking is associated with frequent heavy drinking and risks of injury later in life (NIH in Balkin 2004:52, 54).

In contrast, Dwight Heath, a renowned anthropologist whose decades of research on the cultural norms of drugs and alcohol use is important for this study, concludes differently, saying that factors other than age predispose underage children toward having drinking problems when they become adults. He points out that in the U.S. it is illegal to drink under the age of 21, so that those who are underage drinkers are persons who behave in other risky and deviant ways as well. He cites that in communities where people are socialized to drink at an early age, there are also norms for maintaining sobriety and avoiding drunkenness (Heath 2004:56). The person who deviates from the norms, who is a risk taker, is the person who develops drinking problems. When examining the cultural norms within Esperanza it is important to keep Heath's conclusions in mind. Not all adolescents are drinking, but the ones who are deviant and risk takers, perhaps raised in deviant family environments, are the underage drinkers.

Addicts need medical attention and care, and more research is needed as to why some drug and alcohol users become addicted while others do not. Are some genetic codes at work here? Do environmental factors play a role in addictions? Are some ethnic groups more prone toward addictions? These and many more questions about drug addiction need answers.

Although our study was not designed to find out whether addiction is inherited or is learned behavior, personal views about the issue surfaced in our study. Several participants believe that alcoholism "runs in families" and "it's in your blood." Yet most would agree that genetics, influence from families, and the cultural shaping that occurs from migrating all affect whether a person uses drugs and to what extent.

Drinking and Drugs in Esperanza

Consuming alcoholic beverages has a long history in the southwestern part of the U.S. Historical records note that before the Conquest, the Aztecs used fermented juice from agave plants, calling it pulque. In fact many alcoholic drinks such as tequila and homebrewed beers were made from maize, pods from mesquite trees, and fruit from cacti. The aim for drinking fermented and/or distilled potions was to integrate one's self with the sacred (Bruman 2000). Cultural patterns of alcohol and drug use are part of the fabric of the people living in Esperanza. The people define what "drugs" are; what they are used for; when, why, how much, and with whom they are used; and what kind of behavior is expected and tolerated within the society. These patterns are cultural, not psychological or physical, and are beliefs and values of the people.

As we look at the cultural norms in Esperanza, we are reminded that the majority of the population are poor, undocumented immigrants. A number of studies (Alvarez 1995; Baca 1979; Markides & Coreil 1986; Montiel 1975; Romano 1973) point out that immigrants find rapid assimilation (i.e., learning the language, finding a job, understanding expectations, etc.) into mainstream culture to be extremely stressful. Alcohol and drugs are often used to relieve stress. One immigrant says, "I get drunk to forget my troubles."

Examining patterns of drinking and drug use discloses the emic rules that govern behavior, which all participating members understand and live by (Knipe 1995). For instance, in Mexican families the values of familism and respect perpetuate the influence parental drinking has on the children. If children see drinking as normal behavior, because their parents drink, and associate it with family connectedness, they may start drinking at an early age, or at least not deem alcohol consumption and its effects as unusual or wrong. Those who do protest drinking among family members, do so at the risk of loosening their bonds with their family. Although negative consequences may follow violation of family norms, some children do rebel (Johnson and Johnson 1999), as did Lupita and Isabela (whose narratives appear later in the chapter), who did not want to be drunks like their family members.

Use and Misuse of Alcohol and Drugs

In most societies where everyday consumption of alcohol is common, it is done in very small quantities and is not associated with morality (Knipe 1995:25). As Heath points out, "a major finding, in cross-cultural perspective, is that alcohol-related problems are really rare, even in many societies where drinking is customary, and drunkenness is common place" (1987:45). For instance, when describing the norms of alcohol use in Esperanza, the response usually is:

> Everybody drinks beer, but it's not really a liquor. A hard liquor is dis-
> tilled like tequila or whiskey and used just for holidays—beer is for every
> day—it's not bad—it's normal.

And norms for marijuana use are similar to those for beer.

> Everybody uses marijuana, that's not really a drug 'cause everybody uses
> it—at home, in school, on the street, it's normal. It makes you feel good
> and part of the group." (17-year-old female)

> Drugs like meth or cocaine—or heroin—that's different, that's bad 'cause
> they are illegal and cause problems. They cause you to do stupid things
> and get strung out. You don't think right, and you can go to prison. (18-
> year-old male)

> Some people are different and can use booze just once in a while and oth-
> ers get addicted, they have to have it. It's the same for hard drugs; some
> people get hooked and others never do. Most can stop and start—just
> using now and then. (48-year-old female)

Thus, people do not necessarily base judgments about alcohol and drug use on a broad issue of legality, but instead they look at how drugs and alcohol affect certain people to determine whether they think it's appropriate or normal.

As mentioned previously, the reasons people use alcohol and drugs are hard to explain and include many factors (e.g., genetic, physical predisposition, psychological traits and states, and cultural patterns of use). Lashley (1998), a molecular geneticist, believes the link between substance abuse and biological variation in and between ethnic groups may reveal patterns of propensities. At this time, the relationship is uncertain, so we do not attempt to explain addictions using a genetic model. We, instead, rely on how the people explain use and their guidelines for misuse.

Do Drinking Patterns Exceed National Norms?

Liquor in Esperanza is abundantly available—and has been for a long time. But does Esperanzans' alcohol consumption exceed national norms?

"No" was the answer we found from the household survey. Thirty-two percent of the respondents reported that on a "day of drinking," a special time just for drinking—such as a celebration like a Superbowl game, they would typically consume five (5) drinks. This is the same percentage (32%) and number (5) of drinks that was found as a norm in a national survey done by the National Center for Health Statistics (NIAAA 2003).

Is drinking then a problem if it is a normalized behavior? Douglas, in her anthropological perspective on drinking, says "the most pessimistic estimate is that alcohol-related troubles afflict fewer than 10 percent of those who drink" (1997:3). In Esperanza, 85 percent believe that *their* drinking is normal behavior—that is, "normalized" behavior; however, they and outsiders believe there is overdrinking in Esperanza (by others). These perceptions may stem from seeing other people (usually viewed as "outsiders") drunk in public, on sidewalks and in alleys. Incidents of public drinking are obvious and disturbing, but not necessarily widespread; overdrinking may therefore be exaggerated. Furthermore, determining exactly where overdrinking occurs is difficult. In comparing Esperanzans to more-affluent people living in the area, keep in mind that Esperanzans live in crowded conditions that tend to expose all types of behavior more readily to others. Contrast this to wealthy people living in the foothills, drinking in the privacy of their elegant mansions, undisturbed by police.

Perhaps the cultural norms of Esperanzans are not that different from members of mainstream society. We'll take a look at what Esperanzans believe about drinking and how they explain alcohol use. The townspeople do have opinions about the rules for learning to drink, drinking rituals, and how families and society control overuse. The following perceptions tell you what the cultural norms are.

Who Introduces You to Drinking in Esperanza?

> Parents tend to set an example. Hey, my mom and her boyfriend, my dad and his girlfriend do it; it's okay. (13-year-old female)

> I've seen drinking through my aunts and uncles and stuff like that, so it wasn't just me. It doesn't even matter if it's a family member, it could be your boyfriend—whatever. (17-year-old female)

> Advertisements, they make you curious. (16-year-old male)

What Encourages Drinking in Esperanza?

People view drinking as being available, legal, and encouraged by other people, friends, and family. It is a social act that is used to bring bonding and acceptance.

> Alcohol is out in the open, because it's legal and drugs aren't. (17-year-old female)

> It starts with the friends . . . they're gettin' it at school. They want to be accepted, they want to be liked, in with the crowd. (52-year-old female)

Describe Effects of Overdrinking.

The rules for drinking have diverse perceptions and include how to deal with overuse.

> Women seek religion and men remain at home sleeping off their drunks. (68-year-old female)

> Alcohol damages more than drugs—always drinking beer. I see my sister and her husband—always drinking and there's even an AA [Alcoholics Anonymous] next door. (61-year-old female)

> How ugly is drunkenness—alcohol is not acceptable; life has fallen apart when already they have lost their children, their health, and you lose your ability to reason. (64-year-old female)

What Is Done to Those Who Abuse Alcohol?

The consequences for abusing alcohol range from being ignored to being arrested and put into a drunk tank or being given health care.

> My dad would pass out and my mom would just close the door and say, "leave your dad alone." (23-year old female)

> Nothin', 'cause everybody does it. (20-year-old male)

> Sometimes police pick 'em up and put in the drunk tank just to get them off the sidewalks—but most of the time everyone just looks the other way. (30-year-old male)

Controlling Misuse of Alcohol

The stories of how individuals control misuse of alcohol will be told in several situations. Societal controls are many, such as driving under the influence (DUI) tickets being issued by the police, fines paid, and some jail time given. Roles and status enter into the enforcement of rules; for example, during the study period a couple of elected officials were issued DUI tickets. Nothing was made public about these offenses, and it's unknown if the offenders paid their fines or if their tickets were ignored. In larger society, too, some people with higher status are not held to the same cultural norms as others. Each society chooses limits on unacceptable behavior, according to status and role.

In Esperanza the drunkenness of men may be accepted in homes as a cultural norm—"men are just being men." However, drunkenness of women, especially Hispanic women, is not tolerated. The woman is supposed to be pure and a mother—not poisoning her body. In some cases, people cover up or deny drinking problems. Many families tell of keeping a family secret, allowing the family member to sleep it off, mostly ignoring or tolerating the problem. Often, drunkenness is accepted as part of the lifestyle for certain classes of people. When the rules of tolerance shift to intolerance and stricter rules are enforced, the consequences range from personal shame to punishment.

Alcohol use may be tolerated by law enforcement because prosecuting and incarcerating those who break the law is costly, and the town may avoid prosecuting alcohol misuse to save money. Furthermore, this resource-strapped town depends on tax revenues generated by liquor sales, so monitoring alcohol misuse may not be a high priority. The ambivalence between controlling alcohol abuse and gaining income generated from liquor sales is problematic. This dilemma has existed for a long time, as noted in the quote by Johnson in his historic account of Esperanza in 1975:

> I have been against bars [there were 50 bars and liquor stores in the town] but I was always overruled. Unfortunately, the other fellows thought we needed the tax revenue. It always hurt the town because we get the scum of the drinkers. They chase them out of Tucson and they come down here [to Esperanza] because we don't have enough policemen. (Johnson 1986:8)

In 2006 there were only are six liquor stores and seven bars/restaurants that serve liquor. The reduction in number is significant (that is, from 50 in 1975 to 11 in 2006), but so too is the loss of tax revenue.

Women Won't Take It Anymore

Two events illustrate the action that women in the town took to try to control the availability of alcohol. The first shows how women in the community tried to stop the transfer of a liquor license and the other is an example of how powerful a group of women can be in closing a liquor store.

A large liquor outlet on the main street was closed for over six months during the study, as some townspeople (mostly women) tried to influence the

Liquor store

Arizona State Liquor Control Board of Licensure to deny the transfer of the liquor license. Groups of women from Esperanza took a two-hour bus trip, one way, to the state office in Phoenix. In their words:

> We left in a bus at 8 AM and it was hot then—traveling all the way to downtown Phoenix. We got to the Board Room just as they were getting started. Our names were on the list to give testimony. By noon we weren't called yet, so after the lunch recess we sat and sat until they stopped the hearing at 4:30. They saw us sitting there—waiting to be called, and no one called us—they just ignored us. So we left. We got home at 10 PM . . . so tired and so discouraged, but we tried again six months later. But the same thing happened. We knew we could not win—as money talks—we didn't have $100,000. They say the owner paid the money. That's the way it is.

The women of Esperanza did not appear "passive" or "voiceless" when they objected to a local bar, Amor Libre, staying open.

> We [women of Esperanza]—at least 40 of us—stood side by side, locking our arms together, surrounding that bar for a month, night and day, not letting anyone in. (50-year-old female)

> We were tired of all the fighting that went on in there and all of the used condoms outside, right where our kids from school could see everything—it was disgusting—we had enough. (47-year-old female)

> The police didn't bother us, they knew we were strong—we just didn't take it anymore. The owner tried to sell the place, but no one would buy it, it had such a bad name. (43-year-old female)

The bar building stood empty for several years—a witness to women power. Then it became a depot for a bus terminal (later closed because it was found to be a center for human smuggling). Now it is a brightly painted gallery featuring local native art with a high volume of sales—again producing tax revenue.

The Drugs Most Commonly Used in Esperanza

Drugs used in other parts of the country, such as LSD, Ecstasy, PCP, (phencyclidine), and polydrugs, such as cocaine and methamphetamine, are not used in Esperanza. The five most commonly used drugs are: alcohol (already discussed), marijuana, methamphetamine, cocaine, and heroin. The last four of these are illegal, as is alcohol for people under the age of 21.

Marijuana, also called hemp, weed, or pot, is the second most frequently used drug (after alcohol) in Esperanza. "It comes from the plant, cannabis, whose leaves, stems, and resin contain a variety of psychoactive substances that may be smoked or eaten" (Frisch & Frisch 1998:339). Marijuana can grow in many parts of the world, including the U.S., but because of legal restrictions it is illegally transported into the U.S. from several countries, including: Mexico, Nigeria, South Africa, Afghanistan, Pakistan, Morocco (for hashish), and Jamaica for cannabis oil (Stares 1996:31).

It is used primarily for gaining a tranquil, relaxing feeling, but it is known to impair judgment and motor skills. No report has been received on death from marijuana overdosing, as users go to sleep before consuming or inhaling a great deal (*The Gazette*, March 28, 2005). Using marijuana to control nausea for persons who are being treated for cancer is widely supported in the medical field, and many physicians have promoted legal use for people with multiple sclerosis (Dublin & Kleinman 1991). Whether physical dependency or addiction results from marijuana use is unknown, but psychological dependency seems possible. There is controversy over marijuana being a gateway drug (leading to the use of more-addictive drugs). According to Gray:

> Of the seventy million Americans who smoked the weed, 98 percent didn't wind up on anything harder than martinis. Only a tiny fraction went on to become heroin or cocaine addicts and the cause–effect connection to reefer for this group was no more evident than was the connection to coffee. (Gray, quoted in Singer 2005:81)

Methamphetamine (meth) is the third most frequently used drug in Esperanza. Its use is a recent epidemic. It can be produced anywhere. An ethnographic study found that meth began being noticed as a drug of choice at the border where its use remains high, but the epidemic has moved north, to the Midwest, and to big cities on the East Coast (Glittenberg & Anderson 1999:1997). It is easily manufactured at home or in motel rooms from chemicals available in over-the-corner drugs, like decongestants. Larger quantities are manufactured in "meth labs" from illegal purchases of the base materials in Mexico. These ingredients are transported in relatively small quantities across the border, easily hidden in automobile tire rims, and the odor is undetected by dogs trained to find other drugs, such as marijuana and cocaine (Glittenberg & Anderson 1999).

Not only is meth used for pleasure and to get a high, but it also used by people who work long hours to keep awake, such as nurses, truck drivers, and soldiers (Glittenberg & Anderson 1999). People who use meth may go without sleep for days at a time and then crash, neither eating nor drinking for days. Users desire the substance because it makes them feel sharper (more alert), and it increases physical strength and sexual staying power. Meth is a highly addictive drug with many dangerous side effects, including acute paranoia, hallucinations, and extreme aggression. For instance, during Glittenberg and Anderson's (1999) meth ethnographic study done in 1996, two very brutal murders occurred (the police called them "overkill") in the Tucson area. The homicides, caused by bludgeoning, were blamed on the paranoia and immense physical strength created by the killers' ingestion of meth. Although the cost of manufacturing meth is low, the risks are high. The materials are highly explosive and almost impossible to clean up. Lead poisoning is another risk of use if ingredients are cooked in lead pots, as the lead residue may enter the brain when the meth is injected or smoked.

Cocaine contains addictive properties about which little was known in the early twentieth century. The properties were even sold over the counter as useful medications. Furthermore, cocaine was used in the early production of Coca-Cola, which was offered as the new "temperance drink," and an eight-ounce glass contained 60 mg of cocaine, the amount that Freud suggested for treating depression. Freud, himself a user of cocaine, enthusiastically endorsed it for migraines and depression (Brain & Coward 1989). Chronic cocaine abuse did not seem to be a problem until the 1980s (Gold 1992:206), when its use in crack form (crystallized), commonly inhaled through "snorting" into the nose as a powder, increased cocaine's addictive quality (Frisch & Frisch 1998:335).

The cocaine problem revolves around the chemical's effect on the pleasure center in the brain, especially on the dopamine-rich sites in the basal ganglia (Gold 1992). Seeking the pleasures, the highs, experienced with this stimulation takes over one's life, and these euphoric feelings are very addictive. As Gold notes, the pleasure is so powerful "that sleep, safety, money, morality, loved ones, responsibility, even survival become largely irrelevant to the cocaine user" (Gold 1992:208). Even animal studies have shown the extent to which cocaine was chosen over food or sex. Many physical side effects result from cocaine usage such as perforated nasal septum, weight loss, myocardial infarctions, stroke, and death (Frisch & Frisch 1998:334, 335). Several of the participants in our study commented about the appearance of "crack heads," their fragile physical conditions, and "messed up heads."

Heroin is another highly addictive drug, used somewhat, but not in high quantities, in Esperanza. Heroin is derived from opium, which comes from the opium poppy, grown in and largely trafficked from Mexico, Afghanistan, Pakistan, and Turkey. The poppy produces a seed that contains a milky secretion, which when ingested or injected has a powerful reaction in the neurotransmitter system of the brain, regulating pain and reducing anxiety. Heroin produces a tranquil state of being, making the user feel content and free of worry. The greatest problem with heroin is its addictive qualities (Frisch & Frisch 1998:339).

Narratives of Alcohol and Drug Users

We include five narratives that illustrate how alcohol and drug use affected the lives of some of the townspeople. Alcohol misuse is visible, troublesome, and is often associated with violent acts. Drug use is illegal, and the patterns of use are more covert. Most Esperanzans consider alcohol use to be normal, or at most merely a nuisance. Drug use, on the other hand, is more complex and difficult to unravel and control.

Lupita, a Woman with an Alcohol- and Drug-Free Life

I used alcohol when I was younger and stupid. The first time I got drunk was my freshman year in college—not in high school. We came from a very small town, and I didn't have any need for it there, but in college I had a really tough time coping in the new environment. I felt like a fish out of water. I was scared all the time, and I found that drinking took the edge off—so I started drinking. What rescued me was finding my soul mate and being happy in love, having a very strong marriage, and starting my family. I wiped out my depression. I was a heavy marijuana user, too, but I have been drug free and alcohol free, and cigarette free since I turned 23.

I have a zero-tolerance attitude now, because I have seen so little moderation of it. If anybody is taking a few beers, there is potential they could go overboard. I've never seen anybody because they took two or three drinks or smoked a joint become more creative or a better human being or did their job better. We should really pay attention to Native Americans in our population. Alcohol is such a devastating problem for that entire group. When you talk about Hispanics you are talking about a mixture of Native Americans and Spanish. We're two bloods combined, and we carry that gene, too.

My husband was an alcoholic when he was younger. He started when he was about 14 or 15 years old, and the first time he had it, he loved it. He was very young and he could easily drink two 6-packs of beer and a quart of tequila a day, and he looked stone sober—that's dangerous! One time he got really, really drunk and now he doesn't drink a drop. We stopped together.

Signs of drunkenness start with slurred speech, so the minute I hear that, I'm not interested in that person, that's the first indicator to me. When you have impaired reactions, I consider you a danger. I find people who are alcoholics tend to do things, like be verbally abusive. My own father, when he gets drunk, becomes the creepiest person. I can't stand to be around him.

It isn't just men who get drunk, women do, too. I remember going to a party, and a very attractive woman, probably in her late 30s or early 40s came in all dressed in a wonderful groove, nice hair, and she just walked with a real special presence, "God, what a lovely woman," you'd say. I really admired the way she looked as an older woman—she really cared about herself. When I saw her two hours later she looked like crap—it was disgusting. Everything about her just fell hard; she became flat faced, her hair was crap, her clothing was all rumbled, and she couldn't talk, just slobbered. She went from this vision of loveliness to this piece of shit at the end of two hours of drinking.

The more you tolerate drunks the more they expect you to tolerate them. I don't tolerate them and don't have much respect for them. For instance at my mother's funeral, my father was getting very, very drunk, and he was gross. It really angered me because it was so disrespectful of my beautiful mother's memory and what she stood for. It was also symbolic of what hell she had to tolerate. Alcohol played such a horrible role in our family.

There were tons of people at the house, but I didn't show any anger until my dad was so drunk and then some relative asshole came and handed him yet another pint of whisky. I started coming and intercepted it. I said, "You're not giving him this, goddamn it! He's already drunk. He's just sitting there slobbering, not even making sense, and you want to get him drunker?" There were a lot of men, Mexican men, all standing around. I looked at all of them and said, "You guys are not here to clean the shit in his pants and watch him piss on himself, because he is so goddamn drunk he doesn't know what he's doing. You are not going to be here to take care of him, when he gets the runs for the next week, and we have to carry him around. It is me and my sisters that are going to have to do this." The whole time I'm screaming—then I threw the goddamn bottle and shattered it up against the wall.

"I know you guys shit in your pants, too, and your wives have to clean it up, too. My mother who did so much for all of you, and right now you're disrespecting her by bringing more booze into this house. This is not something she would have liked one goddamn bit." Everybody got real quiet—and a guy came back a little later, to apologize to me. He said, "I really respect what you said, and I'm sorry."

Violence can crush your heart and your sense of well-being, and it is as much as a blow to the face. When people get drunk they no longer have control over their own being, their own sense of who they are. They take it out on somebody else.

You become less responsible with what you're doing, and it gives you that freedom to hit someone or hurt someone verbally. The persons feel inadequate in some aspect of their life—will look for someone to blame that inadequacy on. Drinking makes you forget about it, but it's still there, if you're drunk and violate someone, verbally, sexually, physically, if it's a son, a daughter, wife, a parent, that person no longer trusts you. You have to rebuild that trust.

Lupita is an expressive Mexican American woman who represents someone who has overcome the use of alcohol and drugs. She downplays any stereotype of Mexican American substance abuse but emphasizes how alcohol destroys relationships.

RICARDO, A MEXICAN IMMIGRANT, ABUSER, AND ALCOHOLIC

Ricardo, a 50-year-old male, is a monolingual Mexican immigrant who was convicted of domestic violence. When he got out of jail, he rented space and lived in the back of a store where he sold religious artifacts. He also continued working in the evenings with his estranged wife for a janitorial service. In 2000 he lost his store lease, so he moved into a shelter for the homeless. (This interview was done in Spanish, and the translation is modified for a more concise understanding in English.)

I was raised in Mexico where a man is head of the house. My teachers were nuns who used rulers or paddles for spanking. They were very strict, and I think that is good. They would hit you when you did something wrong, and it worked. I think the church should be a source of discipline. I think there's such a thing as parent abuse. You see my wife is very Americanized, and her way of dealing with our kids isn't my way.

Kids now run the parents and that's not right—parents should run the show. I believe all the disorder in the world comes from the home. My oldest lives in New Mexico. He was addicted to drugs—always in trouble as a teenager. My other son is 24 years old—hasn't gotten his act together. He's on probation and has been in trouble with the law many times. Neither son graduated from school. I think they need discipline but my wife is Americanized and she just talks to them. I'm not the head of the house like I should be—I am not in control of anything. I feel so angry.

I've been told I'm an alcoholic, but I don't think so. I've been drinking most of my life, and I do get angry—hit my wife a couple times, but just on her arm. She won't listen and I just try to make her listen—she needs discipline, too. I'm head of the house, so she needs to obey. She put a restraining order on me so I can't go home. The reason I drink is because I want to get my 24-year-old son out of the house. I don't like his girlfriend, and she doesn't even let me eat in my own home.

Ricardo represents a middle-aged, marginalized man with a drinking problem and a conviction for domestic abuse. His early socialization into a patriarchal system limits his ability to change, and he blames drinking on his wife and on forcing her Americanized ways on him. He may be an archetype of an angry, macho man who needs to control his environment, and when he drinks he becomes abusive. Ricardo has few social supports in addition to lacking the language skills necessary to fit into the new culture.

ISABELA, A HUD MOTHER FROM AN ALCOHOLIC FAMILY

Isabela is a neighbor in the HUD housing. She is an active, well-liked woman who tells her story of being from an alcoholic family.

I grew up in an alcoholic family for most of my life. For the last 15 years I have tried to have no alcohol. I have three brothers, and I am the only girl. I married early, somewhat to get out of the house. My parents both were drunkards; they would visit bars a lot while I babysat my cousins. I started drinking early, especially at parties, because my dad worked for Big Beer Company, and he would buy the beer really cheap and store it in our basement. My older brothers and I would steal cases of beer and take them to parties. I just drink now and then, but I don't want to become like my parents—they were drunks.

My first husband was a drinker, and he beat me. We had two kids, and one lives with me now. I needed to get away, so I got a divorce. My second husband, Cesar, is an illegal immigrant. He applied for a green card, but now that he is in prison for assault and battery, I don't think he'll get the card. He got a whole five years. I had to call the police a lot here at the HUD housing. When Cesar drinks he gets out of control and he's so strong. He does drugs, too, especially coke. Cesar's never violent unless he's been drinking or on drugs—then nothing will stop him; he's angry and suspicious about everything. Since he isn't working he would take my paycheck and that's the only way Cesar can get the drugs. I'm afraid of him; he's so strong. I don't know if I can live with him when he gets out of prison. [Living in the same housing area, we saw evidence of Cesar's violence on several occasions as he would damage cars, HUD property, and he beat Isabela once with a chain. Cesar was a pleasant neighbor when he wasn't drinking or on drugs.]

Isabela represents a typical woman in HUD housing who deals with trying to make a living and with a violent alcohol- and drug-abusing husband.

Her second marriage to an addicted person is a repeated pattern. She lives in fear and cannot prevent Cesar from taking her paycheck to pay for his addictions. Fear is difficult to overcome. Isabela's options at this point are very few, but she has shown resilience in keeping a job and also in not using alcohol or drugs herself.

DIEGO, A RECOVERING ALCOHOLIC IN TREATMENT

Diego is a person in a treatment center for alcoholism. He tells his story of early induction into drinking and womanizing.

> I'm 48 years old and a recovering alcoholic. I've been a patient twice in a treatment center because I had D.T.'s [delirium tremens]. I've been drinking since I was about 10 years old. My dad and uncles always drank a lot, and they wanted me to be a "man," so I started. I think the addiction runs in our family as everyone on my dad's side drinks a lot. My dad died at 62 from cirrhosis of the liver; he was also a diabetic and blind. I don't want to go that direction. My mom never drank that I know of, maybe a beer now and then, but I have a sister and brother who are alcoholics. My mom died broke and bitter about my dad—I don't want that.
>
> I started high school but never finished as I met Cristina, a real beauty. She was only 15 and I was 16, and I loved her so much. We had two babies, but I wasn't a good father. I tried to be a good provider and worked as much as I could, but never steady and with my drinking there were problems. I was good looking and a mariachi bass fiddler and singer. I can't play with the group anymore 'cause I caused problems, never fights, but I just wouldn't show up, as I was always drunk. There were temptations—at one time I had three women. I never got religion—that never was my thing. I'm really trying this time to not start drinking again.
>
> This time I feel stronger because I'm afraid, and I have diabetes now. I worry about my eyesight. I'm used to playing games with the therapists, like I'd tell that I had quit, but I hadn't. But now I'm serious because I'm afraid. Joe, the counselor, tells me straight, no bull shit. I trust him and will stay on AA after I leave. They're helping me find a job with Goodwill. I never was in trouble with the law—that helps. I'll try living at the Salvation Army for awhile so I can get on my feet as I don't have any money.

Diego represents the group of people who are longtime alcoholics and are in denial of their problem until they have other physical problems. He patterned his life in accordance with the expectations of his role models, his father and uncles, who, along with people in his workplace, encouraged macho norms. Diego's losses in life are many but he now is willing to work on his alcoholism. His comorbidities, like diabetes, are permanent. Although he is still young, the damage may be permanent because of the duration of his heavy drinking.

MARK, A VIETNAM VETERAN AND AN ADDICT

Interviewing someone while he is shooting up was not the usual circumstance in which we collected data for our study. Roberto had met Mark on the street and in their conversation found out that Mark was an addict. Roberto asked if he could be present when Mark shot up. "Sure why not," said Mark. "I'd like to tell my story as it might help some other old vet know he's not alone." The interview takes place in Mark's dilapidated apartment in one of the more rundown parts of Esperanza. Mark is 52 years old, graying, and of slight build. He says he's been in and out of drug treatment for about 30 years. While his hands are shaking he rolls up his sleeve and exposes his very infected left arm where veins are exposed from the open wound. Mark doesn't take long to find a vein for injecting, and with a nearly full syringe, he plunges the needle right in. Within a minute the liquid is injected, and he lies down on a worn-out couch to tell his story of his Vietnam War experience and hospitalization.

I'm a vet from the Nam War—I was 20 when I was drafted and saw a lot of action. I was wounded in my shoulder, lucky they didn't hit my spinal cord, just a shoulder blade, the arm, and some muscles. I got sent home for treatment at the VA hospital in Tucson. That's where I got addicted to morphine—I had lots of pain and several surgeries. It took me three years to get out but I couldn't work, not like I had before. So I went to school at the University of Arizona in business and actually I did finish, took me about six years. I had my pension from the Marines but never had enough money.

I got married—that lasted just two years. My wife, Sara, couldn't take my moods. I just couldn't control them, sometimes I'd cry and cry and then I'd pound on things. I even hurt her a couple of times. I was in a lot of therapy to handle my nightmares and stuff, but she couldn't take it any more. I really don't blame her. Now I'm even a worse bastard—look at me—I'm just a wreck.

After Sara left me I tried to get it together. I lived with my folks for about five years. They put up with a lot of crap, and they're gone now. I have a brother and sister, but they're fed up with me, too. I was without any drugs for 15 years. I had a steady job as an accountant, and that was good as I could be by myself—other people bother me a lot.

I was 48 when the axe fell. My company went belly up—all of us had to look for other jobs. I tried, but I get nervous in front of others and I couldn't find another job. I started drinking and living here in Esperanza in this crappy, awful place. It's what I can afford. I went twice a week to the VA for therapy, group therapy with other Nam vets. We lost a couple of guys; they'd been bad off for a long time. One was a double amputee and another had diabetes so bad he was blind. We just leaned on each other—that war left a lot of scars. One guy said shooting up heroin helped him sleep and stuff—so I started to use it. The nightmares—that's what gets me. I keep living it over and over again, and I worry about going to sleep because of what I see, but then I get so tired I can't stay awake.

Shooting heroin has eased all of that and I feel mellow. I get my stuff here in town. I won't say where, but it has been steady. I don't know what I'd do if I didn't have that coming in. Of course I pay—my whole pension check almost. I get food at Casa María and the Food Bank, but that's about it. Then I get infected like I am now, then I have to go to the VA to get it taken care of. They know me and don't preach. Sometimes I want to just end it all—maybe shoot up too much—and just go to sleep, but then I get scared 'cause I've seen lots of dead people. I'll be gone one of these days. I suppose if I could I'd change things, but I can't seem to forget. War is a bad thing and I hope we never have another one.

As Roberto leaves the apartment Mark is dozing off. Mark was found dead in his apartment about a month later, his nightmares perhaps are finally gone.

Mark suffered from posttraumatic stress disorder (PTSD), and it is not uncommon for people with this disorder to use drugs. Treatment to prevent PTSD is now available to people while they're at war, rather than having to wait until they return home. Mark was hampered in his personal life with a long-term addiction. He harmed and destroyed some of his interpersonal relationships. Mark was not a drug dealer, but he participated in a culture of veterans—a drug using community—(Singer 2006b) who shared similar experiences and solutions to their problems. The VA Hospital system was not an enabler and tried to be responsive to his needs, even though the therapy did not remove his fears.

Summary of All the Narratives

These narratives illustrate different contexts within which cultural rules operate and within which people develop addictions. None of the participants stood out as being a deviant in his or her cultural context. Each person had some work experience; none spoke of the church influencing their use of alcohol or drugs; and it appears that family played a more prominent role in shaping their cultural context. Each person (except Mark) had a family member or friend as a user.

Cultural Patterns

First we sample some of the viewpoints of ordinary townspeople to learn how culture shapes ongoing views of alcohol and drug use. Most of these quotes are taken from focus groups, and some are from individual interviews. The age and gender of the speaker are noted to give a sense of how broadly based these comments are. Next, we explore the power of *corridos*—Mexican ballads—to shape and explore cultural norms.

Townspeople's Views

During the 1970s this was a riotous place; there wasn't a night when we didn't stitch up someone—the worst place was at Bar Macho. The number of male heroin users and overdosers especially struck me. We would simply have to give them some antidotes to save them, as they were just thrown on the ground outside the hospital, and their companions would just rush off. There were lots of bodies found in the riverbed by Craycroft and River—drug dealers whose deals went wrong. We dealt with victims.

We always had problems dealing with scum trying to make a buck by selling some kind of drug to the poor people. Sometimes it was heroin, crack cocaine, meth, and always marijuana. We get the dealers from the border and also from Tucson. We were always caught in the middle with not enough police to cover it all. (retired male physician)

Why and How Do People Get Started Using Drugs?

For teenagers "fitting in" is a cultural pressure—wanting to part of the in-crowd or popular may lead to getting started. Compliance and experimentation are two other features linking drug use with teenagers.

> Drinking and getting high—it's glamorous—you see it everywhere—on TV, radio, in our house, everywhere. (13-year-old male)

> It's so popular—I want to be cool—I want to fit in—you're going to try to do all that stuff. You might just try it for one time—maybe you're doing it for the hell of it—to see how bad it was. (14-year-old male)

> Parties are the place—my neighbors have quite a few, and they're putting stuff up their noses, I've seen it a lot. (13-year-old female)

What Are the Drugs of Choice?

In each culture certain rules shape the type of drugs used, with whom, and how often. In Esperanza, a town of poor people, the culture is shaped by the economics, as the people tell.

> Marijuana—it's cheaper and you can get some anyplace; meth and cocaine cost more and are harder to get. (15-year-old male)

> Pot is everywhere. It's cheaper and cocaine is hard to get. Pot is the drug of tradition—it's used for medical stuff. (23-year-old female)

> We don't use "designers" [mixed concoctions] here in our neighborhood—they're just for Anglos—the rich guys. (18-year-old male)

What Are the Dangers in Using Drugs?

In spite of the desire to use drugs, the people tell of rules and dangers of using them.

> Crack's gotten worse—it's bad. (26-year-old female)

> I just think people pretend they don't do it but they do Rochas and they get high, high, high, and you don't know anything at all. It's really common among younger people, they can get only so high, and they want to try something different, and they keep doing it. People will try this stuff, but some will stick to weed. I know a lot of girls—that you know in 10 years will look like crack heads. A lot of girls hide it, but guys don't. It makes a girl look dirty—real nasty, especially if they do coke, they are considered—nasty—it's not proper, if girls do it, it's not proper in the guys' eyes to see that. You get real shaky—all strung out—a guy's different. A woman is like a mother type—she's to be pure. You don't see your mother strung out. A woman is supposed to take care of everybody—especially of a man. (19-year-old male)

Only once in a while there is one who can't control it, most use only for
fun and quit when they want to—or run out of dough. (18-year-old male)

How Do You Get Drugs in Esperanza?

Drugs seem readily available and people know the rules for buying or
trading.

There are no regulations—you can buy beer any time. I see kids smoking
marijuana and using drugs in the schools. Nobody pays any attention to
them; they're drinking behind the stores. You see people just selling right
on the street with no arrests. [Why not?] Because there aren't enough
police. (62-year-old female)

There are different kinds of groups and different kinds of drugs for every
group. Not every group's going to use the same drug. Some like the less
harmful or the most harmful. It depends on the group. Some are more
risky and more violent. You know what you're getting into, but sometimes it's hard to get out. Most kids just try it for a while and don't get
addicted. (23-year-old male)

People do become users who lose perspective and break cultural rules.

Some need to use more drugs, but older people too; they inject themselves anyplace—right in front of the market. I saw a woman do it and
she was pregnant—poor innocent children. (24-year-old female)

Girls are just as bad as boys—they hang around males—all female gangs
use dope and heroin and crack—they all use drugs. (18-year-old male)

Do Hispanic People Use More Drugs?

Some issues remain related to ethnicity, and the people voice their views
about Hispanic usage.

Just like other people, some people are just plain dumb—I could name you
quite a few dumb people and they aren't all Mexicans. (58-year-old male)

I don't know if it's different for us Mexicans, but some people just seem
to need to get high. I think there's a streak in machos, especially, always
wantin' excitement, pickin' fights, drivin' fast. I seen it all sittin' here on
my porch at night. Girls, too, are gettin' wilder. (40-year-old female)

What Opinions Do the People Have about the Issue of Legalizing Drugs?

Drugs need to be controlled as they affect everyone—it does damage to
society. It gives me sadness because the children are the ones that suffer.
(62-year-old male)

I believe them to be criminal people that sell to children—are murderers—
they kill and violate innocent people. It's an addiction. (60-year-old female)

A paradox in the data appears where small-time drug trafficking is widespread but only a minority of people say they are or have been users. The
2000 household survey showed that 23 percent had used illegal drugs at some
point in their lives and that 33 percent had seen kids under the age of 16 years

of age using drugs, mainly marijuana (Glittenberg 2001). This means that 77 percent have never used *illegal* drugs and 67 percent have never seen underage children using them. The paradox involves what people perceive as being "illegal." The emic meaning of "legal" and "illegal" drugs is the key to unlocking the paradox. How some townspeople define legal and illegal drugs is an important emic distinction. "Marijuana is used everywhere, so I don't think it really is 'illegal' but rather the 'normal' thing to use" (24-year-old female). The emic definition of what is legal or illegal is at odds with the etic definition. Hence illegal drug use is perceived as being very minimal when the people consider using marijuana as legal.

Corridos

The *corridos* or Mexican native ballads (whose themes are similar to country and western songs in the U.S., which describe human vulnerabilities and sensitivities), describe the culture of drug use in the larger Mexican culture. What are the messages about the value of drugs in these songs? The messages are friendly, extolling the power of using drugs especially for allaying fears and insecurities. Heard nightly, blaring from low-riders, in restaurants, bars, and houses throughout Esperanza, the ballads openly promote the prestige of underground drug trafficking.

For example. a patron saint of drug dealers in the border area is honored and petitioned to protect the traffickers in their illegal trade. Also a number of songs recommend taking a certain drug to achieve a particular goal, such as "taking cocaine makes me able to drink liquor longer and harder with my friends," or "drinking wine may make me feel more macho." For the female, drugs are advocated for passively accepting or denying the reality that a love relationship is ending (e.g., "my heart is breaking and drugs help me forget").

Many songs have reference to heroin as "*la fina*" (the finest, the best). Ballads give a general acceptance of using drugs and alcohol as well as using violence in protecting one's reputation, as seen in this line from a ballad, "Bastard! You dirtied my name. Be on the lookout as I'm takin' ya down." The songs, in general, denigrate weakness and indecision and promote the cultural ideals of aggression and fearlessness. With regard to drug use, these emic viewpoints reveal a level of accepting illegal activity.

Summary

Alcohol and drugs affect the functioning of the brain, and their misuse can result in adaptive and maladaptive psychological outcomes. Alcohol and drug use follow cultural norms that vary by roles, statuses, families, and communities. The use of alcohol in Esperanza is within the national norm. However, people display various reactions to the public display of drinking and drunkenness—from bragging about it to rejection of anyone who drinks at all. Such comments about people who use excessive amounts of alcohol include: "It's just the Mexican way"; "He's so macho"; "Just ignore it"; "Throw the drunken bastard out!" Also in small, crowded households, as found in the town, private drinking is rare, so the visibility of drinking is enhanced. Many people associate violent behavior with alcohol and drug use.

People who misuse drugs (e.g., Mark, the Vietnam vet) as well as people who use drugs but are in certain roles (e.g., women and mothers) are judged harshly by community members. Drug use is associated with being macho, and men who use drugs can retain the image of an aggressive macho man.

Perceptions are that today there is less drinking and drug use in the town than there was in the 1970s. Back then, 50 bars filled the town and bodies, limp from drug overdoses, were dumped nightly near a hospital. Today there are only six bars in town and no record of people overdosing as frequently as every night. Personal responsibility for controlling abuse seems limited; instead responsibility is given to the police, as people complain, "we don't have enough police." Women show more responsibility both in the private places as well as in public in confronting alcohol abuse (there is an example of one woman being drunk in a public place). Overall, women are more public about their objection to alcohol and drug abuse.

Beer is not viewed as liquor (because it is fermented and not distilled)—it is "something you drink everyday." Marijuana "is a normal thing to use," but heroin, crack, and meth are viewed as illegal, dangerous, hard to get—"don't get caught with them," as possession might put you in prison.

The attempt to control misuse or abuse is projected to be in the hands of the law or medicine, but also several examples are given in how individuals matured and quit using drugs or alcohol. Others recognized they have an addiction and are being treated professionally, not completely from choice but from fear.

Chapter 4

Prostitutes and Gangs

> Those of us who seek to understand and to rethink the meaning of social
> suffering cannot but stay on the path that is no path at all. Broken words,
> fragments of metaphors, snippets of survivor testimony are all we have to
> guide us. . . . By examining and reexamining the way in which commu-
> nal and individual sorrows shade into each other, a way may yet appear.
> —Vera Schwarcz, "The Pane of Sorrow"

Patterns of living become more discernible the longer we are in Esperanza. One pattern of particular interest is that of prostitutes and gangs making profits illegally. Both groups are similar in that they find opportunities to
make a profit at the expense of the stable population. Yet, they are opposite
in some characteristics as well: Prostitutes are usually streetwalking females
who overtly attract customers; in contrast, gang members are mostly males
who are more covert with regard to their illegal activities.

Sexual Behavior as Culture

Sexual behavior is culturally shaped. How a society views prostitution—
sex that is an economic transaction—is also culturally guided (Santos-Ortiz,
Lao-Melendez, & Torres-Sanchez 1998:208). In some cultures these rules are
explicit and legal and in others they are underground and illegal. In Esperanza
prostituting/streetwalking/soliciting sex for money, booze, or drugs is illegal.

Although it's illegal in the U.S., prostitution often has been called the
world's oldest profession, especially where women face few choices of
income-producing occupations. Where poverty is persistent, prostitution has
been a long-standing dilemma. In patriarchal countries, some women lacking
a husband, father, or brother to support or protect them have been able to survive only by prostituting themselves (Elias, Bullough, Elias, & Brewer 1998).

75

> Yes, the streetwalkers—I see them, too. They are really a sad group of women; most are sick and they're stuck and don't see a way out. Most are abused. They just keep getting arrested and not treated. They have emotional problems and pass them on to their kids. (mid-50-year-old female)

Some form of prostitution has been found in all societies and throughout history. In Esperanza in the twenty-first century, views about prostitution and prostitutes in general are negative.

> Streetwalkers, prostitutes, hookers call 'em what you want. I'm sick of them—and the weak men who feed on their pussies; what am I to tell my daughters and sons? They see the sluts come out every night, walking by our house, and all the cars with guys hanging out—hoping to find some quick trick for a couple of bucks. Some are just young and others are old hags like me. (60-year-old female)

> They all look pretty dirty to me. (42-year-old female)

> Yeah, some are carrying guns now. (16-year-old male)

In Esperanza, prostitutes are not Hispanic. One Hispanic male said, "You won't see any Mexican women walking the streets because we (males) protect them, and they should be staying at home." At police headquarters we examined a collection of photographs of "known" prostitutes in Esperanza. None appears to have Hispanic features. All seem to be Anglo or African American females.[1] The prostitutes currently being held in jail, and those who have court appearances, all appear to be Anglos and African American females.

In an interview, an older Hispanic male gives his cultural views of prostitutes:

> I paid a *puta* [whore] to teach my son his first sexual experience. I hired the best one. It's important that a man knows the best techniques for being a great lover. Why not be taught by someone with lots of experience? That's how I was taught, so you don't make mistakes and fumble around. No, never a Hispanic woman, they aren't putas, never—as they are to be faithful, pure—to one man alone. They're like Madonna, they don't sell their bodies like an Anglo or Black woman.

Several other males echo this perception about Hispanic women not being prostitutes. For the most part this perception is an ideal, not reality, as the story of Maria (see chapter 1) demonstrates. Although she says, "I'm no 'ho," obtaining drugs for sex was a common practice for her.

Streetwalkers in Esperanza are likely to use drugs. Most prostitutes who work to support their drug habit are polydrug users, primarily using cocaine, heroin, and methamphetamine. Bromberg (1998) claims that 84–100 percent of streetwalkers have at one time or another used heroin. Esperanza's prostitutes are the lowest on the hierarchical rung of sex-workers, streetwalkers, and crack house "ho's." They charge about $15–$25 for genital sex and $2–$5 for fellatio (oral sex). These charges are very low compared to call girls at resort hotels that charge $1,000 for a night of sex or $100 for one act. The majority of prostitutes are female, but there is one well-known she/he prostitute in Esperanza who operates as a male prostitute. In almost all of the transactions drug dealing is involved, with the prostitute as a supplier or user. "Can't think of a trick I did, if it wasn't for crack—in one way or another" (38-year-old female prostitute).

Problems of Prostitution in Esperanza

The problems of prostitution in Esperanza consist of four components: (1) the conspicuousness of prostitutes walking on the streets soliciting tricks creates a negative town image; (2) prostitutes, along with gangs and drug dealers, perpetuate illegal drug trafficking; (3) prostitutes spread HIV; and (4) the high cost of prosecuting streetwalkers drains the town's meager budget.

The overtness of prostitutes gives the town a negative image. Streetwalkers come out onto the streets later in the evening, dressed provocatively, and aggressively approach people in cars and trucks with invitations to entertain them. The slow-driving cars and the flaunting women give a picture of the process of negotiation and of titillation. Sometimes college students as well as people living in Tucson make the trip to Esperanza for no other reason than to tell their friends at home provocative stories about seeing prostitutes. Others are serious customers, interested in negotiating a trick or purchasing drugs.

The paying customers, called "johns," know they can get both from a streetwalker. Few johns are arrested in Esperanza, as it is difficult to "catch" them in the act of negotiation. Johns come from all walks of life, from rural areas, small towns, and big cities; all populations are relatively equally represented. "We caught one john—he was a physician practicing in the wealthy foothills. His response to 'Why are you doing this?' was, 'I really wanted to help rehabilitate this poor woman'" (police officer comments 2000).

An account given by Charlie describes a typical night scene.

OBSERVING NEGOTIATIONS FOR SEXUAL TRANSACTIONS: CHARLIE'S FIELD NOTES, OCTOBER 1997

I saw one white gal looking like a "bus stop blonde." She was dressed like a teenager with a halter top and low-rise jeans, but her face looked old, and real puffy like you get from alcohol abuse. I saw another walking near by flipping her shoulder length hair, in shorts and a halter-top. They were walking up and down what is known as the "whore stroll." About then, an older Anglo driving a late model brown car drove past her and pulled into the parking lot where I was sitting in my truck. The girl with long hair came over and began knocking on the window asking the guy if he needed anything. The older man saw me in my truck, looked agitated, and pulled out of the parking place, probably not sure if I was a cop. He sped off. The girl yelled at the top of her voice, "fuck you, fuck you—you old cock sucker." Then began her walking again. Next, I saw two white gals dressed in shorts and halter-tops walking around the "stroll" by the Salvation Army residential building. Both wore a lot of makeup and weren't particularly pretty. One looked strung out. Soon a young Anglo man in a black, late-model car drove up, parked, and began talking with the two gals. He got out of his car and with the two gals entered the back door of the building—I didn't see them again.

Most prostitutes in Esperanza perform sexually for cash to buy drugs or for drugs themselves. A "pimp" is a male who "middle manages" the prostitute in securing johns, but in Esperanza pimps are seldom used, as the streetwalkers solicit directly on the streets. The interaction between johns and streetwalkers is open on certain streets, such as the "whore stroll," the street with the low-budget motels. But our contacts told us that the most frequent sexual liaisons take place in pickups, cars, or alleys, rather than in motel rooms or houses. The women usually are strung out on some drug and the john often is also a frequent user or a "wino." The woman gets paid a couple of dollars or a joint or bottle of booze up front for fellatio. Fellatio is often the preferred sexual act, because it is fast and less risky (Campbell 1998). Contacts also told us of "crack whores," who are not streetwalkers but are women who have sex in the crack houses in exchange for crack.

OBSERVING A CRACK HOUSE RAID:
CHARLIE AND ROBERTO'S FIELD NOTES, FEBRUARY 1999

We entered the crack house, a beat-up old place with four rooms near Main Street. The cops made arrests of six people—two women and four guys. We could see lots of hypodermic needles and drug paraphernalia laying around on tables and such. The walls were filled with graffiti, and the place really smelled of drugs and sex. We could tell lots of sex was performed here and were told it was women performing with several males at once and sometimes with other females as well.

In general, townspeople have negative views about both streetwalkers and crack house whores. An older woman says, "It's just a disgrace to see the streetwalkers out every night and the men who try to find some pleasure. It's hard to explain to the younger kids, and it gives our town a black eye." Another woman comments, "It's the same as always. It's always been in the alleys. I just don't even notice it anymore. I don't think it's a good image for our town, but I guess no one cares." A young female warns, "It's gotten worse as prostitutes carry guns now and knives. They'll jack you. They'll jack their johns for their wallets, for their guns or a car." (This comment relates to a widely publicized murder of an older man by a young prostitute who took his money and pickup after shooting him in the head and dumping his body in the desert. She received a second-degree murder conviction). Another negative reaction comes from an older HUD neighbor.

I saw some woman on my sidewalk, she can't even walk straight, she lookin' at me, "What the fuck are you looking at?" she screamed. "Well ma'am, I'll be honest, what I'm lookin' at stinks like shit. You need to go back across the street or I'm going to call the cops." She started cursin' at me and her boyfriend gets out of the car, but he can't even walk straight, so I went back inside my house. That's what we live with! (65-year-old female)

Prostitution is a risky, dangerous business, and violence is a constant threat and a viable reality. It has been reported that 33 percent of prostitutes have been raped prior to becoming a prostitute; 44 percent have been sexually abused; 35 percent are physically abused; and 30 percent have been raped an average of four times while prostituting (Gemme 1998:483). Not only are streetwalkers subjected to violence and abuse, but they are also at risk of getting HIV because they often have sex with injection drug users who carry the virus. In Esperanza, few streetwalkers are now injecting drugs, but their knowledge about safe sex and their abilities to negotiate it are dismal.

The following comments reveal their ignorance and powerlessness: "I can't ask a guy to use a condom. They pay for the extra feeling without it." "I just make sure he's clean." "I try not to have sex when I have the 'curse.'" "I had the test once, so I know I'm okay." And a curious remark by a crack house ho, "I'm faithful, and I know he is, too. He'd better be" (Glittenberg 2001). Although to a majority of people, "faithful" means having one sexual partner, this woman does not equate having sex with multiple partners as being unfaithful; in other words having sex for crack does not make her unfaithful.

The potential of HIV infection from having many sexual partners is high. One former prostitute told of her many partners; she was a methamphetamine addict for several years. "I had sex with dozens of men night and day. Couldn't even count them all—it was just a steady stream." In the four years of study, because of confidentiality, we do not know the serological status (HIV positive or negative) of arrested prostitutes in the Esperanza jail. Rumors abound that the majority of prisoners are HIV positive.

With the high activity of prostitutes in the town and active drug use as seen on the street corners and in crack houses, what is the status of HIV infection among the population? In a survey of prevalence of symptomatic HIV infection, Galper (2000) found 26 percent of those were Hispanic and 19 percent of these were due to injection drug use. A needle exchange program has operated in the area since 1997; it is called Lifepoints. It operates twice a week in Esperanza. It is a harm-reduction program supported by the Health department and Esperanzan police. No further statistics are known about how successful this harm-reduction program is, but it is a move in the right direction.

The High Cost of Prosecuting Prostitutes

In a poverty-laden town with a poor tax base, arresting and prosecuting prostitutes is such an economic burden that it is easy for police to ignore this type of illegal activity. The sentence for being convicted of prostitution is a $160 fine with 36 months of probation; if the prostitute also carries drug paraphernalia, the fine is automatically raised to $260, but the probation stays the same. If the fine is not paid, the convicted prostitute serves six months (180 days) in jail.

> About half the time I can pay the fine but it's always the big whack [$260]. The probation is a pain in the butt—always checking in. (28-year-old female)

The cost of housing a person in jail is $42 a day, so a sentence of 180 days would cost the town $7,560. Even if the prostitute serves no jail time, the legal process still entails expenses. Therefore, law enforcement authorities must weigh the cost of arresting prostitutes against spending time and money on other crimes.

To help reduce the expenses of arresting and convicting prostitutes, Esperanza legally controls prostitution by designating certain areas as "restricted" zones. When prostitutes are released from custody, they are given a map of the town, which shows the restricted zones. A convicted prostitute cannot enter these zones for a specific duration of time as determined by the judge. If a prostitute even steps across the line, she or he can be arrested, without the police having to spend time and money on building a case against the prostitute.

Streetwalkers have a system of helping each other. When a prostitute is arrested, one of her friends steps in to serve her customers until she is released. In this tightly knit network, such an exchange keeps out competition from other hookers seeking to make a hit in Esperanza. As one streetwalker said,

> We also switch with a group of ho's near Miracle Mile [another known whore stroll].We do this 'bout every six months to throw the police off our trails. This way cops get to look for new faces, and we have different johns—it works for us; keeps up the trade and keeps us out of jail—sometimes. (32-year-old female)

In 2000, the police force was increased, and as a result, they had enough personnel to shut down the sex trade and crack houses. By 2006, streetwalkers were seldom seen in Esperanza, and parks replaced crack houses. These changes occurred because the townspeople, the police, and the courts took action.

A Covert Menace: Gangs

Most Hispanic youths living in Esperanza are not gang members: out of approximately 2,000 youths, 400 belong to a gang or about 20%. Nevertheless, this is double the percentage reported in one study that showed less than 10 percent of Hispanic males and an even smaller percentage of females in Los Angles Hispanic barrios are affiliated with gangs (Vigil 1988). Indeed the percentage of gang members in Esperanza is estimated to be very high, but it is not the majority of youth. For this reason the Weed and Seed projects that began in 1998 focus on reducing gangs by providing youth clubs for at-risk youth such as the four Safe Havens. Las Artes (described in chapter 2) as well as other social agencies, churches, schools, and businesses also provide options for youth activities and act as barriers against gangs.

Tony, a former gang member, works in one of those agencies. He is now middle aged, but goes right into the middle of gang conflicts and speaks street talk in an honest and convincing manner. As he says:

> If I can make one young kid think through what being jumped into a gang means, and he or she avoids it, my mission is a success. I had one brother killed in a gang street fight, I don't want that. I've had many close calls myself. I'm a former gang member and I know what goes on. Now I talk to 'em and remove their tattoos if they want them off. I take off about 75 or more tattoos every year. It's something—but not enough. I'll keep working on 'em as long as I have breath.

History of Gangs in the United States

Juvenile gangs, neither a new phenomenon in this country nor restricted to urban areas, now number an estimated 8,000 gangs with over 400,000 members spread across nearly all 50 states. Members live in suburban and rural areas, but most live in cities (Vigil and Yun 1996). Gang membership is not illegal, but dangers arise because of their covertness and involvement in illegal activities. Membership includes youth from diverse socioeconomic and ethnic groups, but gangs proliferate most rapidly in communities marked by poverty and social disadvantage (Fagan 1996)—such a setting would be Esperanza. Today's gangs have emerged from "loosely knit groups into established organized crime groups" (Douglas, Burgess, Burgess, & Ressler 1997:102).

The majority of Hispanic gang members come from families with lower levels of education and higher levels of spousal and substance abuse, especially caused by the fathers (Vélez-Ibáñez 1996). Hispanic youth have a low educational achievement and the highest national dropout rates from high school (U.S. Census 2001). Dropout rates are linked to the inability to read and write. Low-level educational achievement in Esperanza correlates with high levels of gang activity and violence.

In Esperanza, gang members tend to come from families that have many children, are poor, and whose cultural values include holding grudges and packing guns. Also, some youth who join gangs are drawn to violence as a result of craving excitement and risk taking. Family trauma, such as a parent being imprisoned or parents getting divorced, triggers some youth to seek the solace of peers, who often are other adolescents involved in gang activities. Joining a gang seems to lessen loneliness and focus anger. Females who join gangs tend to come from disorganized and abusive homes where they have often experienced sexual abuse (Chesney-Lind, Shelden & Joe 1996; Moore & Hagedorn 1996).

For gang members, violence is a normal occurrence. Most gang members have seen so much in their lives that they know few alternatives to solving problems. Gang violence terrorizes people. Over half of the people surveyed viewed gangs as a fearful problem in the town, and 59 percent reported knowing of or witnessing gang violence (Glittenberg 2001). Fear is also generated by the fact that gangs are covert and secret. "Not knowing who they are and where they are—that's scary" (63-year-old male).

Types of Gangs in Esperanza

In Esperanza, gangs are diverse, ranging from being social to violent (Yablonsky 1997). Social gangs are found most commonly in middle schools. They are nonviolent; they engage in pranks but not in any dangerous activities. Social gangs have only a sketchy notion of territory. Seldom do they have characteristics that differ from youth social clubs. Adolescents join gangs in order to become aligned with other adolescents and friends. A continuum of acceptable risk-taking activities in this age group sets norms of behavior (Thomas 2001). Being socialized into ritual behaviors of risk taking is part of adolescent behavior. For example a Saturday night ritual in Esperanza is a crush of young people cruising all over town, converging on main street, flirting, displaying dominant behaviors such as flashing gang colors, and looking for dates. Sometimes the competitive behaviors erupt into fighting, and guns have been drawn and too often used.

Gangs that are more troublesome have a definite territory, use gang names, wear special clothing, use secret hand signals, and have rituals. Such gangs are involved in a number of more serious misdemeanors, such as painting graffiti on walls; vandalism at schools; small-level thefts, like shoplifting. It is common for troublesome gang members to escalate risky behaviors and become more violent. Violent gangs have even more ritual, secretive behaviors and rites of passage, for example gang raping a girl, conducting a robbery, or committing an assault or even murder. They participate in criminal acts such as drug trafficking and using guns in these transactions (Yablonsky 1997). Violent gang members are the tough ones, but out of approximately 400 gang members in Esperanza, about 25 males and a couple of females are considered to be violent, and they range in age between 15 and 22. Unfortunately, law enforcement and the justice system have a tendency to lump all types of gangs together and then label them all as violent (Glittenberg 2001).

Some gangs in Esperanza are viewed as vigilantes, protecting the neighborhood. Maureen Campesino did her doctoral dissertation on gang violence in Esperanza, and her work is described further in the next chapter. A participant in Campesino's study says, "A gang will guard the neighborhood from other gangs or from anybody else coming in and robbing their houses; they pretty much take care of their own. The community in that area pretty much supports their local gang" (Campesino 2003:190). As one gang member put it, "We're keeping out the bad gangs from our 'hood." But not all residents are comfortable with gang protection: "You have to be careful if you walk down the street; you can't show any weakness; you have to show that you can do it" (17-year-old male). The uneasiness expressed by this young man illustrates the fear and tension that many people living in Esperanzans feel when there is a gang presence in the neighborhood.

Some gangs reflect an intergenerational membership. In Esperanza, we heard of family connections in gangs; these gangs seem to have a more violent history. For example, one mother of three sons in an intergenerational gang family said, "Someday they are going to kill me. It's been awful. It's fighting all the time. They only have drugs on their mind. I try to control them, but I can't. I wish the police could." She sat crying in the courtroom where a son was being tried for assault and battery (Glittenberg 2001).

Gang Leadership

Who leads gangs? Do leaders exist for a specific activity and once this event is over they revert back into the body of the gang? No one knows for sure. Leadership has been fractionalized because some of the leaders are now incarcerated (such as Maria's husband). When a gang leader is gone, from death or incarceration, violence sometimes increases as new leaders try to take over. Also, other rival gangs may try to capitalize on the destabilization within the gang that lost its leader.

As told in the focus groups, the violent gangs such as the Bloods and Crips have a three-man council at the head. Members of the council need to be the most violent, such as having committed a murder to qualify for leadership. Gang members may also fight for the position as leader, and sometimes gangs disintegrate due to a lack of leadership.

Drug Trafficking, Money, and Guns

For gangs in low-income neighborhoods where legitimate economic opportunities are slim, finding viable income in illegal economies such as auto theft, residential and commercial burglary, and drug trafficking becomes a way of life (Campesino 2003:52).

A slightly different twist is put on Hispanic gangs making money.

> Drug selling risks and rewards are evidence of a "culture of resistance" preferring the "more dignified workplace" of drug selling than the low wages and "subtle humiliations" of secondary labor markets where racism dominates work conditions and social interactions. (Bourgois quoted in Fagan 1996:54)

Could this be true? How can we find out? Ask a gang member. He says, "You don't see any Hispanic homeless men—[laughing]—we're out selling drugs. It's our way of doing things" (22-year-old male). This comment was heard from others and is a distinct mark of a "culture of resistance," as Bourgois also found.

For the past 20 years, gangs have focused on making money from trafficking illegal drugs and transporting undocumented immigrants across the Mexican border. Because the business is expanding, gang members are being recruited from the outside, especially from California; growth in business means more money for the greedy drug kingpins.

Conflicts in illegal drug trafficking are the most frequent cause of violence. Violence may also be motivated by a need to eliminate eyewitnesses of a crime or defend a barrio. Although buying guns is controlled, they can be purchased through an older family member, like a mother, brother, sister who does not have a criminal record. Flea markets and gun shows offer easy access to guns, and if they are not bought, guns are stolen. The overabundance of guns in Esperanza stymies control and as the stories will unfold, these deadly weapons are used too often.[2]

Substance abuse is another major contributory factor in gang homicide. "Drug or alcohol intoxication was present in every gang-related homicide a police officer had seen" (Campesino 2003:181). Gang violence accounts for 60 times more homicides for gang members than for the general population (Hutson, Anglin, Kyriacou, Hart, & Spears, 1995). This statistic parallels the ratio between the number of gang homicides (7) to the number of general homicides (11) that occurred in Esperanza during the period of our study—63 percent were gang related. All victims were below the age of 24. The level of hate expressed by some gang members is so profound that death itself is sometimes not sufficient enough for retaliation as Campesino found. "In one incident gang members broke into a local funeral home and desecrated the casket and the body of the dead gang rival" (Campesino 2003:182).

Murders are almost always within the same racial/ethnic group. "We do it to ourselves," said a Hispanic mother when her son was murdered in a Hispanic gang-related gun battle (Campesino 2003:193, 453). White on white, brown on brown, and black on black are cultural patterns of vengeance. What triggers violence within gangs—within the same ethnic groups? The major reasons are fighting over a girlfriend, driving through rival gang territory, or showing any number of displays of disrespect, including hand signals. "Acts of disrespect are a major cause for gang retaliation" (Campesino 2003:181). In the gang subculture, respect is "pretty much what they live or die for," (15-year-old male focus group member) "Dissing," or showing disrespect in any of its many forms, may initiate gang conflict. Now with gun power, gang members not only kill each other, but also they threaten the community and police with unintended deaths in drive-by shootings, which are often conducted for the purposes of retaliation.

Controlling Gangs and Gang Violence

How can the gangs be controlled in a community with limited financial resources? One way is through better tracking of gang members in and out of prison. While gang members are incarcerated, the Arizona State Department of Corrections tracks them from the outside, meaning they are identified before entering prisons as security risks and are confined to areas where special surveillance is maintained for safety purposes. Another means of tracking is a vertical prosecution method. This means that the same prosecutor is always handling the same gang member from the time of arrest and, if convicted, then to incarceration. The prosecutor stays informed about the incarceration. For instance, if a gang member is moved from one prison to another, even out of state due to overcrowding, the original prosecutor is informed of the move. Tracking is a method of control so the gang member doesn't just fall out and become lost in the system.

Community policing also has been successful in controlling gangs. In Esperanza, officers have formed a task force specifically aimed at eliminating drug-related, gang-related violence. Better enforcement at the U.S. and Mexico border also has helped, and an occasional "sting" operation conducted by police (usually several forces joining together, like Tucson and Esperanza) in Esperanza underscores that the police and the judges mean business. Police also conduct sting operations to find truant youths. During the first years of our study, the number of truant adolescents was high, but at the end in 2001, some stings found no one absent from school. That finding indicates the stings are having an effect on keeping kids in school.

Tough sentencing has also worked to control gangs. A highly publicized trial of a drug kingpin who operated a drug smuggling system in a tunnel between Mexico and the U.S. ended with a lifetime prison sentence. "This will send a message that we mean business," remarked the judge (*Arizona Daily Star Citizen,* March 24, 2001). Controlling drug traffic has largely focused on controlling the supply side, so capturing the kingpin and incarcerating him for life is one means of breaking the network. Gangs without a supplier (e.g., kingpin) have been cut off from smuggling—and need to develop new networks. Some gangs look elsewhere for drugs while others break up.

Controlling Gangs in Prisons

One means of controlling gangs in prison is to move a convicted gang leader to a prison in another state, thus breaking easy communication between the imprisoned leader and any gang followers. The success of such an action is debatable. "If you cut off the head of the Hydra, will it grow another?" asked Hammond, a Phoenix-based attorney. Another spokesperson agreed, "Someone will always emerge to take over the job when [leaders] leave." The plan is still being used in Arizona prisons (Field Notes 2000). Another plan being tried in Arizona is giving the more than 320 gang members who are being held in an Arizona prison a choice: "Renounce the gang and reveal everything you know or be sent to a maximum-security unit." This renouncement must be made during intake at the prison and sometimes is lapsed during incarceration. Sometimes former gang members "rejoin" prison gangs for their own protection and safety. In maximum-security units, inmates are locked in their cells 24 hours a day, except for three one-hour shower and recreation breaks every week (*Arizona Daily Star Citizen* 2000). We do not know how successful this plan currently is.

Perceptions and Opinions about Gangs

The context within which gangs form and flourish is one of poverty, undereducation, underemployment, family dysfunction, and social disconnections with high rates of imprisonment and separation. Maureen Campesino (2003) believes gang violence is a response to feelings of powerlessness, disintegration of social organization, and loss of social control that occur when families and entire communities live in multiple generations of poverty.

"I'm going down like that," a gang member said as he peered down at his homeboy in the casket (Campesino 2003:453). His statement was an admission of hopelessness. And sadly this 17-year-old, who saw no positive future, was killed in a gang fight just two weeks later. "We've seen it before and it's all happened again. It's never gonna stop; there's no hope for us" (14-year-old male). What do the people of Esperanza believe about gangs? Two focus groups of former gang members, one for males and the other for females, were held twice. They told us why they got into a gang, why they got out, and the reasons for violence in a gang. We also tapped older residents for their views of gangs and the changes they've seen.

Views from Former Gang Members

Why Did You Join a Gang?

I wasn't popular in my class, sort of always left out of things, and I thought I would get some friends, and I did for a while. I stayed in for two years, then gave it up. But I did get some friends and some are here today. (16-year-old male)

I wanted to be popular, like other girls. I was lonely and wanted to be part of a group. I felt okay for a while, and like everyone was my friend, but I didn't need them after I got my boyfriend. (15-year-old female)

I wanted to do things, like risky things, and have some wild times, but then I got to find out that it wasn't so much fun. I have other things I like better to do now, and I'm planning on going to nursing school and get a job so I don't want to do risky things anymore. (18-year-old female)

Reasons for Getting Out.

Choices need to be made to stay in or get out, and having other goals than making money seems to be a deciding point. The most common reason for getting out seems to be maturation—not liking that violent life any longer. Three views express those sentiments.

I saw some bad things—like beatin' up some old guys for money and stuff. That's why I stay in school and think about going to school, finishing school, doing it all legit; 'cause even though there's parole and all that there's no money in prisons. (15-year-old male)

It's better to be yourself and not just a homey—share with the people you know, first, like your family and then like the people you care about.

And then go help the people that need help. Can't really change anything by yourself, even if you try. If you go to school, go—smokin' and messin' just gets you into trouble. Get a good job—Help your family. (16-year-old female)

It's even worse if you're really poor or middle class—they can't bail you out. Finish school and become somethin' and do it all legit and don't have to worry about somebody coming repossessin' your car, your house. You won't have to worry about spendin' time in prison. (18-year-old male)

Culture of the Gang.

Those who have renounced gang membership tell their negative views of gangs.

Gangs—they're just shit. I mean they're shit . . . made up 'hoods there ain't even such a 'hood. (18-year-old male)

Gang—ha—they don't have a lifestyle. I mean no regular positive lifestyle. They just struggle. How you gonna make it a life without no education or nothin'. Why are you gonna be down for your 'hood and shit when you know; like all your friends, what are you when you're so down 'n all this shit 'n you kill somebody? Nobody is goin' to give a fuck. You're goin' to do your 25 years, nobody's gonna care. A 'hood that doesn't even belong to you, just cause you live there. That don't mean nothing. (19-year-old male)

Violence that occurs for various infractions are also deterrents along with possible imprisonment. As stated:

People are stabbed, people getting locked up because they stabbed somebody. Now there's killing, they just start killing each other. Everybody wants to use a gun. Nobody wants to fight no more, but it's bullshit. You think your homeys are all down for you and shit, but when you kill somebody and you get 25 years, they don't give a fuck. They're not goin' to be there. They're not gonna go visit and your family has to go through that. It's just bullshit. (17-year-old male)

Drug Trafficking: The Major Focus of Gangs.

Today the major reason for gangs is drug trafficking and making money from this trade. Members relate how important it is to be loyal to their gang and to expect violence only when disrespect is shown.

Now you don't see gang members out there trying to kill nobody now. You see them trying to make money you know what I mean. Homicides went down and drugs went up. (18-year-old female)

They sell drugs here 'n shit 'n they think it's all cool. Like nobody in the hood is going to say somethin'. That's what causes problems. (19-year-old male)

Views from Older Townspeople

Older townspeople gave some historical opinions. They owned their homes and most were monolingual Spanish speakers. These are representative comments:

> In the past 30 years there have been changes in gangs. In the seventies we had gangs but they didn't have guns. Now and then you'd hear about a rumble or something like that—a fight over a girl or territory, but no guns. Now it is scary, as they have bigger guns than the police. (73-year-old male)

> My sons all were part of gangs and my husband, too. They just did it to be social and be Mexican. It was more like Scouts for Anglos, I think. They talk that things are so violent in gangs. Sometimes the gangs steal the social checks from mailboxes and really frighten old people. There are drugs, too. There's a group of police who just fight gangs—nothing else—but it's not enough. I don't know what we can do as it's all over. I'm afraid to go out of my house alone. (75-year-old female)

There is a sense of fatalism, futility among the older people; none suggested any community action but rather depended on the police for security.

An earlier symbiotic relationship between the gangs and the community made it difficult to curb gangs, as some people saw gangs as protective. However, guns and drug trafficking have changed the nature of gangs, and fear in the community has increased.

Summary

The underlying base of poverty continues to challenge everyone, and the outside power of endless inequalities and opportunity to make "easy" money creates an unstable and challenged community, ripe for prostitution and gangs. The activities of prostitutes and gangs create disgust and fear in the townspeople. Prostitution is part of a long-standing illegal economy that impacts the whole town. The zone violation strategy has worked to keep prostitutes off the streets, and few streetwalkers have been seen during the past few years. Prostitutes give the town a negative image, but gangs give them fear. Both are loosely linked through drug trafficking; prostitutes are users and small time dealers. Gang members are more violent and are involved in making money from drug trafficking.

Gangs in Esperanza are another challenge as they are not illegal but their covert nature and informal, long-standing community structure is ideal for opportunistic drug dealers and human traffickers to prey on. Gang membership remains around 400, or about 20 percent of the youth population in the town of 5,600 people, with approximately 25 gang members classified as violent. Gangs are feared because of their use of guns and violence.

Cultural norms for ignoring, accepting, or promoting the irritating or dangerous subgroups are inscribed in the minds of the townspeople. Some levels of illegal dealings, especially within the immediate and extended family, are accepted as part of the informal economy, and maybe they are even promoted (e.g., dealing drugs). But the norms may be changing as the people endorse the controls such as zone restrictions so that known dealers can be arrested if they enter the town, "stings" to curb truancy and loitering, camera surveillance, more community policing such as bike patrols, and a larger force of police officers. Reducing and controlling illegal activities takes enormous human and economic resources that can be impeded by the community itself.

Notes

[1] A collection of full faced photographs of known, prosecuted prostitutes is kept in the police department for purposes of identifying persons who were violating their zone restrictions. There are about 100 photographs in this collection.

[2] In the past, gangs used fists and knives instead of guns. The transition to using guns began in the mid-1980s when an increase in drug trafficking reached epidemic proportions.

Chapter 5

Drug and
Human Trafficking

> I look at myself. I watch my brother. I shed tears of sorrow. I sow seeds of
> hate. I withdraw to the safety within the circle of life—MY OWN PEOPLE.
> —Corky Gonzales, *I Am Joaquín*

For people who feel they have no options for making much money, drug
and human trafficking offer opportunities to get extra money, fine jewelry, a
new car, and drugs for one's habit. Much research on drug and human smuggling fails to consider the entire cultural context within which such illegal
behavior takes place. According to Ed Knipe (1995), the cultural patterns of
manufacturing, supplying, and using drugs reflect the broadly shared beliefs
in a society. People in the U.S. believe in individual success, which is measured by the amount of money one earns and the possessions one has. Most
people living in Esperanza live below the poverty line, with poor education,
and few opportunities for upward mobility. In order to achieve success, which
is highly valued in the larger culture, some Esperanzans feel compelled to
participate in an illegal economy whenever possible, covertly and risking danger. We illuminate trafficking and smuggling by describing the current connections from the local to the global level.

Conspiracy and Illegality

The overlapping, covert networks of drug trafficking and human trafficking create dense but also fragile, often dangerous, competitive connections.
They have roots in an illegal economy linked with international crime cartels
and individuals who profit from human suffering. These underworld cultures

91

undermine civil society and counter the positive work done by resilient people—families and social institutions in Esperanza. Curbing the crimes takes so much intense energy, attention, commitment, and capital that, too often, the resilient citizens and victims become weary, complacent, and compliant.

Trafficking in drugs and humans is about making money and, for some, the rush of adrenaline that comes from making the deals and from the risk of being caught. Greed and power drive drug kingpins and human traffickers. So strong are these drives that violence may be an end result of illicit associations with these people. An example of this web of connections comes from Pedro, a small-time dealer in Esperanza.

PEDRO'S WEB OF MEANING

I am Pedro. I was born in Jalisco, Mexico, about 43 years ago. A lifetime drug dealer, smuggler, whatever—I am what some would call a *puchador* [a small-time dealer]. I grew up in a family of dealers. My dad, four older brothers, several uncles, and lots of cousins were all dealers. No women though, just us men. Women get too emotional, crying and jealous—all that stuff. You can't have it. Some women and men do small-time stuff out of their houses; they're called *tienditas* [small neighborhood store owners who sell drugs]. You gotta trust your family—like your life is in their hands at all times. You gotta be sharp and show no emotions, just cool, alert never trustin' anyone—other than family.

My first time dealin' was when I was about nine. My Tío Julio [Tío means uncle in Spanish] was makin' a drug run to Veracruz; he took a van that carried cash and guns. I got to sit in the back where I could see what was goin' on. I saw it all. Tío had the back of the van full of *dinero*, lots and lots of cash. I could tell what it was, but it was all covered with peaches and papers between the peaches—crates of them. Tío had two armed guards—all related to us somehow—that sat one in front and one beside me in the back with large machine guns across their knees. Neither talked to me, just looked straight ahead and side to side, watchin' all the time for trouble. Tío met other vans—five of them—along the way; he didn't have a cell phone or nothin'—just knew where they would be. It was all prearranged. It was an adrenaline rush, seeing every van had armed guards—with lots'a machine guns. The guards was all around, so I knew it was a big stash, and we'd make a bundle of money.

We was never stopped by anyone, but the guns were ready at all times, (but I didn't get one 'til I was 10. By then I knew all about guns and knives and where to hit so you'd drop 'em right away). It was nighttime. I wasn't afraid, more excited and proud that they included me in. Tío said I did fine and would be a puchador. He liked it that I was calm and quiet.

We met at a cantina near Veracruz, as the ship had just come in from somewhere nearby in the Yucatan, carryin' cocaine and heroin, I guess. They had boxes of bananas, sort of a banana boat with a false bottom where they stored the stash. Bananas aren't too heavy, and [they are] sort of bulky to cover up stuff. I stayed near the van and didn't go on the boat. Guards stood outside and told me that if there was trouble to just run as fast as I could. It didn't happen. We loaded boxes and boxes into the vans.

Each van went a different route out of Veracruz. We met outside of El Paso a couple days later. More cars arrived with Mexicans, and I knew it was a big deal because there were more guards circlin' near the vans. Tío was the leader and everyone trusted him. He lived to be 89—a very big influence on my life. There was never any drinkin'—everyone looked serious, but when it was over—everyone was laughin' and singin'. We made a lot of money that day. Tío was rich. He gave away a lot of money to his family. Don't know how much money they made, as Tío never dealt me in—I was too young. My dad was very proud, but he didn't say much. My mom didn't know, that I know of anyway.

Not all the deals was without bloodshed. Two of my brothers murdered a couple of guys durin' a handoff, and they was put away for life. Another brother was shot and killed durin' a trade, so our family set out for revenge. I don't want to talk about that, okay? as it is still goin' on, you know—an eye for an eye. I was shot twice in a leg and an arm. I've been knifed once and I've knifed at least five, don't know if they lived or died, and I don't care. They was trash—SOBs. I never shot anyone. Some was known killers, and others was just plain thieves, ready to take more than their share. I was never scared, 'cause you couldn't show a bit of fear, and you had to stand your ground and always be fair. They respected that and respected my family, especially Tío Julio.

I went to prison twice for dealin', just got caught at the wrong place, wrong time, and spent time in the big house. I did some dealin' while there, but not big time, just weed—to get my own stuff. I didn't want to compete with some of the mafia that was there; they didn't stand for no competition and killed off a couple guys who tried, made it look like an accident. You can get anythin' in the joint—any time. I took care of myself always findin' someone dealin' and tradin', but I never had my wife bring it in, as some guys did. I didn't want her to risk it, as the guards watched the chicanas, always wantin' to poke around for stash. I wanted her clean. I taught my sons to be good people—not to trust anyone but family. Both have real jobs, and I hope they don't do what I did.

But I got religion while I was in the big house. Yeah, it sounds rather made up, but there was one guy who had been a dealer himself. He had been a hard-time criminal until he found religion in the joint. He kept comin' around and preachin' on Sundays and talkin' about the better life. I kept goin' and likin' him better all the time. He could tell it as it is and didn't have fancy words at all for being a faith person. His name was Joe—"Just plain Joe," he'd say. He showed no fear but lots of carin' for some sick bastards. So I saw a priest, since I'm Catholic, by birth, and confessed and took communion. I really felt I would be faithful all my life, but that didn't always happen.

When I got out, I had temptations and fell off, goin' back to heroin, my choice. Don't think I'm an addict—but guess maybe I am—a *tecato*—an old heroin addict. At times I get regretful. I've made a pilgrimage to Magdalena [a town with religious shrines in northern Mexico where crowds of religious Mexicans come on October 3 to receive forgiveness for past transgressions] to confess my sins and even crawled a mile on my knees and let my hair grow—to show my repentance for sins. But then after a time, I fall off and start usin' again.

Why do I do it? For the money mostly. I've made millions and lost millions, but it is also the adrenaline rush that really keeps me goin'. I get a rush when I break into someone's car or into their house. It makes me feel really powerful to pull such a trick on the Anglos. I had a gringa boss who was too naive for words! I got her once to loan me a couple thousand dollars. I cried like a baby for money to pay my mortgage, and she, sweetly, handed it over thinkin' I'd pay her back. Jeez, I never planned to do that at all! I just wanted to see if I could do it, and I did. I never stole big money, just here and there, mostly as a dare to myself, and sometimes just for the hellavit.

Now I've got a regular job, as a salesman of fertilizer. I drive around the country, and see opportunities, especially when I go across the border. There's always some place to make a buck or more. I like the freedom to come 'n go and to see places where I can take advantage of a situation. I'm not usin' now, but maybe some time soon I'll go back to buyin' the good stuff, cut it, use half, and sell half. Yeah, I'm a tecato. Now and then I'm really off the stuff and go to mass every day, and then I get so I need a fix and I'm on it again. I probably will be like this 'til I die. It's a habit I can't seem to break.

Pedro's story is one we heard several versions of while in Esperanza: the lack of fear, the close family/friend ties, trust, and rules for being part of the drug business. If these cultural rules are broken, the consequences are known. Pedro seems to have three motivations: live by family rules, make money, and enjoy the adrenaline rush of the deal. We can also predict that he'll be involved in some illicit trading as his new "job" gives him opportunities and he cannot seem to break his heroin habit. Human smuggling also operates within these same cultural rules, especially making money.

The Network of Drugs and Dealing

How do people see drugs and dealing as part of the cultural pattern? Responses to the questions below illuminate a pattern of rules of drug dealing and ways to control them.

Who Deals Drugs and Why Is There Dealing in Esperanza?

The comments shared by focus group members about the pervasive selling and complicity bring into question how drug dealing can be controlled.

Age has nothin' to do with it; if you're 10 or 13, kids are getting' high and 10 year olds are sellin' crack and 50 year olds are sellin' crack. (19-year-old male)

Everyone doing it—like the kid on the bike, or the fellow pickin' up trash—or the Avon lady—they're all over town. The big drug kingpins from Mexico are the ones that scare me, and who knows where they are. Some are officials dressed up nice. You don't see them walkin' on the streets of Esperanza—no way—they're not stupid! (22-year-old female)

For most of us live here, we're used to it. Some of us deal on the side— well I know I do, just to get by, just dealin', but there's nothin' new that I haven't seen before—I mean everything is the same. Nothin' has increased in my eyes as far as violence or drug dealin'—same as before. (67-year-old male)

We just look the other way. It goes on in every alley and street corner. Some are all in the family, everybody sellin'. (63-year-old female)

It's all about money. You see somebody selling drugs and they're makin' a lot of money—and you envy that person so you want to do the same—it's all about money. (17-year-old male)

I think it's good, say you're poor and your family needs money, just go out there and hustle. (15-year-old female)

I sell so I can get my fix—it's my only way. (25-year-old male)

Although people acknowledge the illegality of drug dealing and their need to be part of the action, they also have views on how to control the dealing, as follows.

Catch more drug dealers. This might not happen quick like, but once you get rid of 'em they will come back. They're everywhere. You've got to have police who stick around for a couple of years to make sure it [drug dealing] doesn't come back. (43-year-old male)

They're all scared so they lock their doors, lock themselves in and don't want to see what is happenin'. Maybe only the police or if we could all be organized, not just families, then maybe it could change. (60-year-old male)

The organized criminal structure associated with drug trafficking poses many threats to societies like Esperanza. The threat of violence related to the drug trade is often as hidden as the informal economy itself: "oftentimes the threat is subtle and insidious" (Fuentes & Kelly 1999:338). Trafficking violence in Esperanza is pernicious and disruptive, making a life of fear for all citizens. Drug dealers make every effort to manipulate the local-level legal and political systems without fanfare so that no attention is called to themselves. If one decides not to play by these rules, the threat of violence looms. The all-too-familiar tactic is used throughout the world. Esperanza is no exception.

Drug dealing was going on almost night and day in the HUD apartments. Hardly any party was given without the presence of marijuana. The apartment next door was alive with dealers with their own system.

DRUG-DEALING EVENTS IN THE HUD APARTMENTS: FIELD NOTES 1997

About 11:30 AM steady action was going on next door; individuals would arrive on foot or several would come in a car. The signal for entry was a whistle; they then went in the front, but came out the back door. From time to time we'd catch strong odors of pot and cocaine; we'd heard that the lady dealt mostly with pot, but what we saw were hardcore junkies, not pot users.

The rush was greater in the morning: four high school-aged males (Anglos) arrived one after the other; three knew the whistle signal and the fourth, a girl, came up but didn't know the signal, so she left. They had their schoolbooks with them, and they went out through the back door. One kid went over our fence, as the front gate was locked, and he went to the side. Five other individuals came, including two Hispanic females, one African American female, and two African American males; all looked to be in their 20s and 30s, clearly heavier users than just for pot.

One African American female, about 23, drove up, parked in front and tried to get inside; her actions were criminal because she did everything to gain entry but leap the blue iron fence that was almost six feet high and with spikes at the top. It was meant to *keep out* intruders. She picked up handfuls of stones and threw them against the windows and doors; after six tries she gave up, got into her car and drove off. About 20 minutes later she came back and went through the routine again, gradually throwing larger and larger stones against the window. Failing to get attention she went to her car and began tooting the horn. Talk about drawing attention! Finally she got frustrated and left again—later she was seen driving back, and she met two African American males, about 28–30, and they whistled loudly for about two minutes and a young African American came out (still obviously high from the night before) and let them in. [Police were waiting for more evidence and trying to catch the bigger dealer; later they did arrest the son and the mother. We heard they both did time.]

Drug trafficking, as heard from a number of informants, was not just in the family apartments—the young residents—but very active in the senior HUD housing, and we saw known dealers going in and out, usually during the evening.

Yes, you can get anything there, about any time day or night, but at night the outside doors are propped open with a little piece of paper, and I hear them coming and going all times of the night—there's a lot of dealing going on. (74-year-old male resident)

Drug sales took place almost constantly, and openly, during our four-year study.

You can see people just selling right on the street, but there used to be a time when the town was tranquil and you could walk on the streets, but now there are drug dealers everywhere; even the woman who sells tortillas also sells drugs. (48-year-old male)

The Business of Drug Trafficking

Drug trafficking in Esperanza is a thriving business, but it is also very complex. Addicts have full-time jobs and are not necessarily visibly obvious. Customers also deal, so it is often difficult to discern the dealer from the customer. The drugs of choice, marijuana and cocaine ("coke"), are readily available. Also, hustlers and mid-level dealers may not have a legal income, so dealing is a way of getting their own drugs. Street dealers are always working on decreasing their debt, and they take "kickbacks" or "flush backs" to sustain their habit, and sometimes they need to cut down. The accuracy of reported profit from drugs should be questioned, as in Esperanza, we considered all of the drug dealers as small-time, mostly those making a little extra and getting their own dope. A clutch (small bag, about a teaspoonful or 15 ml) of cocaine sells for $20 in Esperanza. The usual runner or *pucharo* (small drug dealer) makes $100–$300 a day when selling. But the sales are erratic, and most said that the total amount they make per month is about $300.

I use it for getting by, been doing it for about 15 years now and never caught. I just sell to those I know and in my family. (54-year-old male)

I just sell so I can buy my own stash. Some weeks I don't use much, depends on how I'm feeling. I use about a clutch a day, I'd guess, sometimes a lot more and sometimes none at all. Seems to me I do more in the summer, when it's hot—I like to simmer down. It takes a couple hundred a month to keep me happy. I have to be more careful as I was busted once and spent six months in jail for possession—next time it would be more. I trade sex for a clutch and that works okay and then I sell to customers, too. I don't have a big habit like some, and I've been doing the same thing for about five years now. I want to quit it all and lead a good life, but I keep coming back to the same gang and doing the drugs. (48-year-old female)

Stares (1996) illustrates the immense profit that is made in drug smuggling: a kilogram of heroin bought in Burma for $70 is traded in Bangkok for $3,000 and then sold for export for $6,000–$10,000 and again sold wholesale in the U.S. for $90,000 to $200,000, which then is further diluted and sold in grams at the street level. The coca farmer in Colombia may make $1,000 a year on their coca leaves, while the traffickers take in over $10 billion from smuggling cocaine eventually into the U.S. The cost for actually transporting the drugs is low, but costs related to the bribes given along the way to keep the drugs moving through the system may be high. Tariffs and other constraints in transporting have been lifted with many recent treaties, like the North America Free Trade Agreement (NAFTA), making it profitable to do risky business.

Drug trafficking plays an integral role in the total borderland economic environment (Glittenberg & Anderson 1999). In Esperanza, there have been attempts to curtail the underground drug economy; however, these efforts have been generally unsuccessful because there are too many stakeholders involved, including those in the largely unidentified upper echelons of production and distribution to those at the bottom of the hierarchy—the street dealers and runners. The network remains secret, and connections are maintained for protection and profit.

The illegality of drug trafficking fosters many complications. For instance, where do you store large quantities of drugs or what happens if you overproduce and cannot find buyers? Markets are unpredictable. How does a drug trafficker market or advertise that he/she has drugs for sale? Traffickers have to avoid the legal channels of doing business and instead rely on bribery and corrupt practices that often lead to violence. No quality control measures exist, so adulterated drugs or diluted drugs may enter the marketplace. These are, after all, illegal products. Trust is a critical component of doing business for traffickers, as was learned in the story of Pedro. Cultural rules maintain drug networks—there are no official laws. But then there is no legal recourse for a dealer who suspects he or she is being cheated, so murder may be one way to even a score.

Yet, the profits outweigh the risks. Handling large quantities of money from transactions also has risks. Money laundering on the global scene is so sophisticated that it is difficult to trace as drug transactions cross national boundaries. Hence money is laundered into many layers and the origins are quickly disguised. Money laundering occurs in Esperanza where drug transactions rapidly become part of the informal economy. Tracing the money is an enormous challenge (we tried—and failed). No studies focus strictly on how drug trafficking affects the economics of specific communities. Few clues are uncovered in this covert, complicit money laundering scheme (Bagley 1997; O'Day & Venecia 1999; Poppa 1990). Some get rich and some get little; the distribution of money is not equal, as can be seen by the mansions next to hovels across the borderland.

Controlling Drug Trafficking in Esperanza

Untangling the illegal drug network may not decrease the level of violence and revenge, but the complicity can be understood and curtailed. The original size of the drug load must be divided up among many people (as we discovered with Pedro's multiple truckloads), thus increasing the number of people involved in the collusion. On one level are the people who carry drugs across the border in automobiles, on trains, on foot, and through tunnels and culverts. The big drug lords don't do this lowly work; rather they use medium- to low-level smugglers to hide the drugs in a vehicle or on the body. But the people involved must be trustworthy. When one source of trafficking is shut down, another pops up to take its place. Changing the culture in this tightly knit group is precarious, for covertness and trust are the glue that holds the group together. Change must come from within, through a new direction or belief that legitimate employment can offer satisfactory rewards—that the benefits of legitimate work outweigh the risks of trafficking.

Lisa, who is a registered nurse in her 50s with a master's degree, is married to a psychiatrist who works in the prison system. Lisa shares her insights about trafficking and bringing about change:

> The drug trafficking? That I know goes on all over Esperanza, that's different. It is all for money, illegal, and there's blood on that money. The territorial fights are not going to end until the profit is taken away from the trafficking. It could be done. I also see a lot of addicts. Some have open veins, they've nothing in life. My husband treats hundreds in prison. They shouldn't be there as they are sick. He's testified many times to change the laws.
>
> We are all uptight about the moral issues of drugs. It's not that way. Look at me; I'm not addicted now but I was a heavy user in the 60s, but if I were, would I be thrown in prison when I should be treated for an illness?

Opinions about controlling drug trafficking shifted during the time of our study. Toward the end of the four years, locals acknowledged that there were fewer drug dealers, and there were higher levels of trust with the police. However, given the large economic disparity of most of the local residents vis-à-vis the surrounding community, the drug trade has continued to be part of an extensive informal economy.

During the study period, Esperanza police conducted three local Safe Street Sweeps and seven joint operations with the sheriff's department. They targeted drug-dealing gang members and other known violent crime offenders. During one local operation, 8 felony and 35 misdemeanor arrests were made. Twenty-eight narcotic operations resulted in the seizure of more than $1,127,000 in drugs with 73 felony and 75 misdemeanor arrests. Raids were made on crack houses, and eventually, all known, abandoned houses were destroyed. The U.S. Marine Corps, stationed nearby, took part in tearing down abandoned crack houses and assisted police and town leaders in educating youth about dangers of drug use (Field Notes May 20, 2000).

Investigating drug deals requires a lot of undercover agents. One investigation took nine months, and it linked with Federal Drug Administration (FDA) agents, county sheriff's deputies, the State Department of Public Safety Gang Task Force, and Esperanza police. The chief of police reported, "It was like the drug dealers were paralyzed—their little house of cards collapsed. Now our guys are having trouble finding drug dealers on the street; before they were there every time we turned around." Police surveillance and arrests have reduced drug trafficking in the town, although it is a very expensive undertaking.

The use of zones as an effective method of controlling drug trafficking is widely known. Just as we learned in the previous chapter prostitution is controlled by zone restrictions, so is drug trafficking. Upon sentencing, the con-

Demolishing a burned building

victed person is informed of zone restrictions and the length of time for the restriction. Hence, if convicted dealers are found in those restricted areas they can be re-arrested without further cause.

Bringing down some big-time dealers is one thing, but it is hard to change the long-standing culture of complicity and making money quickly. As long as people see drug dealing as a way to make money and as long as the necessary covert networks exist throughout the country, it will take constant attention to reduce and curb drug trafficking as a way of living in Esperanza.

Controlling drug trafficking is a major concern for the police. For the law officers, safety and security for the townspeople is their first priority, but for change to occur, the people themselves must take a proactive stance. In some instances, community members are making efforts to curtail drug use. For example, in the HUD housing a zero tolerance for drug use and dealing has been put into effect, meaning if you, or anyone in your household, is found to be using or selling drugs, you are evicted. We saw some enforcement of this rule.

Human Trafficking: A Long-Standing Problem

The network of illegal activities and the greed that drives it includes the growing "business" of human trafficking. People often leave their countries of birth because they are experiencing strife, economic disaster, or displacement. They move from a poorer country to one with greater wealth. The desire for the opportunities afforded by another country often overshadows going through the proper channels to obtain visas and work permits—acquiring the documentation to migrate legally—which is becoming harder and harder for those wanting to immigrate to the U.S. Thus, many people enter the U.S. clandestinely and illegally.

Illegal crossing in various places along the 2,000-mile border between Mexico and the U.S. has been risky, and it is growing more so as the numbers of crossers have increased, and the dangers as well. Ellingwood, in *Hard Line: Life and Death on the U.S.–Mexico Border* (2004), describes graphically the dangers from the brutal desert crossing saying, "it's the home to criminal operations of every stripe—smugglers, drug lords, fugitives and crooked cops—and some of the most unforgiving natural surroundings in either country" (2004:4). At least 300 die annually, as many immigrants get lost in the blistering desert, or die in crashes when being illegally transported in crowded trucks or vans driven by inexperienced drivers, trying to avoid the ever-present border patrol (*la migra*). To surmount the dangers, illegal immigrants hire people to escort and guide them across the border. The guide is called *coyote*; coyotes only get paid when they successfully escort their charges across the border, so coyotes try to plan a safe, covert journey (Ellingwood 2004). But it does not always happen this way.

Because of the increased numbers and the high risk of crossing, entrepreneurs have seized on the opportunity to charge substantial sums to smuggle people into the U.S. Now instead of smuggling drugs, they are smuggling human beings, charging about $2,000 per person—reaping an estimated annual sum of $7–$8 billion for all smugglers combined. Although no match for the more lucrative drug trafficking, human smuggling amounts to a large sum of illegal money (Ellingwood 2004:84).

Since Esperanza is a border town, it is a key location for illegal underground networks that handle smuggling of humans (Achary 2004). Although people migrated back and forth across the border for hundreds of years, currently there is a cycle of control and fear at the border. A recent article in *Time* focuses on the subject. The foreboding national crisis is portrayed nightly on the media (*Time* 2006). Debates have grown around this controversial movement, and borderlands such as Esperanza are battlegrounds in this controversy.

Crossing the distance of 45 miles from the border to Esperanza has always been risky, fighting the heat, the gangs, and the thugs. Now the intensity of trafficking has increased significantly because of the tightened border security. Coming unescorted by foot has many dangers, such as becoming lost and dying of thirst; even though hiring a smuggler is expensive, the smuggler's expertise serves as an insurance policy for safety.

An indication of the many pros and cons in the national debate over how the U.S. government should handle illegal immigrants is found in the statements of two leading citizens made in a *Time* magazine article. Frank Sharry, Executive Director of National Immigration Forum, states:

> America is permanently evolving—that scares some people, but that's what we're all about. Do you keep it [immigration] the way it is (illegal) or do you keep re-energizing the country with fresh people and fresh ideas? (2006:40)

And the other side of the argument, George Borjas, a Harvard University economist, states:

> The kinds of immigration policy we have been pursuing, both legal and illegal, lead to an economic outcome where those on the low end of the labor market are suffering and all that extra wealth is being redistributed to the employers. Such a huge amount of wealth is being redistributed away from the poor toward the upper middle class and people who use immigrant service workers—the rich. So what immigration is doing is pouring more poor people into the U.S. and making the poor who are already here even poorer. (2006:41)

Both arguments have relevancy for the people in Esperanza, where poverty, violence, and hope continue to be part of everyday life.

Lest we forget, the border has been crossed millions of times by those seeking refuge—not only for work but also for rescue from dictators, torture, and political restrictions on life. John Fife, pastor of the Southside Presbyterian Church (that sits on the edge of Esperanza) is internationally renowned for his 1980's stand on providing sanctuary for persecuted people, mainly from Central America but also from other places. For over 30 years, Fife (and others) has provided safe shelter, food, and water for thousands of Mexicans who have crossed the border.

In response to the current situation, John Fife has joined other humane groups to lend a humane hand by placing water jugs along routes in the desert—an operation called Humane Borders. These humane groups have goals of caring for the immigrants, so tension is high between these groups and the armed volunteers who guard the border (Ellingwood 2004:227). The vigilantes claim they are defending U.S. sovereignty from illegal invasion of undocumented Mexicans. The debate and tension between the humane groups and the vigilantes will likely be ongoing, because their views reflect the diversity and convictions within the U.S.

In many countries, including the U.S., human trafficking also involves people leaving their homeland, either willingly or by kidnapping, and being forced into prostitution. At the U.S.–Mexico border both types of human trafficking exists—assisting illegal, undocumented immigrants to enter the U.S. and participating in international sex rings. International sex trafficking has been a growing problem worldwide, especially since World War II (Altink 1995:20). International rings of predators do exist at the border. The following example of Mona—possibly a pawn in sex trafficking—underscores the risks people take in life.

MONA, A POSSIBLE SEX TRAFFICKING ENCOUNTER: FIELD NOTES, JUNE 2001

As the research is finishing and I [Jody] am completing the final report to NIDA, I often go back to Esperanza for a good Mexican luncheon. It is a very hot day in June, and I have a burrito at my favorite restaurant. As I am paying my bill, a small Asian woman enters—the place is nearly empty at that hour. Dressed in a long black skirt and a long-sleeved white blouse she stands at the register and speaks to a waitress in very broken English, "Boss?" When the owner comes to the register she says, "Work?—work hard." That is what I think she says. The owner looks puzzled, "Do you have papers?" The Asian woman looks away and the owner says, "We don't need any help now," shaking his head and probably brushing her off. She doesn't say anything but looks down again, and then goes slowly to the door. I pay my bill and begin walking to my car, suffering in the intense heat. I see the child/woman standing in the shade near the edge of the building staring across the highway.

Realizing she doesn't have any transportation, I say, "It's really hot out here, do you need a ride?" pointing to my car. I know she understands, as I smile at her and open the car door. She gets in—I realize that she is very young and quite pretty except for her excessive makeup, for this time of day and the torrid weather. She smiles and says, "Thanks." I ask, "Where do you live?" She points south, so I drive that direction. We reach an intersection, and she points to the left. I turn and we drive a couple of blocks, and following her directions, turn to the right. We are now behind the racetracks—I'm not sure there are any houses nearby. She gestures again and points toward an abandoned motel—at least I thought it was abandoned. Paint is coming off the sides of the building and the neon sign says only O—E as the M, T, L are long gone. It looks deserted. As we drive around the side, she points to a door at the rear of the building. I drive there and park the car—there is a bit of shade—a little cooler. "Name?" I ask slowly. She responds, "Mona." "You—live—here?" She nods and smiles.

Then she smiles again and gets out of the car saying, "Wait"—and motions for me to stay. I do—wondering what to expect. Mona quickly runs through the back door and into the building. A moment later she returns with two small packages in her hand. "You—good." One is a perfumed sachet and the other, a package of Chinese noodles. "You—good," Mona repeats, smiling and pointing at me. I assume it is for giving her a lift on a very, very hot day. "You—work?" I ask slowly. "Men," she answers, smiling. "Who—boss?" "Boss—bye," she waves her hands southward. I try to put 2 and 2 together. "How—you—get—here?" "Mexico," she smiles again. Mona does not look frightened, but instead waves goodbye, smiling and turning around, she runs back into the rundown motel. I think about going in after her, and then think better of it—as this part of town isn't really in Esperanza—and I didn't know what I'd do if I entered the place.

Not knowing exactly what to do, I drive to the police department and seeing a detective friend, Mike, sitting at his desk, I say, "I've just had an unusual experience that might be something for you to look into." I tell him about encountering Mona. He seems puzzled and says, "I didn't think anyone lived in that place. I thought it was abandoned. That's in the county and out of our jurisdiction, but I'll check it out with the sheriff." Mike calls me the next day, "A deputy went out to check on that Mona person, but found no one there—only a couple packages of Chinese noodles in an empty room. You know that place doesn't have any running water or electricity—and in this heat—Whew!!" He says, "It looks like some homeless people might have been living there, but there is no Mona." What a puzzle I think. "Perhaps it's a new ring of international sex traders, human traffickers, in the area," I remark. "Could be, that's all we need," he responds weakly.

I did not follow up on this unexpected encounter, but thought that it wouldn't be too surprising to have an international sex ring in this border town, as any pattern of illegal economy is hard to destroy—it continues to find roots in Esperanza. Weed out the bad, seed in the good; it is a constant adaptation, a continuing battle.

Summary

Reducing and controlling covert illegal activities takes enormous human and economic resources that are impeded by the complicity and complacency of the town itself. The big international drug dealers pass through the porous border, laundering their money in faraway places. But the small-time dealers are often local people, part of the informal network that impacts the whole town. Open dealing and using can be controlled at enormous expense of arresting, prosecuting, and incarcerating. "Zone" restrictions seem to have controlled some illegal actions while still protecting the legal individual rights of those arrested. Zone restrictions have been a major arm of control for both drug dealing and prostituting.

Another illegal problem local people face is the human trafficking of undocumented, illegal immigrants, which includes trafficking sex workers who are either willing participants or have been kidnapped.

Ignoring, accepting, and promoting drug and human trafficking all are part of the cultural norms of the townspeople. "Everybody does it" signifies a cultural norm that is difficult to change. Family and kinship systems are like *cartelito*—small cartels—a very tightly knit group that builds upon family ties for trust and security. These cultural norms are complicit and covert—equally hard to change. Some levels of illegal dealings, especially within the family and extended kinship, are accepted as part of the informal economy. This accepted behavior has been in place for several generations. The underlying base of poverty continues to challenge everyone, and the outside power of endless inequalities and opportunity to make "easy" money relentlessly creates an unstable and challenged community.

But the norms may be changing. People talk about their fears and how things could be different. They trust the new chief of police and the police force— more in recent years than in the past. There is an increase in promoting personal responsibility for changing the norms. Local people talk about, "We've got to clean up this town." "We've got to get involved."

Chapter 6

The Structure of Violence

> Violence has become a common feature of contemporary life, and our society often is said to be caught in a cycle of intergenerational transmission of violence that produces evermore violent generations over time.
>
> —Merrill Singer, *Something Dangerous*

Violence is a human condition just as are joy, fear, and sorrow (Scheper-Hughes & Bourgois 2004:4). It is a social construct built by cultural ideas of otherness, power, and suppression. But how do we explain intragroup violence, a happenstance that circumvents the cultural construction of "otherness"? Homicides in Esperanza have been brown on brown, black on black, white on white. We find that in the same area and time period the rate of Hispanic youth murders were five times as great as Anglo youth murders. Why? This is a tough question to answer, so we approach the problem as we have the others: by going to the people, observing the whole context, gathering all the facts or events, not just one fact or event taken out of context.

Violence is cyclical with the rates rising and falling as related to the clustering of social events. Agar believes that "systems don't just move randomly through time, they change by self-reorganizing" (2004:413). Following the nation's "Summer of Violence in 1993," and the drive-by murder of Oscar, the people said, "No more!" The homicide rates in Esperanza dropped over 50 percent in two years. That's a significant change.

Some violent acts are easily visible, like a murdered person lying on the pavement, but other acts are subtle and covert, like ignoring or shunning unwanted people of the town. That, too, is violence, resulting from the desire of those with power to suppress those without. This type of violence is seen in societies in which the distribution of wealth and opportunities is unequal. In this chapter we will describe some visible events, such as violence from drunkenness and drug abuse, also domestic and gang violence. In chapter 7 we will uncover the shunned, unwanted people and see violence from their perspectives.

105

The Criminal Mind and the Violent Family

Multiple theories exist about what causes violence. For example, Desmond Morris's zoological notion of aggression was popularized during the 1960s. Morris (1967) views the basic nature of violence as originating in our animal background and in the natural tendency to defend territory. Others in agreement with Morris's argument that violence is biologically determined include Freud, who viewed human beings as fixating on instinctive reactions. According to Freud, "Men are not gentle, friendly creatures wishing for love, [they] defend themselves if they are attacked, [this is] part of their instinctual endowment" (Freud 1929:30).

Others have looked for the roots of violence in genetics or biology but find little evidence that such a link exists (Lashley 1998). Instead, they see violence linked with cognitive dysfunction, changes in personalities, and increased feelings of depression and paranoia, which can lead to violent behavior. As discussed previously, oftentimes psychoactive drugs may give rise to these types of violent states. People may commit violent acts when they feel their reputations, possessions, and/or privileges are threatened. People, such as dictators and bullies, may use violence because they feel threatened and wish to control the situation.

To explain violent behavior, our study uses a cultural explanatory model, a systematic view of the interactions of all components in a culture that inflame violence or, on the other hand, control it. We described in chapter 1 the use of a cultural consensus model that indicated a range of behavior associated with individuals, families, and society—the entire system. Below, we provide two stories of violence, one of an individual and the other of a family. In spite of resilient people being a counterforce, violence still occurs in Esperanza, as illustrated in the following story of Ana, a girl gangbanger, now in prison for murder.

ANA, A GIRL GANGBANGER IN PRISON FOR MURDER

I've now been in prison for six years; I got locked up when I was 14 and I'll be here until I'm 41, that's 20 to 30 years for second-degree murder. I'm now 20, and lookin' back, I was a bad teen. I was always in trouble. I didn't know nothin'; I didn't go to school much, as I was always skippin' school. I was havin' a good time with my homeys—been in juvenile detention and all that, and everyone thought I was cool 'cause I was mean. We was driving around Friday night, drinkin' beer, smokin' weed. Was lookin' for excitement, action 'n trouble. There was five of us—just cruisin' when we come up to another car of girl gangers. We'd known 'em from school and just messin' around. I threw some hand signals; they got mad and started talk'n spank 'n dissing. We started talk'n back and it got hott'r and hott'r—we was gettin' mad. They yelled, "stop 'n let's fight it out." They was five, too—was a tough bunch of bitches.

I took out my loaded 45 that I'd had since I was 12 'n started unload'n it at them's car, smash'n a couple windows—then we made a get away. It wasn't long 'til the cops stopped us. I was arrested, the only one with a gun. Guess I'd shot one, Myrna. I didn't meant to. I was just shoot'n at the car. She died on the spot. She was 18 'n had a little girl.

During the trial Ana was belligerent and unrepentant. The judge was not impressed with the potential of rehabilitating her. However, while in prison Ana made progress toward completing her GED, and her attitude changed. She still has 20 more years before she can be considered for parole. Often a speaker to teens who are in trouble, Ana tells them of her life. "I hope what I done they can learn from—I wish I hadn't done it—and maybe this will wake somebody up so they won't do the same" (Field Notes, July 17, 2000).

Ana was a gangbanger, bragging and showing immature judgment. She was trying to show superiority and to be admired by the gang. In her act of arrogance, Ana committed a murder affecting permanently the lives of many. Violence does not just follow clear borders but, like a mudslide, it spills over from one place to another. The next example is of a family of killers from a neighborhood nearby Esperanza.

THE BENITO FAMILY, A VIOLENT FAMILY

Mateo, head of the Benito family, is only 46 years old but has a reputation as a "mean bastard" and as a drug-abusing wife batterer. He is the father of four sons, all in prison at this time. One 19-year-old son, Henri, had eight arrests from juvenile crimes including: burglary, theft, assault, trespassing, and disorderly conduct. He was placed on probation at age 18 but then murdered a neighbor at age 19. A younger brother, Juan, was arrested at 15 for drug abuse and beating a mentally retarded boy; he was sent to prison and released two years later. Soon after being released, Juan and his father were both charged with beating and savagely killing a 72-year-old man, then stealing his pickup. Two older brothers, Manuel and Miguel, were convicted of murdering a man by brutally beating him with their fists and a jackhammer, and finally killing him with a rock. The reason given for the killing was "we made the mistake of eatin' his pizza." In each incident, each perpetrator had consumed large quantities of beer and hard liquor as well as smoked marijuana and crack cocaine. The father and four sons, Henri, Juan, Miguel and Manuel, are doing prison time, all for violent murders. Alcohol and drugs were used often in their violent home environment (*Arizona Daily Star Citizen*, August 2000).

Murder Statistics

Homicide refers to the act of killing another human being. Not all homicides are criminal acts, however; a homicide is committed when a four-year-old child, out of curiosity, picks up a gun, not understanding that it is a dangerous weapon, points it a his two-year-old brother, pulls the trigger, and the two-year-old dies. Murder, a subcategory of homicide, is a criminal act. It is the intentional and unlawful act of one human being killing another (Douglas, Burgess, Burgess & Ressler 1997:18).

Murder represents about 1 percent of all crimes in the U.S., but it is considered the most serious of all them. Murder is the tenth leading cause of death for men in the United States. Seventy-six percent of murder victims are male and 90 percent are persons 18 years of age or older. Only 5 percent of all murders are gang related, and 20 percent of murders are linked to felonies such as rape, theft, or narcotic trafficking. Cycles of murder occur; for instance, in 2003, the percentage of men murdered by intimates (spouse, ex-spouse, boyfriend, and girlfriend) dropped by 71 percent since 1976—a 30-year low. For women, murder declined to its lowest rate in 2001–2002 (Uniform Crime Reports 2004). Males are 10 times more likely to commit murders than are females. Forty percent of white males kill other white males, and 40 percent of black males kill other black males: white on white and black on black (Best 2003), or as we find in this chapter, "we kill our own." There were no specific national data on Hispanic murders.

In the 2003, the United States' prevalence rate for murder was 8.8 per 100,000 (Uniform Crime Report 2004), and Arizona was ranked among the top 10 most violent states as measured by prevalence rate for murder. In Esperanza, the rate of murder was 25.2 per 100,000 for Mexican Americans but only 4.9 per 100,000 for Anglos—a five times greater rate for Mexican Americans.

Many murders in Esperanza are drug related. A drug dealer could be murdered in Esperanza as punishment for being an informant, during a robbery, or for infringing on another's territory (Douglas et al.1997:47). Drug-related murders are hard to solve and prosecute, as most witnesses have unstable backgrounds, and their truthfulness is often questionable. These murders are often very brutal, probably because the characters involved have long histories of crime and tend to be callused. Gangs are frequently involved in murder in Esperanza. A border patrol officer was killed just outside of Esperanza during the study, targeted by gang members. Gang shootings may be about drug trafficking or revenge and involve gang conflicts, "dissing," or competition for a female. If you are a drug dealer, a prostitute, or a gang member, your chances of becoming a statistic, that is being hurt or killed, are very high. If you are a law-abiding citizen, the chance of being a random victim is pretty minuscule, although it does occur, like the drive-by shooting of Oscar.

Homicide Survivors' Support Group

Homicide Survivors—what could that mean? Homicide victims do *not* survive—so why the name and what does this have to do with violence? This was a question I asked myself as I went to attend a meeting held at Project YES, a social agency that provides support for people whose loved ones have been murdered. We were a small group—varying from 10 to 16 members—meeting for two hours every week. Sad and strained faces, tears and sobbing—yes, these *were* the survivors, for every murder there are at least five people who survived. They have to. They are the mothers, fathers, wives, husbands, and children of the murdered victim. Too often they, the homicide survivors, are left to grieve alone for people just don't understand how to talk with them about *murder.* Perhaps people fear they, too, will be targeted or in some way tarnished by such violence.

But being left alone to mourn is seen also as violence. "My husband was murdered, beaten to death by a mad man on meth; I couldn't even take his wedding ring off—as it might be 'evidence'—I could not touch my beloved. I was separated from my grief. And the murderer, what does he have? A nice cell in a warm prison with 'loving' people bringing him Christmas presents, writing him letters of hope while I have no one to even talk to about my pain!" the widow cries hopelessly, angrily.

"When Oscar was killed, my life stopped," cries his mother, speaking only in Spanish. "Yet the newspapers and the TV showed his picture, our family, our home—without thinking of our pain." Each of the survivors reviews over and over again how the media ripped their families apart, leaving nonhealing scars. "It seemed the reporters got some joy from catching our tears and sobs on camera. I just wanted to disappear—to run away—but I had to go to work, I had to make 'normal,' but my heart will never heal," sobs a gray-haired father.

As I sat week after week listening to the sorrow, I see how important this support group is to the survivors. Here they are heard—listened to—not asked more questions—but their sorrow is heard. I could feel, as the hours went by, that closure to the pain is being sought and perhaps answers are found. I saw they are surviving with this support—at least for another day—or a week.

I also attended, in Esperanza, a fund-raiser for the Homicide Survivors, Inc. "Why are there so few people here?" I ask of an organizer. "We never have many come out to help the cause. I think they are afraid that this group will bring bad luck to them—sort of like a curse." How sad I thought as I know the needs of this group. For instance in addition to emotional support, families also need financial help, such as with housing when the wage-earner is murdered, for the cost of a funeral, or for child care when a mother is killed. There are so many needs that I had never considered before I became a part of the support group.

Homicide Survivors, Inc., began in 1982 as a national support group headquartered in Cincinnati using the name Parents of Murdered Children. In some places this name is still used, but a broader, more inclusive name was used in Arizona. In 1997, the beginning of the research grant, the organization began in Esperanza using the current name. It is a self-help support group for emotional re-integration and some financial support for those in need. Trauma and turmoil of murder creates a battle for survival of family and friends. The support group counters the burden and pain of police investigations and the criminal justice system during trials and convictions. Survivors have additional pain when they believe justice was not served when the killer is not apprehended, tried, or convicted. "I just know the killer is still out there and may kill another little girl. How can I ever forget?" sobbed a mother, aged by grief. Yes, survivors are the murder victims as well. When considering that in the U.S. there are over 20,000 murders annually (Talking Points 2003), there are at least 100,000 "survivors," grieving and struggling with losses. This is an example of ongoing violence with no cure for the aftermath.

Rape and Sexual Assault: Violent Acts Feared in Esperanza

Using the Uniform Crime Report of 1996, only 37 percent of rape offenses were reported, and the estimate is there were 72 rapes per 100,000 population. In 2004, 65,510 completed rapes were reported in the U.S. (Uniform Crime Report 2004). Two-thirds of the victims knew their offenders. Since 1993, rape and sexual assaults have fallen by over 64 percent, possibly due to the use of DNA testing in forensic investigations, anger-reduction educational programs, zero tolerance by the public, and the empowerment of women (Uniform Crime Report 2004). Rapes and sexual assaults still are underreported because victims feel social shame and fear.

Rape and sexual assaults are violent acts and are feared in the town. An extensive literature exists about the rape. The resource used to illuminate the topic in this book is *The Crime Classification Manual*. The authors of this reference manual note, "sexual assault includes criminal offenses in which victims are forced or coerced to participate in sexual activity. Physical violence may or may not be involved" (Douglas et al. 1997:193). What constitutes rape or sexual assault varies by state, so there are marked differences in the reported rates and frequency. Because of these variations, the authors use the terms *rape* and *sexual assault* interchangeably. In this book the term "rape" will be used, for it is the term used by the townspeople. In the manual there are fifteen major categories of rape including: felony rape, domestic sexual assault, child domestic sexual abuse, entitlement rape, subordinate rape, power-reassurance rape, anger rape, sadistic rape, abduction rape, and gang rape (Douglas et al. 1997:191–246). Several categories of rape were described by the study participants, but the most feared are entitlement, abduction, and gang rape. These violent acts will be explained through the viewpoints of the people.

While in Esperanza we did not hear of any rape event; however, we learned that a fear of rape persists throughout the town. In our survey, 60 percent of those surveyed (this includes both men and women) responded they knew of rape occurring in Esperanza. Teenaged former gang members describe their fear of rape:

> I don't want to have kids 'cause I'd be afraid my daughter would be raped. (16-year-old female)

> I don't want my sister to be on the streets or run with gang's 'cause I'd worry she'd be raped. (18-year-old male)

> It happens a lot; it's a way of jumping a homegirl into the gang—to gang rape her. (16-year-old male)

> Girls—they know what to expect; it's just part of being in. They don't like it, but they know to keep their mouths shut or they'll get it, too. (16-year-old male)

> It's [rape] a reason why I'm not in anymore—I'm afraid of that sort of thing. (17-year-old female)

Gang rape appears prevalent as a ritualized bonding. As described in the focus group, "In some gangs, if a female wants to become part of it, she must be raped by the gang. It's sort of a group thing" (17-year-old male). Philippe Bourgois, a noted anthropologist who studies drug use and gang behavior, relates an informant's remarks about an organized gang rape, a ritual that is part of voyeuristic bonding, sexual celebrating, and socialization for this segment of the population:

> The bitch is gonna have to pass through the wild thing—she gets beat down—I own you now, bitch, whoever never came back to hang out at the club passed through some trauma, and it's gonna be hidden within their life—they go home—and keep a dark secret for their life. (2004:344)

Society seems to have few means of controlling rape. Rape is too often kept secret. According to Bourgois, "Rape runs rampant around us in a terrifying conspiracy of silence. It becomes a public secret that enforces an important dimension of the oppression of women in everyday life" (2004:345). In focus groups and privately, older monolingual women covertly described their fears and disgust about spousal sexual assault by describing how they, as women, were powerless to resist sexual encounters with their husbands. "Wives that provided everything for their husbands even when they don't want to." As one woman said, "I'd never marry a man from Mexico; they are so macho. They think we [women] are just property for them to do with as they want when they want it." These comments reveal hidden fears. As will be described later in this chapter, monolingual women cried, in a group session on domestic violence, about how they had been kept in seclusion and had not known that other women suffered sexual abuse as well.

During the study period, three very young Hispanic girls, 7–8 years old, who lived outside of Esperanza but in a nearby neighborhood, were targets of a serial kidnapper, sexual molester, and murderer. The bodies of two of the girls were found, and both had been raped—the other young girl's body was never found, so the case was still unsolved at the end of the study in 2001.

Violence as Perceived by People in Esperanza

The mayor and other leaders raised the question: "Is Esperanza more violent than other towns?" Yes, as was indicated by the murder prevalence rates mentioned previously. But what do the townspeople perceive as violence in their own lives? What do people believe creates the violence? A majority (73 percent) of surveyed people believe they live in a violent community. They have seen all kinds of violence—perpetrated especially against victims who are very vulnerable. For instance, 40 percent have seen elder abuse, 74 percent have witnessed spousal abuse, 77 percent have seen child abuse, 60 percent have seen sexual abuse against women, and 59 percent have seen gang violent crimes.

> Hit a girl—a woman sure if she's gonna hit, it's an eye for an eye. I think she gettin' it right back. (17-year-old male)

> You hit a police officer, you're going to jail for awhile. But I think you should be able to hit a cop, because if they could hit you then, same thing back at them. (15-year-old male)

However, there are cultural rules, such as whom you can hit or can't, such as:

> It's not all right to go and hit your mom or grandma or someone like that. You have to respect your elders, can't go and smack them, but like your little brother, it's okay when they mess with you. (14-year-old female)

Seventy-nine percent believe that violence is learned in childhood, in the home, and 58 percent believe people are violent because of anger about their poverty status. Seventy-six percent say that as children they were abused themselves or they witnessed a parent being abused. In their own families, 42 percent report someone has been violent, 33 percent have had someone in their household arrested for a violent act, and 30 percent have had someone spend time in jail for violence. Forty-six percent have intervened in a fight in Esperanza (Glittenberg 2001). The household survey reveals that people perceive violence to be prevalent throughout the life span and experienced both in the home and on the streets. Most believe that imprisonment is one means of controlling violence.

> Many hate their parents 'cause they saw their mother being hit, and even then they would also strike their girlfriends, wives, and even their children. Children learned it from their parents. (22-year-old female)

> I believe it comes from the family. I used to hit my husband, too, I saw my father do it to my mother. He did a lot of harm, he beat her, he cut her face. It was enough, I said, "no one is going to touch me." So I hit him if he is out of line—I'm not going to be a victim. (51-year-old female)

Alcohol and drug abuse are consistently viewed as the "cause" of a violent event. "They aren't themselves when they're drinking or on dope [cocaine or meth are most common]." This perception was also discussed in chapter 3, and it agrees with Best's report in the 2003 Uniform Crime Reports that alcohol and drugs are the major causes of violence (Best 2003). The other most frequent cause of violence is drug trafficking, where gunfire seems the preferable way to settle accounts rather than going through the appropriate legal channels.

Another frequent cause of violence is losing face or being dissed—or disrespected. A number of events occurred in which one person took offense at another's remarks, and getting revenge for these actions seems to have local approval. The Hispanic macho persona is brave, fearless, and revengeful; an eye for an eye is the underlying cultural norm fueling violence.

Do people live in constant fear? Fear is a disabling response to violence. As one single mother said:

> No one told me that I rented a damn crack house when I moved here [Esperanza] with my three kids. Every night someone comes knocking on the door—at all hours—trying to buy crack. When I say, "this ain't a crack house" a couple of shots are fired at the house—so we all sleep in the middle of the living room floor—it's really scary. My 14-year-old doesn't want to go to school, she's scared all the time, and I have to go to work. We don't go out at all at night.

This family is paralyzed by fear. Dealing with violence and related fear create ways in which the people take action to feel safer. Things began to change in 2000 when more financial resources in town focused on increasing safety and protection. Since then, more police have been added to the force and crack houses have been torn down. Nevertheless, people are still cautious. As one says, "I just look down at the sidewalk when I walk" (17-year-old male). Another mentions, "I just don't look for trouble; I don't look at other people. I just keep to myself" (35-year-old female). "I know who to talk with, just my neighbors and my family—I don't trust anyone else" (54-year-old male).

Many of the local people remain under a cloak of fear. However, the majority of people believe that in recent years violence has lessened in Esperanza.

> Violence has decreased. There's more patrol. (24-year-old female)

> There's still homicides but not as bad as they had before. I don't know, there was like a person dying every week. So they're getting stricter—like they're cutting down. (32-year-old male)

> It's gotten better—the bad guys are locked up and don't live here anymore. Everything's quiet now. (26-year-old female)

Former gang members describe their perspectives of violence and rules of behavior. As you can see from the remarks below, it is a cultural norm to use violence to protect self, property, and territory.

> If some boy from another neighborhood comes in, we'd beat him up. It's okay. Well, if they're cool, just like they risk their own, then kick back but if they're bad and start talking spank to other people, I think they should get it. (15-year-old male)

> You gotta think about territory. It's your neighborhood, and you're inside their neighborhood—bad news. Don't you think they jump you, too— like a black guy in a white neighborhood? (16-year-old male)

> Gangs, if they get into a fight—I think if they're talking spank and to other people they should get it. (14-year-old female)

> This is fighting like being harassed by somebody you don't know. It's been going on a long time. (30-year-old female)

> Violence, that's reality. If you play with the dog you might get bit. If you act a fool, you'll get your ass whooped. It just happens. (58-year-old male)

> Violence is acceptable in self-defense—wherever it takes place, like somebody going to do somethin'. You may have a police department, but you still have to fight to defend yourself if that other person starts an argument or fight. In school there a lot of fights and some of them are pretty cool. (16-year-old male)

Such responses place cultural rules as primary reasons for violence as they point to behavior as justified, such as "you have to defend yourself" or "it's just part of life." No solutions seem forthcoming as ways to control such ways of responding to challenges.

Summary of Perceptions

Opinions vary; some differences may be due to where the people live in the town as some sections are more violent than others, or to age, as people experience and interpret events differently at various times in their lives. The majority believes that Esperanza has become a more peaceful town, probably due to more police surveillance. People themselves do not seem to take responsibility for controlling violence as we will see in the case studies that follow.

Violence on the Streets

Themes of violence have been threaded throughout this book, creating a mosaic of violence and drug trafficking, drug overuse, and alcohol abuse. The following narrative of a male study participant, Mario, who is now an active youth counselor, illustrates how values are built from a life that includes alcohol and drug use and from being part of a family whose members were drug dealers and violent.

MARIO, A FORMER DRUG USER AND HIS VIOLENT FAMILY

Mario is a 52-year-old Mexican national who is now an American citizen who works for a social service agency in Esperanza.

> I think violence, anger is the same thing to everybody—Anglo or Mexican. One thing I do see different—it's our fault—as a Hispanic, if you have a son, he grows up in your house until he's turning 50. Anglos, once they're 18—they've got to move out of the house and look for a job or go to college. I like that. 'Cause you see they're doing, their own life instead of us as parents being with them and giving them everything. My grandpas are very good friends to myself. They tried to talk to me—nowadays we don't talk with our kids. I see gang violence now. Kids can't walk certain places; there's the gangs controllin' the area.

When the Cubans came in, there was a lot of violence. They came out of prison and came over here—carryin' guns; they were carryin' knives. One tried to stab me, one Cuban. I think those from Mexico are more into drugs. They're lookin' for more money, by sellin' drugs and all that. The norteños [people from the northern part of Mexico] are cold-blooded; they don't care what they do. They come and murder somebody, and they just go back across the border and the police'll never find them. It's the same thing, the machismo. That's been going on in Mexico for a long time, it's very strong there, the machismo.

But here we have a lot of young kids being murdered, and the older ones into drugs, the drug dealers are the problem. I think heavy sentences for the dealers. I've seen elder abuse with the young kids, 14, 15 doin' it. They see elders as easy targets, so they take their monthly checks. It's—not right.

I think we should stop it when they're growin' up. Machismo, it's violence. The stronger you feel the more violent you're gonna be doin' it. From my culture I see a lot of violence. It's too much machismo. I see a lot of violence—they're not afraid to use the weapons, they're not afraid to use the knife, drugs, there's more of it. It's like they like to abuse themselves—I see a lot of it in Hispanics.

Alcohol and drugs have somethin' to do with violence—'cause when you're using, you're not the same person. Alcohol and drugs make you angry, your pressure—peer pressure you have—worries and all those things will cause violence.

My family, I've had them convicted of violent offenses—yes, fightin' and stabbin'. As a matter of fact my uncle was in prison for almost five years. I had some of my cousins do the same thing—gang related. They got convicted and they were in jail in California. I have a son who has been a victim.

My uncle in Santa Ana, California, was involved in drugs. The big drug kings went after him 'cause he wasn't dealing right. They caught him and put him on his knees, forced him down until he died to make an example of him—no cheating. They got him. People just stay clear of getting involved. Like there was someone murdered right here—they burned him in that car. I think it was drug-related. A lot of people were passin' in the alley, seein' that car burning, they just kept lookin' down at the ground and walkin' on by. Pretty sad.

To change things, we've got to start early with the kids—talk to them. Keep the bike police, they are helpful, as they can go into the alleys and everywhere, see what is going on. We need more community police to work with the kids, if you can talk with them you'll find they will change. They're all in need of help if it's not drugs, it's for something else.

Mario is a man with experience on both sides of the issue, is a victim and perpetrator of violence, but also is a man now involved in finding ways for people to cope—especially children. He views violent behavior, especially from the macho role models in the Hispanic culture. To curtail violent behavior, involvement is needed by all. Community policing is valuable.

Domestic Violence

Domestic violence is one of the biggest problems in Esperanza (as will be described further in this chapter). It can escalate into murder—a spontaneous event (a sudden angry outburst resulting in murder) or a staged killing (a well-planned and executed murder). Spontaneous domestic murder is unstaged. It is triggered by recent stressful events or by a build up of stress and anger that finally reaches a climax. A history of prior abuse is common, but often it is kept as a secret. Abusive events usually start off as verbal arguments then escalate to physical beating and eventually intensify into killing. The murder weapon can be any instrument, like a hammer, stick, gun, or knife. Staged violence is planned and covered up to look accidental—like falling down stairs or off a cliff or having brakes fail. An assault may be staged to make it appear like a break-in where a stranger robbed or raped the victim and then killed her. The following case has many key elements of domestic violence.

PRISCILLA, A VICTIM OF DOMESTIC VIOLENCE

Priscilla was 42 years old with a 9-year-old daughter, Angela, who often stayed with her maternal grandmother who lived a few blocks away. Priscilla had been married to Pepe for 12 years when we met her through the Domestic Violence Zero Tolerance Program. Because of physical and emotional abuse, Priscilla had been separated from her husband for six months.

Early Dating

During an early date, we got into an argument and he took me to the desert in his truck and told me, "If you ever leave me, I will kill you," and he pulled out a knife he had in his pocket and slit my throat. I remember gasping for air, then he took me out of the truck and told me it was an accident, and he was very sorry. I remember passing out while we were still in the desert. He then must have carried me back into the truck, because he was crying when my nose started to bleed. I passed out. And my nose bled a lot [Priscilla becomes very quiet and looks away].

Another date we had, we were at a nightclub and Pepe went to the restroom, and another man came up to me and complimented me on my legs. Pepe overheard that and he became incensed and pulled me out of the nightclub (he didn't mess with the other man), and when we got to the car he punched me in the face. My nose started to bleed. Pepe took me home. My father confronted him and called the police, and they took a report, but I didn't file charges. I was too afraid.

Marriage and Womanizing

When we weren't drinking he was so good to me, but after we got married and I was pregnant I knew he had other women, like most macho men. I cried and cried. He would say he was sorry, and after Angela was born, he was better for a while. But Pepe was soon in the streets again. I tried to always have a clean house and gave him all he wanted from a wife, but when he was drinking he got real mean. I remember one time he got upset with me. I don't remember why but he chased me into the backyard, and he pushed me on to the ground— kicked me on the back. It hurt me so much, but I didn't want to make him more angry, so I laid down on our bed for a while. Later that night I had lots of pain in my back and blood in my urine. Pepe got scared and took me to the General Hospital; he told me not to tell anyone what happened. He told the doctors that I had fallen out of a chair. When Pepe left the room, I told the doctor what really happened; I was so scared.

Cycles of Violence and Repentance

He was better for a long time, but another time, Pepe was yelling at me, then he went to the bedroom and returned with a revolver. He put his hand around my neck and picked me up off the floor and smashed me into the wall. I felt so faint and afraid. Then he pointed the gun at me and began pulling the trigger, Russian roulette, and he was laughing saying he was going to kill me. I guess there weren't any bullets in the gun, but I didn't know—I was so scared. Angela wasn't there, thank God.

Husband Arrested with a Restraining Order

Another time he choked me so bad that I had bruises on my neck, and he kept me hostage in the house for several days, locking me in. I called my neighbor, Gracela, and pretended to ask for sugar and for Gracela to call me back. Gracela knew about Pepe; she was my friend. He picked up the phone when it rang, and threatened me not to go over to her house. I did though. I went. He came after me and pulled me home—I cried all the time. Later Gracela told me that I had to call the police as I was going to be killed by Pepe. She didn't want that to happen.

I made up my mind to do that, so I did. I still had bruises on my neck, arms, and legs where he kicked me, as he pulled me home. They arrested him, and I had a restraining order put on him. He isn't to come into the house. The other night he did come in when I was sleeping and I woke up. He was standing over me, laughing and said I couldn't do anything to keep him from coming in. I told him I was calling 911, as I was strong and I wasn't afraid anymore. I had help and the police knew what he really was like. He left—I think he knew I wouldn't take it anymore. Now I'm getting ready to file for divorce. I'm stronger now. I've got a job and I'm going to start my life over—I'm 42 and I have my rights. I'm talking to the social worker at the Mental Health Center—I have my rights.

Priscilla: Murdered by Her Husband

Two months after this interview was recorded, Gracela tried to contact Priscilla after she didn't answer her telephone. The house was deserted as Angela was staying with her grandmother. The police searched the house, but they found no trace of Priscilla. Two days later her car was found in front of a grocery store, in a parking lot outside the town limits. The police opened the trunk and found Priscilla's body with her throat cut and her body showing signs of having been beaten. She had been dead about three days.

The police arrested Pepe. He denied having seen her and claimed he had been obeying the restraining orders. When the police searched Priscilla's house again, they found a copy of a "Do it Yourself Divorce Kit" on the kitchen table. At Pepe's trial, the evidence showed that he came into the house through a back window. When finding the divorce kit, he became enraged and proceeded to beat Priscilla. Pepe then took Priscilla's unconscious body to the desert where he slit her throat (just like he had done over 14 years before). He dumped her body into the trunk of her car, then drove to the parking lot in Tucson, and left it. Pepe was convicted of first-degree murder and sentenced to life in prison without parole.

The story might have had a positive ending. The system was not failing, but rather it was enforcing a domestic violence zero tolerance policy. Pepe had been arrested and a restraining order was in place. He was mandated to attend anger management control classes. Yet Priscilla lost her life just as she believed she was gaining it back—perhaps she could have benefited from a more aggressive protective system, or not been left alone during the most dangerous period of time—filing for divorce. Maybe training in self-protection and the use of a call system or a stronger security and alarm system in her house would have given Priscilla that chance for her life. It has been a lesson for the CEPP team that controlling domestic violence is one of the most urgent goals of public health. In this case alcohol was involved, but the people involved were not part of the drug trafficking scene. To control and prevent further homicides due to jealousy and rage, multiple social agencies must be involved. This type of violence cannot be controlled only through the police and judicial systems.

Other Victims of Domestic Violence

Angela, their daughter, did not actually see the violence resulting in the murder, as she was staying with her grandmother. Children of domestic violence are traumatized. We do have an eyewitness account of a 10-year-old boy who watched his father kill his mother. He said, "We—my 7-year-old brother—ran next door to the Gomez's when dad was beatin' mom. They'd helped before when there were fights." The boys were fortunate to have a safe haven so close or they also might have been killed. The police were trained to care for the children present, and Victim Witness volunteers gave emotional support for the children. How effective these measures are in preventing PTSD or other long-term emotional distress is unknown, but an evaluation showed the program was effective in preventing recidivism.

Zero Tolerance for Domestic Violence

"This has got to change! Every holiday, every weekend we seem to be picking up the same guys, and their women are always beaten up . . . same way—too much booze—fights and then the blood and tears. What can we do to change this?" asks the Chief of Police. Living at the HUD apartment, we can testify to the fact that fights are ongoing, and it seems the same people are involved over and over again. Could the pattern change? How could it? It seems from what we are learning—the whole community is involved. Could this be a cultural pattern? Yes, as the older women share, "We're expected to just take it—these macho men!" "Not so," says the judge, "that's no way to treat a woman."

Things began to change. The biggest plus came with a federal grant that put a halt to accepting domestic violence as just being the way it is. The 15-month grant paid for training a detective on how to handle arresting someone in a violent fight, protecting the couple but also himself. It is known that domestic violence calls are the most dangerous for any police officer, because when he/she enters a home to break up a fight, the officer may become a victim. That is what happened in the well-known case in Esperanza of John Valenzuela, the young police officer who went to a home to control a fight and was shot and killed by the husband (some details were given in chapter 2 of this tragedy).

Once trained, the detective trained other officers and organized a community support group that met monthly. The group designed and implemented means of support for victims of violence. For instance the community group formed a hot-line for people (usually women) in need of someone to talk with; supplied women with cell phones and answering machines, so they had access to outside help; and helped get new door locks for women without resources who needed protection.

Strong support also came to the children of domestic violence in a program called Victim Witness. This national program involves volunteers who become part of the judicial system but in a nonlegal, supportive manner. As volunteers they are trained to become advocates for victims of crimes, providing a variety of services, like transportation to and from court hearings, assuring that dependent children are cared for if a parent needs to be absent because of legal transactions, and being present in judicial hearings as witnesses to justice. The federal grant received by Esperanza also helped in training a full-time Victim Witness in domestic violence cases. This advocate, Jenny, said:

> I'm really the eyes and ears for someone stressed out by all that has happened. I'm sort of a case manager as I help organize their lives again. Being a victim needs change, support for change, and someone who just is a friend. That's who I am. I've seen some really hurt people, especially the frightened children. Just being there for them makes a difference. For instance in the Gomez case, I was the one who helped those kids get connected with their grandma who lives in Mexico—things like that. Without such support people just fall deeper into a hole.

Another powerful conduit for change was the Hispanic judge who put teeth into the zero tolerance for domestic violence grant. He was a man of valor, and when a perpetrator entered the courtroom, the judge demanded respect. He accepted no excuses from a man for beating a woman. The judge would say, "Shame upon you—how could you, a Mexican man, do such a thing . . . shame on you! Women are to be respected, to be honored, and you—a low-down coward—have brought shame to the Mexican family." He continued, "You have a choice—either go into anger management classes or be put into jail for 180 days . . . which will it be?" All of the perpetrators chose the treatment. This was a course held at the La Frontera Mental Health Center that focused on cognitive restructuring, learning how to deal with low self-esteem and anger. By the end of the 15-month grant period, 44 men had entered treatment and 16 had already finished the 16-week course. The others were in the process. There was no recidivism—none at all. If the perpetrator missed a class, a police officer showed up at his home with an arrest warrant. "We don't tolerate—zero—any domestic violence," declared the judge.

We conclude that it does take a whole community to change a long-standing pattern, but we also believe that it is the cultural respect for authority—such as that for the judge—that made the difference. The Hispanic culture has a deep respect for authority and when the judge shamed the perpetrator, this seemed to be a more painful punishment than any other kind would have been. Did all the problems with domestic violence disappear with this small grant? Definitely not, as you will learn in the next example, a women's consciousness raising conference.

Mi Voz Vale (My Voice Counts): A Community Effort to Empower Women

"Women—you have the power to change things—to stop this violence—to be proud mothers and women of Esperanza!" Thus was the call to action from Fere Feria, a fiery Hispanic woman from Hermosilla, Mexico. Dressed in a powerful purple dress, her long black hair shone with the pride of a Mexican woman. Fere, herself an attorney, knew the need for power, as three thieving thugs had invaded her home, shot and killed her husband, and shot Fere. She lived to tell the story of nearly dying from five shots to the chest; after about a year of recovery from a near-death experience, she gained her full power to speak out. Having three small sons herself, Fere challenged the 300 women at the conference, to "set the standard of respect in your home—you are the ones who raise the macho man—or not—we women must change this, but you have to stand up and speak out . . . your voice counts." The women rose as one long plank against the wall, singing, shouting, and some crying in a positive response to her call for action.

Cosponsored by CEPP and La Luz, a social agency for the underserved, women from Esperanza and surrounding barrios came to an all-day conference on reducing violence in the home. Food and child care were provided. Small breakout sessions were held for more intimate discussions. I led one on domestic violence. Here, older monolingual Hispanic women openly cried, saying, "I never knew other women had the same problem, that their husbands beat them, too. I was ashamed, thinking I was the only one, and that I deserved to be beaten." Clearly this group of women longed to talk about ways of stopping their powerlessness and fear. The conference ended with all the women standing in the auditorium, clapping and singing Hispanic songs. They were excited about returning in a month for a repeat discussion, but the next time bringing their husbands and sons.

Plans were made for the follow-up conference. High expectations were held of continuing the dialogues and planning some action in which these women could have greater participation in strategies for change. The next conference day finally arrived. We waited for the auditorium to fill, but it did not. Only a handful of women came, maybe 60, and only three men. What happened? Where was the energy—the power—their voices to be counted? We asked, "Why are there so few people here?" The answer came, "The men did not want us to come again—but some of us did—anyway." "We think they are afraid that we will become too powerful." And so the effort ended— but not as we had wanted. Culture is slow to change and sometimes it simply does not. The success of the Zero Tolerance for Domestic Violence was distinct, for it had power brokers (all male) endorsing the change. My Voice Counts had none—just the common local women. Zero Tolerance also had grant support, and the money aided the educational process, communication, and ongoing feedback. My Voice Counts had none of these essential support mechanisms, plus fragile grassroots support. This is a lesson to be learned when wishing for culture change—go slowly with plenty of broad support— and grant money helps.

Funerals as a Community Integration of Violence

We have seen how individuals and groups cope but how does the community as a whole integrate the loss related to violence? Earlier, we saw how the community coped by uniting in peace marches and attending masses together when Oscar was murdered. How does the community cope in less-public murders? What rituals and rites of passage are used in the grief process? What are some cultural practices that counter the destructive consequences of grief? What symbols unite the community in making meaning out of violent upheavals in the ongoing lives of families and townspeople?

With permission, we use information from the dissertation study done by Maureen Campesino (2003), *Voces de las Madres: Traumatic Bereavement after Gang-related Homicide*. Campesino analyzed the bereavement processes for over two years of two mothers whose sons were murdered in a gang-related event. Her study of funeral rituals gives insight into the Hispanic culture and how the whole community copes and grieves when murders occur.

> Huge numbers of people . . . came to the wake, mass, and burial services . . . anywhere from 200 to over 600 people. All ages are represented at every service from infants to elderly in wheelchairs. Nearly everyone [is] Mexican American . . . all the victims had large extended families . . . some [attending] did not know the family but wanted to show their sympathy . . . [standing] many hours in line . . . sometimes in searing desert heat. (Campesino 2003:350)

Campesino reasons that community support demonstrates the Hispanic cultural value of "what happens to one of us affects all of us" (2003:351). She concludes that rituals enable people to socialize and network. For example, gang members gathered and socialized, maybe 20–25, at a funeral, posing for pictures, showing the colors, and flashing their hand signals to the cameras. Members were very obvious; they were not covert. A funeral director said, "You hear them at the casket say, 'you know what, that's how I'm gonna go. I'm gonna go down shooting'" (Campesino 2003:363). She continues:

> Open casket viewing was at all wakes—the coffins were lined most often in white with a picture of Jesus, the Virgin Mary, or Our Lady of Guadalupe on the inside of the lid of the casket—the deceased often had personal items inside the casket. These included pictures of his or her family and any children they may have had: favorite shirts, such as sport jerseys, a soccer ball, or a small bouquet of flowers. Personal items of the deceased often are placed inside the casket. . . . One young man had a cell phone placed in one hand and a cologne bottle in the other. People often touched or kissed the deceased as they paid their respects. At one wake, there was a TV mounted high on the wall that played a video montage of photographs of the deceased and his family. At many wakes friends and sometimes family members wore white T-shirts that had a photo of the deceased on the back with the phrase: "In loving memory of _____ with the dates of the birth and death. . . . [The] deceased is sometimes honored when the funeral procession drives by his or her favorite locales or stopping at the victim's home for a few minutes. (2003:353–355)

> People expressed their grief through tears or wailing. Women were the most expressive though some adolescents and young men embrace each other and cry. About half of the services included a *mariachi* band at the wake, mass and burial, a cost between $200–400 an hour. Mariachi bands perform popular Mexican songs in Spanish with lively guitar playing. The women wailed loudly as the band began to play. At one wake the wife and mother of the deceased were helped by fellow mourners to leave the chapel area when their crying became too intense and their wailing turned into yelling . . . at the burial the wife tried to jump into the open hole as the casket was being lowered. The father and three other people were holding the wife around her waist to prevent her leap. (2003:356–357)

Campesino found that rival gang members attended the funerals even at the risk of being arrested. Her study also showed one incident in which the body of the deceased was desecrated in the mortuary before the wake. Tombstones and memorabilia left at the graveside of the murdered teenagers were also destroyed repeatedly during the years following the murder. Are these acts of disrespect or are they a means of countering the fear of retaliation from the dead?

Death signifies an important life-cycle transition that requires sanctification by the Catholic Church authorities. This is no less true for gang-related funerals. As Campesino explains:

> A relationship of reciprocity existed between the deceased and the mourners during these services. Mourners helped the dead through repeated

prayers that "cleansed their souls" while the deceased could bring spiritual help to family and friends in their earthly problems (2003:454).

She makes note that even gang leaders, whose deaths were drug-related, and who were demonized by the dominate society, were instead "cleansed of their sins" in the Hispanic community through prayers of forgiveness (2003:455).

It is interesting that in a male-dominated society, it is the women who, through expressing their emotions and keeping the household operating, demonstrate strength and help others cope with the loss. A priest commented:

> [Women] are the great stabilizers; they tend to support one another more than men . . . women tend to be much more emotional about it in terms of expression, but I find women being stronger about the reality of what happened and being able to have a great deal of empathy; they deal with everything else that is going on. Whereas the men are much more reserved. Almost across cultures, when it comes to death I think women tend to be the great healers in the family. . . [they] keep the traditions" (Campesino 2003:371).

Summary

Violence is a complex cultural construct. Cultural rules about violence vary according to the age, role, and status of the individuals involved, and according to contextual factors such as alcohol and drug use. Defending rights and territory, being insulted, or carrying out revenge are reasons for a whole range of violence. Violence within ethnic groups is more common than between them. Close relationships often foster conflict and intrapersonal revenge, as seen in many domestic violence cases.

The cultural rules that seem the most powerful in shaping violence are fear of the other, protection from intruders, and revenge (especially for being insulted). Violence is perceived by Esperanzans as being caused by family—where it is learned—along with misuse of alcohol that flames emotions, and drug trafficking that motivates money making. Programs to eliminate domestic violence by empowering women were initiated, but they need more grassroots support to become effective. Coping with violence increased through some community-wide programs, such as zero tolerance for domestic violence. A federally funded program on reducing domestic violence was used to increase the coping skills and support for over 40 perpetrators and judged successful, as there was no recidivism for one year. A partnership between the police and a grassroots community network continues focusing on this problem.

Rituals and symbols were studied at a funeral to learn how a whole community copes with loss related to violence. These cultural patterns help to protect people from fear and also to mourn the loss of murdered youth. Funeral rites of passage allow rehumanization of those murdered.

Chapter 7

The Culture
of the Shunned

> The very poor are often disconnected from market forces because they lack the requisite human capital—good nutrition and health, and an adequate education.
>
> —Jeffrey D. Sachs, *The End of Poverty*

Not all violence is obvious, like drive-by shootings, or illegal, like murder. Violent acts do not always inflict physical harm, but instead, some inflict emotional pain and violate human rights and human dignity. This type of nonphysical violence may be instigated through subtle, unspoken, even invisible culturally patterned behaviors such as discrimination, scapegoating, or shunning. In this chapter we will describe three subgroups of people who are victims of the nonphysical, hidden violence of shunning.

The longer we lived in Esperanza it became obvious that three groups of people are shunned: the homeless, families in HUD housing, and monolingual Spanish speakers. It is doubtful that these groups would term themselves as "shunned." They would probably describe others' attitudes toward them as unfriendly, rude, or mean. Why in a town where the majority of the people are poverty-stricken Mexican Americans would certain subgroups be shunned? Why would they be targeted? What purpose could this possibly have? What common attribute do these shunned groups have that would explain the purpose of a subtle pattern of being ostracized? What possible messages are being sent by shunning these subgroups? How do these subgroups feel about being treated as outcasts? Do they adapt or become extinct? Do they have cultural rules and norms for surviving in their state of marginalization? How can this type of violence be eliminated or reduced especially when it remains hidden? We intended to find out.

125

Shunning is an insidious type of violence. In this chapter, we have stories of shunned people that describe how they view their ostracized lives and how they view changing their lives—if they do.

The Homeless

Homelessness increased as a problem in the U.S. in the early 1980s when many of the social services, especially for the mentally ill, were slashed and never reinstated. People with mental illness were moved out of large state mental institutions, and many had nowhere to go so they ended up on the streets—homeless. Following the Vietnam War, numerous veterans suffering from PTSD fell out of step with mainstream society. Troubled with addictions, nightmares, and broken marriages, they were often unable to work. Many veterans found no mental health treatment. They wandered the streets. They became—homeless.

Homeless people exist today—the twenty-first century—living in the shadow of home-dwelling people around the world. From an ethnography done in Esperanza by Vincent Stuart for a master's thesis in 1997, we gained insights into their world. With his permission we quote and paraphrase his work (pp. 65–75).

> Sitting in the shade of a tree in a public park, are four homeless men, Tex, Roy, Grady, and Pete (pseudonyms). They tell of their lives on the streets.
>
> "I'm Tex and I'm Black, 53, and divorced, been livin' on the street and in shelters for about 20 years, since about 1980. I never finished high school, just dropped out." "Hi, I'm Grady, I'm Black, 53, and divorced. I've been on the streets for three years and can't get a job. I don't have a high school diploma and move around a lot. I want to get back to my family. My luck will change and one day it will pick up—I'll be all right again." "Hi, I'm Pete, I'm White, 43, a graduate from high school, but haven't had much of a life. I've been on the streets now for 10 months. It's dangerous out here. I just live from shelter to shelter. It is not a life." "I'm Roy, white and 62, divorced and been homeless for 2 1/2 years. I graduated from high school . . . and once upon a time in [a] land far, far away [laughs] I had a house, a wife, kids, but now I have nothing. It's a rough life on the streets [he looks down]."

Strange how few details these men give, like reciting name, rank, and serial number. Perhaps that's all they see of themselves any more—as a short biosketch. Only one says he's homeless, the others say they are living on the streets—perhaps that is a cognitive adaptation to the situation.

> "Sure we have some drinking buddies, but just a couple. We look out for each other. There are thieves everywhere, they'll take your stash and sell it. We have worries out here, like the food. You have people cooking the soup in the kitchens, and you don't know if they're clean. Cold food in the dumpsters can have salmonella or whatever."

"Every morning we get up and go to the park where there is a water fountain, we wash our faces, wash our mouths, take our shoes off and wash our feet. You know you can't wash in the restrooms—so you have to kind of look around to see if you can do that because if you do, you can go to jail or get a ticket."

"I'll get sick and worser because nobody wants to help a poor, homeless man. Health is a good thing to have but without it you die. Who cares about somebody dying?"

Identity: Defined by Others

"They asked me where I lived. I said I didn't have a place to live and that I was homeless. I told them I was . . . living on the street day to day. 'Oh you're one of those tramps?' I told them I wasn't a tramp that I was just down on life. I'm black and homeless—you become immune. Among men you are a man no matter what color, but you are treated like nothing from the work force and higher ups like your boss, the managers, and the supervisors."

Rules of the Shelter

"When I stay at a shelter, I call to get a reservation. The phone numbers of shelters and everything—are on pamphlets that you can get everywhere. You have to have an updated TB card and identification. Go to the Health Department, they'll X-ray you and give you a skin test. You take the white bus that says "Pleasant Valley" on it that will come pick up all the guys at 5:00. You have dinner, take a shower, and wash your clothes. Once you're in there you have to stay the night."

Becoming Homeless and Other Losses

"Out of all these many years, I lost my family, I lost my mother, I lost my daughter, I lost my house, my furniture and I didn't even have enough to pay rent. I'm 53 years old. I ain't got nothin'. I'm a little too old to start over."

"I used to do drugs and I know how to do them. When I was in the round of people doin' drugs, you doin' drugs, he doin' drugs and we all sittin' around here doin' drugs, smokin' crack cocaine. I couldn't see my thing to better myself."

Making It on the Street

"A 'take' is a thing that makes them money. We didn't rob anybody but we just talked somebody out of their money. Panhandling—it's a way of life. It goes two ways. There are some that just panhandle, and they don't want to work. Oh, they might put that on the sign—'work for food'—but they don't want to work. When I was panhandling—I haven't done it for awhile— when someone offered me a job, I took it. I hooked up with several good jobs that way. They call it running a sign, hanging a sign, or flying a sign."

"You go about getting food stamps for the first time—you go to the food stamp office and fill out an application. They ask you all kinds of questions on the application. They ask you if you got money in the bank. Do you own a car? If I had all of that I wouldn't be in there! They [food stamps] are money. You use them just like money only you can't buy things like cigarettes, beer, soap or anything like that. It's strictly for food. You can buy soda or you can buy stuff that has to be cooked. You can buy coffee that you have to cook but not coffee that is already made. It has to be food that is room temperature or below. It can't be anything hot. I can buy ready-made sandwich in there that are cold but I can't buy them heated. They are good for food but most of the guys sell them."

Some Events That Make Life a Surprise

"A friend and me were going down an alley with a shopping cart and we were picking up cans. This lady was in her yard and told us to come over and gave us seven goddamn big black bags full all the way to the top. They could barely be tied and were all crushed and weighed about 25 or 30 pounds each at forty cents a pound. We got $57. About the best is copper—you can get red brass and it pays more than yellow brass. You can recycle silver if you can find some. You can recycle anything."

Keeping Safe

"Safety—you have to watch out in 'certain parts of town'—they aren't safe. They don't just take your stuff, they'll jump you or shoot you. At night they might just take a shot at you. They're very territorial. If you are just coming to buy something like drugs—they love you, they won't do nothing to you. If you're spending money, they won't bother you. If they know you and know that you're just passing through, then they'll let you alone. If they think you're there to steal or to sell drugs or cut into their territory, then they'll get you. It's gangs mostly."

"Shelters are places where everybody is sick to one degree or another. All that coughing and hacking, you end up with nose running, colds, and chest pain. You are in a heavy environment with people who are so sick and have been living out on the streets who never take care of themselves."

Many of today's homeless people are similar to the four men we met in the above stories, some of whom have faced life changes, leading to unemployment and the dissolution of family ties.

The homeless population is not counted in the demographic statistics of Esperanza where over 51 percent of the population lives at the poverty level. The percentage of homeless fluctuates continually without an exact number. In the warm, pleasant winter months, thousands of homeless come from the frigid northern states and then migrate back again when the summer heat makes living outside unbearable. Demand for crisis relief like food boxes, blankets, and other daily needs for people living on the streets jumped 6.5 percent in 2000. Casa María, the soup kitchen, added a third giant pot for feeding about 400 people and 300 families rather than the usual 300 meals for single people and 250 for families (Field Notes 2000). These types of local responses to the homeless address their immediate needs. The social services industry, of which shelters are a part, shape local responses. The sheltering industry receives funding from the government or charities and simply treats the symptoms of homelessness; it does not treat the cause. Instead of doing something about the inequality of opportunity, the sheltering industry normalizes homelessness in order to continue getting funding for programs. There are a few exceptions in the industry, but most "give-away" organizations would rather not address these political-economic causes of homelessness (Lyon-Callo 1998:1–6). We conclude from this study that most of these programs merely perpetuate the problem with their short-term give-aways.

The homeless do not have stable connections to society; for instance, they have no address, telephone, or bank accounts. They are disconnected from society. They are shunned, discarded. Poverty and rootlessness unite this group of people. For those who have worked, their work histories have not been strong most of their lives; they have gone from one sporadic job to another. This type of uncertainty in the workplace has not gotten them out of poverty; instead, it has kept them in it. Entry-level, part-time, and low-wage jobs have replaced career professions, which once provided stable living wages with salary increases and benefits. Employment does not necessarily protect people from precarious living. There may be more jobs, but they are low paying, keeping the poor just as poor as before.

Day labor, the crux of homeless economic support, remains at minimum wage. Expenses, such as transportation to and from work, plus paying for certain things needed for work, like gloves and sun hats, cut into paychecks, reducing the amount of money needed for shelter, food, and the other necessities of life. Without telephones and home addresses, even cashing a paycheck can be costly. In Esperanza, day laborers are an unorganized, migrating group of people who are often taken advantage of. Starting their day at 3 AM in order to get to the Labor Hall by 4:30 AM, their work day is long. The work is often outside, sometimes in the blazing heat or in the bitter cold (it does get cold in the desert) before returning to the shelter or the street. Wages only cover the actual working time, and often the working conditions are very strenuous and demanding. Many homeless workers are not robustly healthy; many have chronic illnesses such as diabetes and hypertension.

Homeless females, if they have children, have even more difficulty getting employment. If they do find work, child care must be found, or they must take the children with them to work. For most employers this is unacceptable. Single mothers often live far away from their family support systems, and their local support system can be very fragile and unpredictable.

If the children of homeless parents are enrolled in school, their attendance is very sporadic. Teachers often remark how a child remains in a school only for a few days; thus, their education is continually interrupted. As discussed before, these children are called "couch kids" for they have no permanent place to live and sleep on different couches on most every night. Of course the disrupted education leaves these children vulnerable to all types of problems and significantly limits their opportunities to get out of poverty. Too many become dropouts or easy targets for drug or human trafficking. Solutions need to be found to minimize the disruption in these children's lives.

The mild winter weather makes the Tucson region attractive to those homeless moving out of the cold climates that prevail in the north. Homeless people congregate in vacant lots and parks in Esperanza. There are two shelters in Esperanza for transients; one has room for 60 men, but no children (Gospel Rescue Mission), and the other can take 20 women and their children (Bethany House). Mission on the Street, established in 2000, closed by 2006. The Salvation Army also is a place for homeless men with alcohol problems, where they feel welcome—or at least they are not kicked out. As one homeless man says, "This is the best place to be in the whole U.S., as the police don't hassle you here, and you can get food."

In Esperanza, the most visible service to the homeless is Casa María, described briefly in chapter 2. This soup kitchen was founded and run by a dedicated man from a privileged family, Brian Flagg, a Catholic in his late 40s: "My whole thing is to put the Gospel into practice in a daily way." Brian has been arrested dozens of times as he stands out like some haunted prophet who's just lurched out of the baking desert. He speaks passionately for the human rights of the homeless (*Arizona Daily Star Citizen* 2004). Flagg began doing this work 20 years ago. Besides providing two hot meals (breakfast and lunch) he has a little building that serves as his home, a clothing bank, first aid station, and stop-off for the homeless. "I feel that what I do is a calling. It's about struggle," Brian remarks. Often an articulate voice at various political and civic settings about the plight of the poor, Brian is admired—and ignored—by some. He lives on the premises in a rundown house, sharing it with others who help him. He takes a salary of $10 a week for his work.

Financial support dribbles in from various agencies. Benefits from a Beggars Banquet nets about $5,000 annually for funding the food and supplies. The food for the soup kitchen is donated and prepared by over 200 churches in Tucson, rotating responsibility for providing soup and sandwiches daily for approximately 500–1,000 meals (depending on the season). Local restaurants and grocery stores also donate food, while the federal government donates some food such as cheese and peanut butter. No one is turned away. Some homeless people also work there. A small free health clinic is held one day a week in the home of a nearby resident who donates his living room for the cause. Professional staff come from the El Rio Health Center, a local Mexican American center, which receives block grants and federal grants for its work. An outreach program from the Center has a group of professionals who daily look in culverts, ditches, and parks and under bridges for ill, mentally incompetent, and injured people and bring those found to shelters or gives them food.

Flagg has strict rules for cleaning up after the meals and for policing the area. The area around Casa María is kept tidy and the portable toilets are clean, but the area between the park (three blocks away) and the soup kitchen is often trashed. Neighbors of Casa María are not thrilled about crowds of homeless who congregate in the neighborhood, some sleeping in their front yards, crawling over their fences, using alleys for bathrooms, leaving trash, and peering in windows. In general the homeless presence is disruptive to the local people's daily lives. One neighbor said:

> Sure I feel sorry for the homeless, but why do they have to park here? You bet people in the foothills [where the wealthy live] would object if they had a soup kitchen in *their* backyards. They think by their "generous" helping with the sandwiches and soup that they are helping the problem, but I believe the rich do this give-away to keep the homeless right here—in Esperanza.

Another program goes beyond feeding the stomach only. It is called the Union of Art and Health Local No. 9, an ex-soup kitchen that provides space for the homeless to create art works, and has a meal program called Work for Food Café. The manager comments, "We focus on building self-esteem and helping disenfranchised people to learn, grow, and become a part of the community. Most who come here are Anglos and African Americans—very few are Hispanic."

While helping to serve meals at Casa María we notice something strange. "Where are the Hispanics?—no one looks Hispanic and you never hear Spanish spoken," questions Roberto. "All people working here seem to be Anglos or African Americans. Where are the Hispanic people—either to serve or to get shelter? They are not here—although the center is in this Mexican American town." One Hispanic participant answers the puzzle, "You won't see us homeless, we have families." He's right; it's a cultural pattern found in extended families—they care for their own. However there is the negative reaction from neighbors to Casa María—and from town leaders.

The leaders of Esperanza take no notice of the homeless; they simply ignore them. Local people do not give gifts to the homeless at Christmas time. The border patrol and police do have a covert agreement not to hassle the homeless, and they have kept that agreement. So the system will continue as it is; the homeless will remain a group of people fed, sheltered, and left alone, unless they have the energy, strength, and will to turn their lives around, as June, whose case study follows, did.

JUNE, A HOMELESS PERSON

June is a former homeless person who has changed her life from call girl to college student.

Growing up Poor in Chicago

> I grew up in Chicago, in the projects, the Robert Taylor projects. I was 17 with three younger brothers when our mother died of a stroke. Mama was only 38 years old, but ancient in living a life filled with sorrow—basically she worked herself to death. We never had a father that I knew—he'd been a day worker in a foundry, then in trouble with the law. He's in prison somewhere in Illinois and has been there since I was five and my youngest brother was less than a year old. Our mother worked all the time, janitorial jobs and as a nurse's aide for private folks. We never went to church—said we didn't have the right clothes—but

she made certain we went to school. She was pretty strict with us and never laughed much. I was doing well in school. My teachers always said I'd make something of myself—I was pretty and loved to read.

Hooking Up with Jerry, a Pimp and Drug Dealer

Mama died suddenly. I was a senior in high school, so we went to live with Grandma. She wasn't happy about having 4 teenagers to raise; can't blame her—so she made sure I went to work part-time until I finished high school. I worked at fast food places. Being pretty I attracted lots of attention, and one day I linked up with Jerry, a black dude—so good lookin' and a real dresser. He was 20 and well-established on the south side as a drug dealer. I knew all about it but didn't use anything—neither did he. Jerry was big, strong, and had a temper to match his size. He always carried a gun and talked tough. He loved to show off, driving his new Corvette and livin' in a high rise apartment in the center of Chicago. Soon he became my boyfriend and I moved in with him—I felt protected.

He had other ideas for me, and he arranged "good dates" for me. I was about 19 when I started prostituting. You'd say I was a call girl—Jerry was my pimp. The johns were mostly businessmen and came in all sizes and shapes. Since I'm black, I think many of them liked the thrill of having sex with a black woman. I had no fear, I was making about $2,000–$4,000 a week. Jerry kept the money. We had a really nice apartment. I had my nails and hair done professionally. Jerry took care of getting me smashing clothes, perfume, jewelry, and so forth, but I wasn't happy. Something inside always seemed empty.

I started out with a little marijuana that Jerry gave me. He didn't want me to do drugs as he said it made you stupid. Then I started on meth so I could work all night. I didn't eat right and didn't sleep much. So I started on coke—to perk me up. I loved it and felt okay. I always had a supply from Jerry. He was into big-time dealing then. I was doing this about four years until I was 23 and in my prime.

Moving to Tucson and Becoming Homeless

One night in February, Jerry came rushing home, frantically saying we had to get out of town as some dealers were out to get him. We packed in an hour, left the Corvette there, all my clothes, caught a plane to Tucson where Jerry knew some guys who would help him out. He said it was warm and I'd love it. I didn't. Things looked bleak as Jerry's friends were no where to be found.

We had been living pretty high and hadn't saved any money, so we moved into this dumpy motel in Esperanza. Jerry thought it was a place to hide out, as he took a different name and grew a beard and [started] wearing glasses. Before long I was back prostituting to help get us a car. Being I was black it didn't help me. Most of the other hookers were white, and they didn't want competition. I linked up with a couple of other black hookers and for a time we looked out for each other.

I got charged with soliciting and went to jail three times, but Jerry paid my fines. I learned about the "zones," places where hookers couldn't go or you'd automatically get picked up for soliciting. I worked some as a waitress. Most of the johns were drunks and weirdos, not like I'd had in Chicago. I hated the work, but I needed the money.

Jerry did some dealing but he was pretty cautious; he was always looking over his shoulder to see if the guys from Chicago would find him. We fought a lot. His temper was still as violent as ever, and he didn't have any friends. I was scared most of the time.

Jerry Goes to Prison and Is Killed

One night in the summer of 1997 it all came crashing down. I guess Jerry was taunted by some white guys at a 7-11; they didn't like blacks. Jerry pulled his gun, shot, and killed one right there in front of the store. He wounded the other. The police pulled him in right away. I didn't know what happened to him for a day. I was worried; then I heard about it on the street so I went to see him in jail—all crumpled over, but still mad. He told me to leave and never come back. He screamed at me. I didn't even go to the trial but read about it in the papers. He pleaded self-defense—the other guys weren't even armed! They gave him life in prison. They found out he was also a dealer. About a year later I heard he'd been killed in prison, probably from a fight he caused or maybe some gang member from Chicago got him—who knows.

Becoming Homeless

Things went from bad to worse. I was still using crack. I lost my job 'cause I was always late and not focused. I made a lot of mistakes. I got kicked out of the motel 'cause I couldn't pay so went to the shelters. There were quite a few, but sometimes I had to sleep in the park. I still did tricks in the alleys and sometimes some dude's pickup. I'd do it just enough to get me a fix. I'd go twice a day to get meals at Casa María. It saved me. I did have a few friends, but it's hard being black in the Southwest.

I didn't know where my two living brothers were. One other brother had been killed in a gang fight shortly after I left Chicago, and my grandma had died. I felt I needed to end it all.

Finding Religion and a Life Change

One day while walking from the park to Casa María, I walked by Victory Outreach, right there on the corner. I'd been by the place a hundred times—just a barn of a building. But that Sunday, the music was coming out loud and jazzy. I stopped a minute and listened. They were singing "Blessed Assurance Jesus Is Mine." I listened to the words. I'd been to church only once—my mother's funeral. They then began singing "Amazing Grace"—to save a wretch like me!! My heart stopped as I thought they were singing about me. I began to cry. I walked into the church—hungry and bedraggled—and afraid. Brother Joe and his wife were at the altar surrounded by about 20 men and women all holding hands and singing. Brother Joe began to talk about how they had all come to know the Lord and given up their drugs and alcohol. I wandered into the circle still crying. They took me in.

Off Drugs and in College

I know it probably doesn't seem true, but that is how I changed and have been off of drugs since that day in 1998. I have not done any tricks. I'm at church every day, go to Narcotics Anonymous (held here at the church). I witness to the Lord and reach out to others in need. I have no past, as my sins are wiped away. I even started classes at the community college. I know it's a long way off, but I hope to have a degree in counseling or in law. Something to help others. I know I'm smart and can work hard. I'm a waitress now and have my own apartment—not much, but it's mine. I pay for the rent myself. I don't own a car. I have no desire to go back to drugs or hooking. I'm safe in the arms of my Lord.

Postscript

I checked on June toward the end of the grant period in 2001. I found that she was still attending Victory Outreach in its new location near the foothills. She had finished course work at the two-year community college and received a minority scholarship toward a degree in psychology at the University of Arizona. June is an exceptional student. This example illustrates that drug addicts can change. It is not a matter of simply deprofitizing or legalizing drugs, but rather also working through social support networks and getting therapy for the addictions.

HUD Apartment Dwellers

Our neighbors in the HUD apartments belong to another group that is shunned. The HUD dwelling is supposed to be a temporary stopgap, an inexpensive place while you try to make it financially to live independently. The HUD unfurnished apartments are well constructed of adobe, usually one-story with one or two bedrooms, with high blue iron fences surrounding the perimeter. At the center are a playground and a place for people to hang their clothes to dry. People park on the streets. It is well lit and not littered with trash.

GLADYS, A HUD MOTHER

Many of our neighbors tell courageous stories of their limited opportunities but also of hope for change. Gladys is one with hope. Gladys is an example of the average head of household living in the HUD family apartments. She is a Hispanic 28-year-old single mother of school-aged daughters. Her husband, whom she calls "a good man," has been in prison for two years for dealing drugs. She gives some insight into living in a HUD apartment and her future plans:

Coming to Esperanza

I was born in Nogales, Arizona, and lived there until I was 19, a citizen and all. I'm now 28. My husband, Simon, is a good man who was caught being a runner for a drug dealer here in Esperanza. It was a first time for him. He was told he would get $300 just to take a grocery bag down the street to a guy sitting in a pickup truck. Simon probably knew there were drugs—but he wasn't dealing— he just wanted to make a little money. But the pickup was on the street next to the school, and the police were on the lookout. They picked him up right away. He got two years in Florence [a prison in Arizona]. I get to see him once a month. I have to take the bus. It takes all day just for a half-hour visit. When he gets out we can't live together here. He's a felon. They can't live in HUD apartments. I could try and hide him, but everyone knows everythin' here—so we'll need to find another place. That's hard when you are a felon—no one wants to rent to you.

Life before Prison

Some days I cry all the time as Simon worked so hard in the fields. He'd go to the Pool pickup at 3 in the morning—so he'd be the first in line to get picked for work. He'd work so hard and not get home until after 7 PM.

In prison Simon's trying to learn to be a mechanic on big trucks—that would be good work. Maybe we could move back home to Nogales. Simon doesn't drink much—is not a macho—he had big ideas of being rich. I didn't know that he was running drugs. We always was struggling to make it.

Life in Prison

Simon says he loves me and won't do dealing again. I believe him and will stick by him. In prison he keeps to himself, but there are temptations there, too. He tells me that gangs rule the place but he stays clear of them. They have connections to the outside dealin' drugs, and are always hurting someone who cheats. One guy was choked and died when four of them sat on him 'til he couldn't breathe. It was in the cell next to Simon's, and he could hear them struggling. He was so scared—he didn't say nothin'. Simon misses the girls and me. Sometimes he cries when I come in as he says he just wants to smell me. It's been a long time and that's not good for a marriage, as I have temptations, too. In prison Simon says there are guys who want to find a "girlfriend" and pressure Simon with lots of "gifts." Simon tells me it makes him sick to think about it, but he tries to keep peace, so he does what he has to do. He is very strong and muscular, but he's not very big, sort of my size. In Mexico in prisons they let husbands and wives have private time together. I wish we could be together here like that.

Making Ends Meet

I clean houses for rich women in the foothills. I have six women that I do their houses every two weeks and make about $700. Sometimes they cancel—then I worry as we don't have anythin' else to live on. I take a bus to the foothills and that isn't easy as I have to walk about three blocks to the bus stop in Esperanza and then about four blocks in the foothills. On hot days that's bad, and in the monsoons I hurry to get done in the morning before the rains start in the day. A neighbor watches my kids. I pay her a little but during school my daughters, María and Josephina, go to after-school programs at House of Neighborly Services. That helps as they have dancing and art classes there, but sometimes the girls don't feel as good as others. Sometimes they get teased 'cause of their dad in prison—it makes me cry.

I can't get food stamps because my husband is a felon, so I go to the Food Bank and sometimes to Casa María, but mostly we just live from day to day. I cry a lot as I thought Simon was going to take care of us. My daughters are 8 and 6 now and they want their dad. I'm not religious and not pretty, and my teeth are falling out. We don't have dentists in Esperanza, so I don't go.

HUD: Learning New Skills, a New Life

I'm pretty smart about numbers and read a lot. The HUD director made me come in to help—like volunteer in the office for my rent. I pay $85 a month. She said it was a policy. It is hard 'cause I work so hard all day and need to be home for my daughters, but I go to the office for eight hours a week. They have a computer that I'm learning to use. The director talked to me 'bout takin' some classes so I can become an office secretary. I'm excited—we start classes next week.

Living in the HUD is okay—all of us are in the same boat—no one has anything but each other. Sometimes the women get jealous and get into fights. There are a lot of drunks and drug dealers but not as bad as before. When you came and asked us about our talents, what we liked to do, that was good, as it started me thinkin' that maybe I could make somethin' of myself. I put down that I could cook real well and when we had that big Halloween party, I made the burritos. We did it all. We found that we could work together.

There are some classes the director is going to have on "dressing for success." We laugh, but I think she has some good ideas. Some rich ladies had a "loan closet" of clothes to try on. We could keep the clothes. I looked pretty good in a couple suits. I'm going to try and learn more about computers, maybe get a job in an office, and get my teeth fixed. Maybe Simon can get a job working on trucks near the border and we can start over. Sometimes I think it is possible.

Long-Standing, Subtle Shunning of HUD Families

The "maybes" and "possibles" are messages of hope, but the web of hope is very fragile in the HUD housing. It took time for the team to comprehend this fragility, for it is very subtle. An example of how shunning destroyed hope is the story about how we tried to create new opportunities for the families at HUD.

After living in the HUD apartment for about six months it became clear that certain patterns of noncommunication or miscommunication from the town leaders seemed confusing. Mary Lou was living full time in the two-bedroom apartment with her teenaged daughter and grand nephew, writing a monthly newsletter, attending HUD housing board meetings, holding weekly coffee klatches with her neighbors, and in general being a good neighbor. She is very attractive and was employed as an administrative assistant at a prestigious university, so she had some status in the apartment complex. Mary Lou, who is very sensitive, began to notice that she was given preferential treatment compared with some of her neighbors. We noticed that the HUD housing units for the elderly had been given a name, but not so for the family units that were across the street. The town leaders had a discriminating, negative pattern of interacting with the people in the family units. Little by little the pattern of shunning of other residents began to be noticeable.

We also noticed that during "Make a Difference Day," a day for cleaning up the whole town, shunning was even more prevalent. On that day volunteers help clean up the town's streets and alleys, so the CEPP team and students from the university were there from early morning to the end of the day, cleaning up tons of trash. Carnations, donated by a flower shop, were delivered by the CEPP team to elders living in the Bernie Sedley HUD apartments to let them know that "they made a difference." "Shall we give flowers to the HUD families, too?" "No, they don't make a difference—in fact, they are just

Bernie Sedley senior HUD apartments

trouble," responded a leader. Such a perception has a long-standing pattern as noted many years earlier in a Tucson daily paper, *The Arizona Star Citizen:*

> December 10, 1975   Problems with HUD in Esperanza are being investigated by a HUD official as to why the city has failed to install a playground and playground equipment in a park partially funded with federal tax money. The Director of the local HUD was asked to resign by the Mayor (of Esperanza) because of mismanagement. [Since then the tenure of other housing managers has been short. During our two-year stay, the HUD Director, a woman, was very sensitive to the needs of the families and was well organized and efficient.] Esperanza officials and HUD are at odds over the funding for a park (at the address of the HUD family units). This project was supposed to be part of a $40,000 HUD grant. The town leaders deny any intentional wrong doing. (Johnson 1986) [But by 2005, to our knowledge, that park has not yet been built, and there are no plans to do so.]

Ignoring the HUD families—especially children—is frequent. For instance HUD children were not given invitations to participate in many of the community social (and funded) activities, such as Drug Education For Youth (DEFY) summer programs. The summer programs are camping experiences with a focus on building social skills and eradicating drugs. Several town leaders led these two-week experiences and glowing reports from the leaders told stories of happy kids learning new skills and finding new friends. Yet no young person from the HUD family units attended the camp during our two-year stay in the apartment. They never even hear about these events. Also, HUD children are not invited to many after-school programs. For example Head Start, a national program that benefits low-income preschool education, has its school directly adjacent to the HUD apartments, yet mothers are given no information about Head Start or the eligibility for their children to attend. This type of shunning is focused and hurtful.

HUD Parties: Building Self-Esteem

The CEPP team saw an opportunity to work with single mothers, helping them build self-esteem. An inventory of talent was made; it showed many women had talents to be shared, like singing, painting, cooking, and sewing. "We have talent" the women would laugh and chant at the weekly coffee klatches held at the CEPP apartment. Talent among these women is abundant and even recognizing that they had talents was a first positive experience for many of them (such as Gladys). Too often these women are blamed for causing their own poverty because they lack talent and ambition.

Maximizing these talents, the women organized four social events: two Halloween parties, an Easter party and a Christmas party, for children (not only the HUD children) and for the HUD elders; all the events would be held on the HUD grounds. The first was a Halloween party, and then there was a Christmas party where over 1,000 children came and were given free gifts from Santa Claus! A local television station covered these events, and the publicity was a powerful reinforcer for the HUD women's self-esteem. Things were said, like, "I never knew I could just call up McDonald's and they would donate to us." Or "Did you notice how everyone was happy? I

Halloween party guest

didn't realize I could make someone that happy!" There was a glow in the HUD family apartments and a buzz about doing more things. The women had accumulated a small balance from donated funds (about $100). They began to organize a co-op for funding "self-start"—micro-banking projects, such as a revolving credit union. The next project, an Easter egg hunt and barbecue with the elders, was equally as successful. Blending the generations was positive for all HUD residents. "Getting to know these families *es que bueno* [is great]," remarked one elderly man. As the summer went by, plans for future events were being made.

When it came time for the next Halloween party, I said, "You know the town's leaders never attend these events although they are invited; that's strange. Perhaps they fear the HUD women are becoming powerful and will be demanding 'things.' I suspect they may ask CEPP to leave." As the day of the party arrived and the HUD women were busy setting up the room for the party, the mayor sent word that the party could not be held in the HUD meeting room, but was to be held at a safe haven near the City Hall. The women were devastated as they worked hard getting the food together and now all the party supplies had to be moved. Furthermore, the mothers did not want their children to walk across the street to the safe haven. "Why not?" we asked. "Because it's gang territory—we can't risk our kids crossing that way." The emic understanding of threat and danger was something we, as outsiders, had not recognized. This is a very important lesson to learn when working to empower people—listen to their concerns.

The event was held at the safe haven, but very few HUD children attended. The HUD mothers were given no credit by the town leaders for their work, and there were no TV cameras. The women became silent and withdrew; their voices no longer seemed valued. Their efforts toward getting donated food and organizing the games were ignored by the mayor, who wanted all the credit given to her—alone. Violence is about power, and shunning is a form of withholding power from marginalized segments of unwanted people—like the HUD families. Certain signs, like the town leaders not attending any of the HUD parties, were clues that many of those *with* power were less than enthusiastic about empowering the HUD families. This power play by the mayor was a sign to the CEPP team she was feeling threatened by CEPP.

Moving into the Storefront

When participating in a study such as this, being invited *into* the community is the first important step in being accepted, trusted, and held accountable. At the same time, a community can *dis-invite* you—asking you to leave the town, village, or even country. It has happened to anthropologists in the past. We were alert to the fact that some of our findings were not positive about the town, especially the governance. Trying to tell the whole story means that certain factions may become disgruntled if they perceive you are favoring one group over the other. This is exactly what we began to feel—that the town hall folks might want some issues kept quiet or undisclosed. But this was not our promise—our contract; we pledged to "tell the truth—even if it hurt." It is wise to have a backup plan in case you are shut off from some activities of a town.

We as a team needed to make new plans. So we relocated our office to a storefront, and we had already moved into our new office when we got a written notice from the mayor's office that we were to vacate our HUD apartment immediately. HUD women came to see us at our new location. We now understood the dynamics of the shunning and discrimination that most of the HUD women had probably experienced most of their lives. We were cast out because we were seen as a threat—a threat caused by telling the truth.

We continued to collect data over the next two years and reported regularly in writing to the town council. We attended the Weed and Seed meetings—they were open to the public. Shunning can only discourage you if you let it—not if you have enough self-esteem to shun the shunning. Many of the fragile women in HUD housing could not rise above being ostracized, so they withdrew and continued being shunned.

Monolingual Spanish Speakers

Recalling facts from the survey, we found about 42 percent of the town's population spoke mostly or only Spanish. So why would a group of Spanish speakers this size be shunned? The shunning of monolingual Spanish speakers is subtle and also selective. Certain venues are exempt from shunning, for example where only older women meet, like in Capilla de Guadalupe or in other neighborhood churches where older people worship, and in neighborhood stores. We also note that at Hispanic political rallies, where Spanish is the only language used, we see no leaders from Esperanza in attendance. Why would this absence be so noticeable when Esperanza is being celebrated as a Mexican American town?

A Poetry Reading: A poetry reading by a locally well-known Hispanic professor was held in the Las Artes building, a public space in Esperanza. At the reading, approximately 50 people—a mixed group of half Anglos and half Hispanic—attended, but only English was spoken. The poems were passionate—about Hispanic conditions and lifestyles—but all were read in English. No one spoke Spanish even after the readings. Was this to be a symbol of acculturation and evidence of such acculturation by speaking only English?

Calling 911: Monolingual Spanish-speaking women report that if they call 911 and speak Spanish, the dispatcher hangs up on them. We never tested that hypothesis, but these reports were frequent and from many different types of people. (However, Señora Martínez, the monolingual Spanish-speaking woman whose case study appeared in chapter 2, says that when a Spanish-speaking person calls the police, they come, so the evidence is mixed.)

Public Hearings: Another piece of evidence of the shunning of Spanish speakers was at one of the Weed and Seed public meetings. With about 100 people in attendance, a woman from the community, speaking in Spanish, chastised the leaders for not conducting the meeting in Spanish. As she said, "That's the language for most of us." She received stony silence as a response to her request. In public meetings in Esperanza and in citywide celebrations (e.g., dedicating the new fire engine), the only language used is English.

Shunning does not seem to affect older women, who live very private lives, leaving their homes only to worship at the local capilla or to shop at a local store. No one seems to bother with them, or is it no one cares? "Why bother," one says. "We're old and going to die soon."

Learning English: One reason there is high prevalence of Spanish speaking in the home is because native Spanish-speakers believe Spanish is the language of the soul; it more nourishing than English and establishes a deeper relationship between the speakers. However, older monolingual women are hungry to learn to speak English. "Please come to our homes and teach us; we're prisoners, we can't get out. We can't go anywhere by ourselves." Or, "We are abused, but we can't tell anyone what is going on." We tell them that classes in English are given at the school on 4th Street, why not go there? They give their reasons, "We're afraid to cross the street." Or, "Our husbands would never let us go alone." As mentioned previously, bilingual education is hotly debated in the town. In 2000 a proposition was passed by the voters in the state to abolish it. The monolingual mothers were happy as they believed bilingual education was keeping their children from advancing, causing them to drop out early. They say:

> Don't let bilingual education be in the elementary schools. It keeps our children prisoners, too. They never learn enough English to study beyond elementary school, so they drop out.

> Do total immersion in English, but not bilingual education. You need teachers who can read and write in English, and I know some bilingual teachers can't do that. They say they're bilingual, but they can't read or write English.

We also found that some fluent Spanish speakers with Master's degrees could not read or write in Spanish; they had learned to speak Spanish at home, but they never had formal classes in order to become literate. It is challenging to teach in a language you poorly grasp or in which you are barely literate.

One significant reason for the pressure to speak only English is because it is the language for business. It is based on economic values, which are shaped and rewarded by those in power. So, shaping the local culture to be English speaking only benefits the town's economy. Knowing that lack of literacy in English causes students to drop out of school, we can see how literacy in English affects getting a good education and therefore also affects earning power, especially when we look at some statistics. According to the

1997 U.S. Census, the median income for people with a high school diploma was $19,851; for people with a bachelor's degree, it was $59,048. The discrepancy is even greater for those without a high school diploma, indicating that those who do not have a high school diploma will live a life of poverty. Hence, there are nested problems in this area of language acquisition that need focused attention.

Not being fluent in English, especially for men, limits where they can work. Without skills and English proficiency the job market is limited to part-time, episodic work, with long hours, often in harsh work environments (Dohan 2003:51). Jobs such as carpenter helpers, janitors, home health care workers, hotel laborers, gardeners, dishwashers, and fast-food cooks can be demanding; the hours of work may be long, and many workers hold down more than one job. This overwork does not allow time to acquire language skills. Often day laborers are working only with other Spanish-speaking employees, a situation that impedes learning English. These employment situations permit little upward mobility and lock families into intergenerational poverty—and being shunned.

The cycle of work for Spanish-speaking women is the same, except more complicated if they have children. Finding safe child care is the hardest task HUD working mothers have. It is difficult as they would say:

> Grandmas, friends, neighbors, or an older brother or sister, those are the dependable ones. We don't make enough to pay for child care, and the hours are so long. I get up before anyone else just to get to work on time. Without a car, what do you do if you have to walk or take a bus? Grandma's old and cross to my kids. They [HUD] cut off our allowances with the program to get off of welfare. I had to donate many hours to the HUD, lots of time, and it cut back on what I could make in my job cleaning houses. I wish I could speak English, but I don't have no time to go to learn it. Then my sister got here from Durango last week, and she's got two kids, she can help Grandma take care of the kids, but there's no more money 'til she can get some work.

In a town with a population of 84 percent self-identified Hispanics, does this pattern of shunning Spanish speakers have an adaptive meaning? Mexican-born spouses represented 81 percent of the population. In 2004 69 percent had less than a high school education (*Arizona Daily Star Citizen* 2004). The majority or 61 percent of the respondents to our survey have lived at their current address less than five years. These statistics represent a very mobile, migrating population, one without established roots in the town. The inability of monolingual Spanish speakers to assimilate quickly and become independent and hopefully out of poverty, we conclude, is the reason for shunning them.

Shaping through shunning also can be linked to the Hispanic cultural pattern of familism, the high value Mexican family places on caring for each other, and *respecto*, the respect of each other. Although the large households of extended family seem ideal, such thick kinships also foster dependency. New arrivals into the family place burdens on the whole household. Dohan (2003) notes that upward mobility is hampered as earnings dribble out to sponsor more family migrants. This dependency pattern, he reasons, perpetuates intergenerational poverty. Closing the door to kin and new immigrants also has its downside—isolation. Mexican immigrants say that isolation from their families is so painful. Rather than choosing painful isolation, most residents of Esperanza open their doors to immigrant kin even though such kindness may keep them all in poverty.

Dependency is especially seen for those living near the border; they maintain close ties with others in Mexico and go back and forth to their homeland. This pattern is called recurrent migration. Recurrent migration disrupts employment and it does not promote the acquisition of English. Both of these conditions lead to poverty.

Summary

The ongoing dynamics of shunning the homeless, HUD families, and monolingual Spanish speakers continue to shift and change the structure of Esperanza. These three subgroups compose a pariah, an unwanted class in Esperanza. Each subgroup lives within a cultural system of subscribed rules and norms. The larger society reinforces their behavior through a series of shunning and rejecting responses. This unwanted class of shunned people is not breaking the law, like drug traffickers, yet subtle pressures are placed upon them to change, be quiet, and stay preferably out of sight. By ignoring them or by not going out of their way for them, the local leaders express an opinion, which seems shared by the townspeople, that this population is a drag on the society. They are not wanted, only tolerated. Only time will tell what happens to these groups of ostracized people, perhaps they will die off, and maybe another group of shunned people will take their place.

Local people would like to change Esperanza's image of poverty to prosperity and tranquility. Understanding the facts and context surrounding poverty and discrimination is one step toward change. In a complex, multifaceted, multidimensional, and dynamic civil society all people must have respect and equal opportunity to participate in their own self-determination. Instead of shunning people, the whole community must recognize and assist rather than ostracize the unwanted.

Chapter 8

A Shift in the Paradigm

> Equality is a very big idea, connected to freedom, but an idea that doesn't come for free. We can choose to shift the responsibility . . . or we can choose to shift the paradigm.
>
> —Bono, "Foreword," *The End of Poverty*

Change is possible. A community can change, propelled by new ideas, or remain stagnant under the weight of controlling norms. To change the profile, all parts must change, not necessarily all at once but in an integrated way, from the outside to the inside and from the inside to the outside. In Esperanza, not all movement is done with consensus, sometimes there are sudden disruptions—starts and stops. Beliefs and behaviors are dynamic, alive, and representative of the pushes and pulls within a natural system. The town is continually self-(re)organizing, at all levels, as people and the social structure keep shifting and shaping responses. Sometimes it feels chaotic and random, but it isn't; there is an emerging pattern that leans toward the positive, resilient side, away from the destructive violent side. In describing cultural change—or a paradigm shift—Agar uses the analogy of birds flocking together, an image proposed by Schelling (1971), each one influencing another in a random pattern until all are content to be where they are.

How have Esperanzans faced the challenges to strategize, change, and survive? Living with them and becoming part of the threads woven into this Hispanic border town, the CEPP team members are cocreators of this ethnography. The findings are not surprising, and understanding them generates the power to continue to change directions. Understanding the causes of violence gives the community an opportunity to adopt new and more liberating strategies for living more freely and without fear.

145

Causes of Violence

Violence is a destructive, maladaptive, unwanted human behavior. Esperanzans are victims of two types of violence: (1) the structural violence of inequality and poverty, and (2) the personal violence of physical and emotional abuse. Structural violence occurs when the larger society prevents (or perpetuates a situation that prevents) marginalized people (such as the poor) from meeting their needs. Structural violence is expressed by the dominant society in racism, sexism, shunning, discrimination, among other ostracizing practices, and it restricts individuals from partaking in the opportunities afforded to those of a higher social status. Structural violence is covert and subtle and is perpetrated by social institutions (e.g., the government). Personal violence, on the other hand, is more openly discussed, and people are more familiar with the behaviors associated with it (e.g., domestic abuse, murder, rape, etc.). It is not uncommon for illegal activities and personal violence to occur as a result of structural violence. We begin by interpreting structural violence through the shared viewpoints of townspeople.

Structural Violence

In Esperanza the cause of structural violence is social inequality, which has a long history in the Southwest. Over the past 400 years, the land has undergone contentious battles for ownership, resulting in the establishment of two unequal nations, Mexico and the U.S. This imbalance has propelled Mexican immigrants (both illegal and legal) to seek a more prosperous life in the U.S. The stability of the border town continues to be undermined by the continual flow of migrating populations in and out of Mexico only 45 miles away. Because it is difficult for them to assimilate into the U.S. culture, immigrants cannot find high-paying jobs, so most of them remain poor and are marginalized in their new country.

Long-standing inequality perpetuates poverty—and poverty gives birth to opportunistic drug lords. Due to poverty and inequality, drug trafficking has become a normalized way to get easy money, and personal violence has followed. Discrimination, disconnections, and fear are three factors at the societal level that underlay poverty. Each will be described briefly.

Discrimination

Whenever there has been a shortage of labor (as there was during several periods in American history, such as during World War II) the welcome sign for cheap Mexican labor is put up. As soon as the crisis is over, the "get out" sign halts and penalizes Mexican workers. This push and pull has created tensions, and these have led often to discrimination and violence. Changing the pattern of this ongoing problem needs new understanding and discussion, not vigilantes with guns patrolling the border or fences to keep people from crossing the border.

Today there is a growing disagreement about Mexican workers in the U.S. In Congress, some legislators promote a guest-worker plan while others argue that these "alien" workers cost the U.S. citizens money. Facts do not support this latter position; immigrants contribute over $40 billion to the social security fund every year and use less "welfare" funding than any comparable minority group (Hayes-Bautista 2004). A guest-worker plan would be modeled after the Bracero Program (described in chapter 1). The worker from Mexico would be invited to the U.S., given a temporary work visa, employed, and given rights and access to education and health care (not free but paid for by the worker and employer). The worker and his/her family could apply for permanent residency, as is true for other immigrants, and if immigration quotas are not exceeded and if all other legal requirements are met, permanent residency or citizenship would be possible. The guest-worker plan is being considered by the U.S. House of Representatives.

As it stands now, Mexicans arrive in the U.S., landless and jobless, and end up working for wages that are lower than what Anglos are paid. This type of discrimination causes low self-esteem and is highly stressful. Furthermore, their homeland is only a few miles away, so a pattern of recurrent migration slows their acculturation and exacerbates discrimination by members of the mainstream culture in the U.S. This pattern of acculturation is different for Esperanzans than for those who cannot migrate recurrently, such as immigrants from Asian or African countries, because their homeland is too far away.

Disconnections

There are several types of disconnections in Esperanza: migrant workers who reside in Esperanza but who are emotionally disconnected from the town; U.S. citizens who work in the town but live elsewhere; and the groups who are shunned by the town leaders.

About two-thirds of Esperanza's population are immigrants; some are legal and others illegal. This migrating population is often a collection of kin and friends who have crossed the border with dreams of a better life, only to find a life of discrimination, hard labor, and continued poverty. They often stay connected to their families in Mexico, sending earnings back to their kin. Many of these migrants are disconnected from Esperanza structurally and emotionally, even though their labor and purchasing power are welcomed. Furthermore, fear of immigration patrol keeps many immigrants in the shadows, not participating in the governance of the town or in their own independence. Self-reliance does not emerge when one is hiding from la migra. To stabilize the town, local leaders need to include immigrants in dialogues and in structuring ordinances and opportunities for legal employment. It can be done.

There are also disconnections on another level: the people who live in Esperanza do not work there, and the people who work there do not live there. Most service jobs, such as banker, information technology specialist, and accountant, require a college education, and the majority of residents (over 60 percent) have less than a high school education (Glittenberg 2001). Most who work in service jobs in town do not live there, saying, "Oh, I wouldn't live here [Esperanza]! I live in the foothills."

Progress for the whole community is still hampered by internal disconnection (as described in chapter 7). Certain marginalized groups—the homeless, HUD apartment dwellers, and monolingual Spanish speakers—are perceived as pariahs and are shunned because they represent what the townspeople do not want to be—poor with limited choices, a drag on upward mobility for people striving to get out of poverty. The shunned groups are not hidden. They are part of the local community but are particularly ignored by the town leaders. For example, town leaders tolerate the large soup kitchen for the homeless in the center of town but make little effort to work with it; they do not inform HUD families of government services available to them and they avoid HUD-sponsored activities; and local leaders show disdain toward those who do not speak English and they, themselves, avoid speaking Spanish in public.

Fear

Societal fear is a consensus by individuals that danger exists throughout the community. In Esperanza, the societal fear comes from the drug trafficking that occurs in the town and from the possibility of being deported. The pervasiveness of these fears undermines initiatives to partake of many of the opportunities afforded to most U.S. citizens such as employment, education, and political participation.

Fear stemming from drug trafficking grows out of the associated violence seen in the streets and in many homes. The way to eliminate this fear is to change the impetus for trafficking—financial gain. If opportunities for making money from the sale of illegal drugs no longer exist, drug trafficking would gradually subside and violence would be reduced. For many decades the townspeople chose to shift the responsibility for controlling drug dealing to officials—like the police. This displacement of responsibility works for only a short period of time; for a long-term solution, all individuals need to be responsible for eliminating trafficking.

Mexicans come to the United States to work in jobs that many residents refuse to do. But the U.S. government also refuses to issue work visas to these workers. The situation is a paradox: laborers are needed, but laborers are illegal and their status is not secure. This lack of security instills fear and uneasiness. When employment of Mexican labor is open, transparent, and legal, fear will be diminished.

Personal Violence

Aspects of the Hispanic culture that shape individual behavior can result in violence. Four cultural factors were identified by the people as causes of violence in Esperanza. They are: (1) patronism, (2) machismo/marianismo, (3) greed, and (4) codependency. Each will be described briefly.

Patronism

Mexican culture has for centuries been built around the issue of patronism: a one-party governance model. At local levels there is a pervasive custom of a "big man" in control, as we found in Esperanza. Patronism was blatant during the study, as one family—that of Ernesto Hanson—ruled the election process and controlled the governance of Esperanza for over 40 years. This fact may not be labeled as negative in outcome for it accounts also for stability, such as resisting annexation by the big city of Tucson. This type of "one party" governance is similar to that of the government of Mexico. It had changed only recently during our study when Vincente Fox was elected president, at that time representing a new political party.

Patronism is an ethos of power and is adaptive for a stagnant culture, where control is important. In a society undergoing rapid change, however, patronism is maladaptive. Despite the changes that have occurred in Esperanza, some patterns of patronism remain in traditional Hispanic families, and in gangs, where revenge and punitive domination are used to maintain control in an authoritarian, patronal system.

Machismo and Marianismo

The townspeople in all venues spoke about how the prevailing macho cultural norm is a cause of violence in Esperanza. "Macho men—they drink, fight, and live in the streets." "It's how we're supposed to be—going to our death with a smile on our face—macho—that's what we are." The other side of the coin—marianismo—idealizes the submissive, obedient woman. Redefining these long-held cultural ideals is slow and painful, as is illustrated by the statements of two people: One female said, "I am beaten because I deserve it—I know he wants me to serve him as any good woman should. I saw my mother beaten and that's what I expect, too, when I'm not obedient." A male expressed his view, "We need to treat our women like Madonna—for they are pure." Another said, "You don't see Mexican women being putas, they are pure, not like Anglos or Cubanos who sell their bodies." In opposition are voices of more modern women saying, "I won't be beaten like my mother because I don't obey some drunken man." "I'll hit him if he tries to make me do things I don't want to do." Such conflict between the traditional and nontraditional cultural rules creates tension and sometimes violence.

On a personal level such cultural norms encourage aggressive behavior. A prevailing norm shapes males to be possessive, authoritarian, and revengeful. Several narratives illustrated that when a male is challenged, violence erupts. The cultural norm of overdrinking and drunkenness, linked with machismo, also often results in violence.

Alcohol misuse may also be part of the expected cultural behaviors of being male or macho. Alcohol is used in 80 percent of the households and if this fact is going to change, then cultural patterns must be altered. Too often the problem of overdrinking is placed into a moral framework that leads to few or no solutions. Broadening the explanatory model for alcohol misuse would include addressing the role of machismo and marianismo in the culture of migration and stress. Community efforts to control drunkenness and domestic violence are beginning.

Greed

Greed is a personal pattern of taking resources for personal benefit at the expense of others. Greed is not more prevalent in Esperanza than in other places, but when interpreting the causes of violence in Esperanza, greed is a factor. Prostitutes, gang members, drug dealers, and coyotes are part of the greed ethos of the town. All of these groups make money off of someone's need or addiction. The common thread of greed in each of these illegal actions seems to continue; when one source is squashed, another pops up. Fighting greed seems an endless challenge.

Codependency

Drug trafficking is a major, widespread problem. Thick kinship systems and neighbor networks also keep the illicit economy complicit. Do you turn your uncle, father, or sister in for selling drugs? The stories of small-time dealing come from a diverse population—from prostitutes to political wizards. Because of the networks of covertness, control is difficult and sporadic. A codependency cultural norm further challenges changing behavior, as people in the community seem to accept drug and alcohol use as normal. The pattern of codependency needs further study; as it remains, the pattern is destructive at the personal, family, and community levels.

Doing Something about Structural and Personal Violence

How might the townspeople deal with structural and personal violence? Just as the causes of violence are multiple and intertwined, dealing with violence is challenging and entails using methods and having expectations that are realistic. We will look at the following aspects of surmounting structural and personal violence in Esperanza: (1) community understanding, (2) sustaining positive cultural connections, (3) valuing positives, and (4) empowering the community.

Community Understanding

In Esperanza, structural violence has led to poverty, and poverty has led to drug and human smuggling—a way to make money at the expense of others' physical and emotional well-being. But it isn't only the person who is illegally smuggled or the drug addict's well-being that is abused; the well-being of the entire community is affected—especially by the violence that surrounds these illegal activities. The mother of a teenager killed in a gang shoot out said, "We do it to ourselves." At the funeral, someone said, "When one of us gets killed, it affects the whole community."

Coming to grips with human rights abuses needs a community understanding and a sense of power to change. This community action is fundamental for removing drug trafficking as a way of life, "a thing we all do to survive." In Esperanza, they cry, "No more violence! We want to change." The people want to hold onto their Hispanic way of life, but they want to be free—of poverty and violence.

To be truly free, Esperanzans need to get to the heart of crime, to change the greed of selling a substance that destroys lives and harms relationships. They need to gather courage and be neither complacent nor complicit. Individuals cannot do it on their own. Being free means becoming a responsive community of people who live in a world of inequality and violence.

Political scientist John E. Schwarz says it well:

> The fundamental sense of freedom involves something far larger than simply being left alone to follow one's own best self-interest. The idea of freedom is considerably more than private value. Individual autonomy is nested within a complex of obligations individuals have toward one another. Obligations are required for freedom to be moral. Far from being individualistic, freedom is an essential social idea. (Schwarz 2005:4)

Furthermore, laws of the nation need to be changed to prevent abuses and to give attention to those with fewer resources and limited opportunities. Esperanzans never need to lose hope.

Sustaining Positive Cultural Connections

There are a number of very positive cultural norms that provide people with the resources to be strong and to develop a nonviolent community. Both the habits of the heart, found in Mexican family culture, and loyalty to Mexico's patron saint, Our Lady of Guadalupe who "never leaves them and grieves with them," provide foundational cultural connections. Connections to Mexico are also found in food, fiestas, home decorations, love of the family.

Misusing alcohol may be a negative part of connections, for drinking together bonds relationships, but overuse of alcohol may result in violence. Breaking the connection between alcohol consumption and violence clearly is a goal of many—especially women. Strong alliances between women are part of the cultural context. For example, women closed a violent bar by surrounding it and standing arm in arm for several weeks, night and day, to keep customers from entering. They also tried to obstruct renewal of liquor licenses, but did not get the support of the town council that wanted the tax dollars received from the liquor sales. In this case, societal needs for financial resources outweighed the need to control the misuse of alcohol.

Valuing Positives

Paulo Freire says, "That dream for a better world requires all these struggles . . . without ever losing hope. No matter what society we may be in, or what society we may belong to, it is urgent that we fight with hope and fearlessness" (Freire 2004:122). One way to fight with hope and fearlessness is to value and promote the positive elements within the community.

In the midst of poverty in Esperanza are children whose talents are awakened when someone cares enough to help them read and write and to find their natural talent in art—as seen at Las Artes. We saw the look of hope, even for a brief moment on the faces of poor HUD mothers who were recognized for their talents. What would the world look like if we only see talents and gifts rather than deficits in people, governments, and global connections? Yes, there are individuals in Esperanza and the world who do see the positives in people rather than only their deficits. They are those who build with hope and fearlessness.

Empowering the Community

Even though resourceful, resilient leaders remain, they are challenged by the networks of illegal activities. Superficial changes are obvious, such as new streetlights, sidewalks, paved streets and alleys, and new houses. Federal grants like Weed and Seed have helped to beautify the streets and homes, create zones where no criminal activity can take place, tear down crack houses, add Safe Havens with programs for at-risk youths, build commemorative parks, add resources for the police, and, in general, establish a network of security and hope. "These changes are dynamic like ice changing into water" (Agar 2004:414).

A future is being built, but how likely are these superficial changes to be permanent? Permanent changes can be seen as the people visualize the *future*—a better town. This shared vision of the future includes: the Peace Garden to be used by generations to come, commemorating the life of Oscar;

Peace Garden in memory of Oscar

the mosaic wall of tiles made by the hands of illiterate older women depicting their lives as migrants crossing a hostile border; a wall honoring veterans of the Korean War; filling the enlarged public Sam Lena library with knowledge seekers of all ages; commemorating the life of John Valenzuela, the young police officer lost in the line of duty, through building a memorial wall and showing respect for the importance of police protection; and, building miniparks on land where abandoned crack houses once stood.

These subtle changes illustrate that communities can build a future without illegal economies. They can sustain hope within their own boundaries by changing their perspectives (or as Bono says, their paradigms)—by seeing new possibilities. Yes, the Weed and Seed grant brought needed money to build—to change—but the real (lasting) hope came when the local people spoke about the future saying, "We want to change," and as several participants claimed, "We can't do it by ourselves—we need each other."

MacDonald and Leary say "humans need to be/feel connected; we are social animals that need integration" (2005:203), and that exclusion is equivalent to death. The leaders and people come together in fiestas with the purpose of celebrating various aspects of their Mexican culture and to insure that the group survives, thrives, and counters the disconnections. But still there are private disconnections when the people say, "Nobody cares." "I don't trust anyone." Hope must begin by rebuilding a town with people connected with one another. Structural connections already in place need continuance, such as the community policing with the bike patrols—police being *with* the people. School activities still need to connect families and build literacy for all—especially the older monolingual women who feel isolated, locked

Crowd at a park dedication

behind their doors. No one should be left shunned. Talents need to be recognized, supported, and celebrated. Small cottage industries hold promise for income and also building self-confidence and self-esteem.

We conclude that eradicating violence involves multiple layers of commitment and change. Overcoming both structural violence created by discrimination, disconnection, and fear will be a collective challenge. Also, culturally held behaviors that promote patronism, greed, and alcohol misuse demand a major change beyond the mere visible improvements in the town's appearance. The true strength of Esperanza is beginning to take shape as the people themselves say, "We want change—no more violence."

A New Paradigm for Transformation

What would the world look like without poverty, drug trafficking, and violence? Can we have a world of justice and fairness? To paraphrase Bono, if you are going to become equal you have to take responsibility for changing the situation or changing the paradigm. This story of violence and hope points to ways of changing the situation and perhaps changing the paradigm. Real hope will come when cultural rules change, when complicity and complacency in drug and human trafficking are no longer accepted as normal. Violence follows the money trail, but until there is a paradigm shift, little long-term progress will be made. A vision, inclusive of all, must be framed and operationalized by good, courageous leaders who care about the well-being of individuals and the community as a whole.

Two people in Esperanza have been named by the townspeople as outstanding leaders. These leaders call for action, for change. John is a parole officer and Sister Serena is the director of a social agency. Their views summarize the situation and what needs to be done to change it. John tells his story of seeing violence perpetuated through the futility of the correctional system (structural violence). Sister Serena addresses the issue of individual cultural change as she speaks of the gift of self-reliance and building hope through being truthful, giving kids a sense of honor, and being a trusted friend.

JOHN, A PAROLE OFFICER

The Drug War

Let's start with the most obvious problem: the war on drugs. People know that the war on drugs has failed because violence and smuggling have not been reduced. We suggest that a two-pronged approach is needed: (1) stop the greed and illegal market by halting prohibition of drugs now known as illegal and regulating sales, as is done with alcohol; and (2) promote an educational and treatment plan to curb and treat addictions. If drug use and trafficking were not prohibited but rather regulated, then imprisonment is not appropriate. What needs to change is to target the real issues.

Our so-called war on drugs is a joke. We need to deprofitize drugs. Do you see those big drug kings suffering, the Mafia, behind bars? No. Why do you think gangs are now focusing on making money? Yes, because there are profits, but you don't see the big ones get caught, it's the little guys who get caught, and we think we've won the war. We could deprofitize drugs. Think about it, the Harris 1914 Drug Act controls provisions of physicians to prescribe drugs legally. Coca Cola originally contained cocaine, but changed to using caffeine—a legal drug. Opium used to be sold over the counter at local pharmacies. We need to legalize the use of drugs, with prescriptions and thus deprofitization. A whole illegal drug industry would go up in fumes; think of the money that would be saved—billions of dollars and millions of lives. The price of drugs goes up when it's illegal—and the public protection with a strong law enforcement and judicial system. But the revolving door syndrome serves no good purpose. We need courage to change this failing war on drugs.

Another real issue is that trafficking is an international problem. At this level radical changes are needed, for instance regulating the whole process rather than separating manufacturing, distribution, and sales as illegal. All are now illegal, and we need to regulate. An organization already in place to establish such a regulated system is the World Health Organization (WHO) with seven regional headquarters worldwide. Such a cultural change would have an immediate reduction in crime, violence, and imprisonment. Counterinterests such as the many manufacturers and growers, drug smugglers, and a whole system of profit takers will resist such changes. It will be a long, involved process, but it can be done.

In large part we live in a culture of violence; we glorify violence. Every kid grows up with a play gun, with violence on video, on television, in newspapers—it's got to stop. If we are a society that takes this seriously we can turn the corner—we did it with cigarette smoking. But we seem to leave it for the next guy to handle or better yet—lock 'em up and throw away the key. Get the violent ones off the streets, yet there is no therapy for the kids and family who remain behind. It really is a very ignorant way to try to change a society.

It would be so much better if we would really get serious and educate society to control violence. If we, as parents, could teach our children to learn that real men and real women will walk away from a fight. We should celebrate the one who walked away or held out a hand to shake, rather than a fist to punch. When will we grow up as a nation? We have people/kids who are so fragile. They need help to grow up and accept responsibility. I recall a prisoner who had killed people—a murderer. He told me that he had been taught by his dad in a brutal way, that when he was a little kid if he came home beaten up, his father would beat him up even more for not being a "real" man"—for not fighting back. This attitude is pervasive throughout our society.

The Failing Prison System

I've been working in the prison system for over 30 years and it has gotten more punitive over the years. In Arizona there has been an increase in the number of prisoners over the past decade when we had perhaps 2,000 in prison, but now we have 30,000. It is incomprehensible. The population has not increased to that extent; it has to do with politics. Politicians play games with the public when seeking election; they say they are going to protect the public by putting every criminal behind bars. But the public is not fully informed of what changes need to be made and how criminals could be handled differently than placing them all behind bars. Resources could/should be reallocated.

Let me give you an example. We had a violent prisoner who was getting ready for release, and he had a 3-day pass with his mother. They spent the pass staying in a nearby motel, and his violence erupted. He killed his mother and cut her up. The point is that the prisoner had not been prepared—with education and therapy—to deal with anger and frustration—and being holed up in a sleazy motel didn't make it any better. Better planning needs to be done.

We lock up violent criminals, but no real effort is made to change them. After serving time, they have no housing, transportation, or employment. This is a costly recycling of crime and punishment. The biggest problem is that the prisons are going in the wrong direction. It is little wonder that the crimes are repeated and reincarceration rates remain high. Prisons should not be the first weapon of defense in fighting drugs but rather the last resort. It's a mystery why we continue to imprison; it's an ineffective way of dealing with drug users, we throw them into prison, and they are worse off. How are they going to make a life that way? We need more halfway houses for drug users. The point remains that the parole system believes it is saving money by not having a therapist on payroll, so there is little help—something is wrong there. Legislators need to come into the prisons and see what is being done. In my history only 4–5 legislators have ever visited the prisons. They don't have a clue as to what is going on and neither do ordinary citizens. It's a crime in a society that values freedom to continue to have a system that builds more crime and less freedom.

Churches—Called to Be a Counterculture

Churches haven't done nearly enough. They need to be a counterculture—to rise up and make/take a stand. We in the church have lost our role as a counterculture; we need to be looking outward to real problems and how to change them rather than just looking inward to ourselves and just feeling good about being so churchly. We need to speak out against all kinds of violence; it is violent to remain silent.

SISTER SERENA, A SOCIAL AGENCY DIRECTOR

Family and Social Support

My parents lived in the same house for all of their married life, so I grew up in that same house; we never moved, and I had a huge extended family; everyone lived in Kansas. There was so much stability in my early life—so different from the kids in Esperanza. I had a lot of love and support.

Programs for Parenting

We're into a second or third generation of parents who were not parented appropriately. We are soon going to be in a fourth generation of kids who haven't had love, support—stability. Programs that seem to make a difference are those working with parents. Parents at some point in time come to terms with who they are, how they were raised, and what's the best they want to keep and pass on to their children. How can they be better? It's not that you don't have hard things to deal with, but you need people in your life who help you deal with stuff in an appropriate way. I do anything I can to help kids realize that there really is a reason to be honorable in life.

Direction and Advice

It's hard to give kids or teenagers advice. The way I grew up, and the things that were most important to me are things they don't have in their lives. So it's hard to encourage them to be something that they haven't really had any experience to be. I think that the most we can offer these kids is a way to learn who they are and to be true to themselves. They are lacking an awareness of other kids—they need to be sensitive to others. The kids who easily hurt other kids don't have that sense that there's a value in being compassionate. So many kids are missing all of that. They need to understand that there are consequences for actions and what responsibility really is.

We need to help give kids a sense of honor and responsibility to themselves, to God, in whatever form that is for them, in whatever religious beliefs they have. They need to come to terms with themselves, how to make choices, live with decisions and their consequences, and to understand what responsibility is. We can work with children to help them realize that there are consequences for everything that they choose to do. The only thing that makes a difference with kids is when you're honest with them. You really care, and you are willing to challenge some of their choices even though that's not easy, [but also] you're willing to support them. Many feel that no one is there for them. They need to know somebody cares.

You can't possibly do these things without help and support. At times it feels like it doesn't matter what we do, it's not going to change, nothing is going to happen. We all feel like we are not making a difference, and it doesn't matter. But at the same time what is the alternative? If you just quit for sure nothing is going to happen.

Two social institutions stand out in the new paradigm suggested by John and Sister Serena, the correctional system and the family system. The correctional system is endorsed as a means to protect society from dangerous people. However, as John points, out the greatest factor in today's path of violence and crime is not dangerous people, it is drug trafficking. He points out that the war on drugs is built on false premises, that controlling drug addicts and dealers with surveillance, arrests, prosecution, and incarceration does not work. In fact, it is a long-standing failure.

He suggests, instead, an alternative plan that will address the public health issues of high-risk behavior and mental health needs; a new paradigm that would shift monies currently used to control people who distribute and sell illegal drugs to a system of regulating drug use and providing treatment for drug and alcohol misuse. Shifting a paradigm is never easy, but it can be done in stages and with a clear plan. It needs to be done with a program of transparency and grassroots involvement.

The second part of the paradigm shift involves personal commitment to return to and retain a covenant of caring. Inequality is built upon an unjust system in which the survival of some is threatened and diminished by the greed of others. Such inequities eat away at the whole. Those who suffer the most are the powerless, such as the children. Understanding, as Sister Serena does, that one generation's suffering shapes the next generation, paradigm shifts need to change through caring for our children, which can be done in school, in church, and by making good jobs available to all. Change will not be without resistance, but if we don't do it now, when will we?

Reflections

At the beginning of ethnographic fieldwork, you do not know what the stories will tell. In this natural study of violence, we could not foresee what changes would occur—like a town being renewed. The unknowns made our journey challenging, baffling, surprising, disappointing, fulfilling, puzzling, and exhilarating—all the emotions of being human. A good ending is always great—but not always the outcome of an ethnography. This story has a good ending.

To end such a study, though, is like placing a comma in a sentence, for the life of the community goes on, continually changing. The fact that the town is changing has been documented through the stories as well as through evidence of structural change. The drop in murders is over 50 percent and for other crimes the same. The people's perceptions are positive, "Violence is down—I don't hear gunfire." "The police are good, and they are here for us." "The town is safer." Perhaps lessons learned through the stories of Esperanza can become a blueprint for other towns, cities, borderlands, and even nations faced with violence within and without. Open leadership, inclusion of all, dialogue, and sensitivity transform myths and overcome fears. Equality is a constant challenge. Overcoming self-centeredness is a first-order goal, as greed blinds even the most noble. Courage is needed to face facts, such as a failed war on drugs. The war on drugs is weakening as the public becomes more informed and weary of the huge budget for punishment and very little slated for rehabilitation and treatment programs.

Solutions must be accepted only when they are empowering for all—not just the privileged few. And some places will need extra help, like bootstraps, to jump-start a transformation. The people of Esperanza have told their stories. They have shown that poverty, discrimination, fear, violence are all qualities that inhibit access to a full life. To change things you simply must begin. As Sister Serena said, "If you just quit, for sure nothing is going to happen. They need to know somebody cares—they need to have hope."

Adios tile sign created by Las Artes students

Appendix A

Questions Posed to Focus Groups

1. What do you believe are the norms for alcohol use in Esperanza? Gender? Age? Role?

2. Is drunkenness permitted at all? When? Where?

3. Are drugs permitted at all? When? Where? Parties? Celebrations? Age? Gender?

4. What makes it not OK to use drugs? What happens if you break that rule? Who can break it? When? Where?

5. When and where is it OK to get violent physically? With whom is it OK or not OK?

6. What do you call violence? Verbal? Physical? Nonverbal?

7. What keeps a person or group of people from getting violent?

8. Is Esperanza more violent now than a year ago? Five years ago? Ten? Will it become better/less violent? How, When? Through what means? Have the rules changed about being violent? Or is it that no one talks about it? Who cares?

9. Who are the role models, gatekeepers, and guards within this community against alcohol and drug misuse? Against violence?

10. What about the economy? What about the church, schools, businesses, liquor stores, and bars? Describe how each contributes to reducing violence.

11. Who has the right to change things and how?

12. Are gangs in Esperanza a problem? Why? When did they start? Fear? What can be changed?

13. Who are the good people in Esperanza? What makes them "good"?

14. What things and activities in Esperanza are positive? What reduces violence? Crime? Alcohol abuse and drug use? Drug trafficking? What would make it a better place in which to live?

Appendix B

Questionnaire Used in Esperanza (a shortened sample)

Q1. What is your date of birth

Q2. How would you identify yourself?
- 01 Mexican
- 02 Chicano
- 03 Mexican American
- 04 Spanish American, Hispanic American, Latino American, American
- 05 Anglo American
- 06 Asian American
- 07 African American

Q3. Which ethnic identification does (did) your mother use? (used same codes)

Q4. Which ethnic identification does (did) your father use? (used same codes)

[Next 15 questions identified cultural patterns such as preferred language, foods, and religion, also birth places of family.]

Q22. Are you now . . .
- 00 Single (never married)
- 01 Married
- 02 Living as married
- 03 Separated
- 04 Divorced
- 05 Widowed
- 06 Other

Q23 How long have you been living at your current address?

Q24. Do you
    Rent your house/apartment
    Own your house/apartment
    Live with someone who rents house/apartment
    Live with someone who owns house/apartment

Q25. Have you always lived in Esperanza? (01)=Yes   (02)=No

[Other questions related to employment, income, and religious practices.]

[Next series of questions deal with seeking help when in need.]

Q27. Who would you turn to if you should have personal problems (check all that apply)
    01 Mother
    02 Father
    03 Grandparents
    04 Aunt/uncle
    05 Friends
    06 Pastor/priest
    07 Other

[Questions 28–44 relate to social life (e.g., work, church).]

[Next questions are about alcohol and drug use.]

Q45. Have you ever drunk alcohol? (01)=Yes   (02)=No

Q46. If yes, why do you drink? (describe)

Q47. Does anyone in your household drink? (01)=Yes   (02)=No

Q48. If you have drunk alcohol, how old were you when you first drank alcohol . . . describe what type.

Q49. If you do drink, why do you? (describe)

Q50. In a typical day of drinking, like on a weekend, how many drinks do you have?

Q51. If you no longer drink, at what age did you stop?

Q52. Do you believe Mexicans have a greater response to alcohol than other ethnic groups?

Q53. Why do you think some people drink so much that it affects their work, family, health?

Q54. At what age do you think it is OK to use alcohol?

Q55. Where do you usually drink alcohol? Describe all places.

Q56. What is your drink of choice?

Q57. With whom do you usually drink?

Q58. Do you think you have a drinking problem?

Q59. Have you ever had treatment for alcohol abuse?

Q60. Do you buy your liquor in Esperanza?

Q61. Do you make it yourself?

Q62. Have you seen children under the age of 16 drinking alcohol?

[Most of the responses are given as "yes" or "no" responses. The same type of questions are asked of drug use—such as drug of choice, sold in Esperanza, cost, and who is selling.]

[The next section contains many questions about violence; included are a sample.]

Q77. In your opinion is there a problem with violence in Esperanza?
   (01)=Yes   (02)=No

Q80. What are some of the reasons you feel people are violent?
   01 Economic (no jobs)
   02 Prejudice
   03 Learn to be violent from childhood
   04 Abused as child or spouse
   05 Drugs and/or alcohol
   06 Other

Q81. Who or what protects Esperanza from drugs, alcohol, and violence? (list all)
   01 Police
   02 Courts
   03 Citizens themselves
   04 Neighborhood watches
   05 Churches—God
   06 Social service agencies
   07 Parents/grandparents
   08 Teachers
   09 City government
   10 No one protects us

[A series of questions was also asked about prostitutes and gangs.]

[A series of questions was then asked about actual violence in their homes and if it was related to alcohol and/or drugs.]

Q97. Have you or anyone in your household ever been arrested for a violent offense?

Q98. Have you or anyone in your household ever been in jail for a violent offense?

Q99. Have you or anyone in your household been in a fight or intervened in a fight?

[The next series of questions deal with social service agencies and churches in Esperanza, asking for opinions about the positive influence on the town; a sample is included.]

Q100. Name three people in Esperanza you believe are good leaders.

Q109. In your opinion what things would make Esperanza a better place
in which to live?

[The respondent is asked to give an opinion about the survey and to ask
any questions.]

Each interviewer signs the information and offers opinions related to
honesty and confidence in the accuracy of the answers.

References

Agar, M. 1983. *Professional stranger: An informal introduction to ethnography.* New York: Academic Press.

Agar, M. 1999. Workshop of Ethnographic Research. International Conference on Qualitative Research, International Center for Qualitative Research. University of Alberta, Edmonton Canada, January 1999.

Agar, M. 2004. An anthropological problem, a complex solution. *Human Organization* 63(4): 411–418.

Altink, S. 1995. *Stolen lives: Trading women into sex and slavery.* New York: Harrington Park Press.

Alvarez, R. R. 1995. Mexican–U.S. Border: The making of an anthropology of borderlands. *Annual Review of Anthropology* 24: 447–70.

Arizona Daily Star Citizen, April 23, 2000.

Arizona Daily Star Citizen, August 2000.

Arizona Daily Star Citizen, March 24, 2001.

Arizona Daily Star Citizen, October 2004.

Arzaladua, G. 1987. *Borderlands/la frontera: The new Mestiza.* San Francisco: Spinsters/ Aunt Lute.

Baca, Z. M. 1979. Chicano family research: Conceptual distortion and alternative directions. *Journal of Ethnic Studies* 7: 59–71.

Berger, P. L., and T. Luckmann. 1966. *The social construction of reality: A treatise in the sociology of knowledge.* New York: Anchor Books.

Best, B. 2004. *Death by murder.* www.benbest.com/lifext/murder.html

Bono. 2005. Foreword. In J. D. Sachs, *The end of poverty: Economic possibilities for our time.* New York: The Penguin Press.

Borchet, J. 1980. *Alley life in Washington.* Chicago: University of Illinois, Chicago.

Borjas, G. 2006. Moving north. *Time,* April 10: 41.

Bourgois, P. 2004. The everyday violence of gang rape. In N. Scheper-Hughes and P. Bourgois (Eds.), *Violence in war and peace: An anthology* (pp. 343–347). Cornwall: Blackwell.

Brain, P. F., and G. A. Coward. 1989. A review of the history, action, and legitimate use of cocaine. *Journal of Substance Abuse* 1: 431–451.

Bromberg, S. 1998. Feminist issues in prostitution. In J. E. Elias et al. (Eds.), *Prostitution: On whores, hustlers, and johns* (pp. 294–321). Amherst, NY: Prometheus.

Bruman, H. J. 2000. *Alcohol in ancient Mexico.* Salt Lake City: University of Utah Press.

Bruns, R. A. 1980. *Knights of the road.* New York: Methuen.

Campbell, R. 1998. Invisible men: Making visible male clients of female prostitutes in Merseyside. In J. E. Elias et al. (Eds.), *Prostitution: On whores, hustlers, and johns* (pp. 155–171). Amherst, NY: Prometheus.

Campesino, M. 2003. Las voces de las madres (The voices of the mothers): Traumatic bereavement after gang-related homicide. Unpublished PhD dissertation. University of Arizona, Tucson, Arizona.

Chesney-Lind, M., R. Shelden, and K. Joe. 1996. Girls, delinquency, and gang members. In C. R. Huff (Ed.), *Gangs in America* (pp. 185–204). Thousand Oaks, CA: Sage.

Dohan, D. 2003. *The price of poverty: Money, work, and culture in the Mexican American barrio.* Berkeley: University of California Press.

Douglas, J. E., Burgess, A. W., Burgess, A. G., and Ressler, R. K. 1997. *Crime classification manual: A standard system for investigating and classifying violent crimes.* San Francisco: Jossey-Bass.

Dublin, R., and M. Kleinman. 1991. Marijuana as antiemetic medicine. *Journal of Clinical Oncology* 9: 1314–1319.

Elias, J. E., V. L. Bullough, V. Elias, G. Brewer, and J. Elders. 1998. *Prostitution: On whores, hustlers, and johns.* Amherst, NY: Prometheus.

Ellingwood, K. 2004. *Hard line: Life and death on the U.S.–Mexico border.* New York: Vintage.

Fagan, J. 1996. Gangs, drugs, neighborhood change. In C. R. Huff (Ed.), *Gangs in America.* Thousand Oaks, CA: Sage.

Field Notes. August 16, 1999. CEPP. Tucson: University of Arizona.

Field Notes. May 20, 2000. CEPP. Tucson: University of Arizona.

Field Notes. July 17, 2000. CEPP. Tucson: University of Arizona.

Field Notes. September 16, 2000. CEPP. Tucson: University of Arizona.

Freire, P. 1986. *Pedagogy of the oppressed.* New York: Continuum.

Freire, P. 2004. *Pedagogy of indignation.* Boulder, CO: Paradigm.

Frisch, N. C., and L. E. Frisch. 1998. *Psychiatric mental health nursing.* Boston: Delmar.

Fuentes, J. R., and R. J. Kelly. 1999. Drug supply and demand: The dynamics of the American drug market and some aspects of Colombian and Mexican drug trafficking. *Journal of Contemporary Criminal Justice* 15(4): 328–351.

Galper, C. 2000. The problem of HIV IV users among Hispanic people. Unpublished term paper. Transcultural Nursing N 607 (summer session), University of Arizona, Tucson, Arizona.

The Gazette (Colorado Springs, Colorado), March 28, 2005. Worry about alcohol, not pot students say. Metro p. 2.

Gemme, R. 1998. Legal and sexological aspects of adult street prostitution: A case of sexual pluralism. In James E. Elias et al. (Eds.), *Prostitution: On whores, hustlers, and johns* (pp. 474–487). Amherst, NY: Prometheus.

Glittenberg, J. 1994. *To the mountain and back.* Long Grove, IL: Waveland Press.

Glittenberg, J. 2001. *Community as slayer: Community as healer.* Final report to the National Institute on Drug Abuse. Tucson, Arizona. University of Arizona.

Glittenberg, J., and C. Anderson. 1999. Methamphetamines: Use and trafficking in the Tucson-Nogales area 1977–1989. *Substance Use and Misuse* 34(14).

Gold, M. A. 1992. Cocaine (and crack): Clinical aspects. In J. Lowinson, P. Ruiz, R. Millman, and J. Langrod (Eds.), *Substance Abuse: A Comprehensive Textbook* (2nd ed.). Baltimore: Williams & Wilkins.

Gonzales, R. 1972. *I am Joaquín: Yo soy Joaquín; an epic poem.* New York: Bantam.

Gozdiak, E. M., and E. A. Collett. 2005. Research on trafficking in North America: A review of the literature. *International Migration* 43(1): 99–128.

Greeley, A. M. 1988. Defection among Hispanics. *America,* July 30: 61–62.

Gutmann, M. 1996. *The meaning of macho: Being a man in Mexico City.* Berkeley: University of California Press.

Hayes-Bautista, D. E. 2004. *La nueva California: Latinos in the Golden State.* Berkeley: University of California Press.

Heath, D. 1987. Alcohol use, 1970–1980. In Mary Douglas (Ed.), *Constructive drinking: Perspectives on drink from anthropology* (pp. 16–69). New York: Cambridge University Press.

Heath, D. B. 2004. Early age drinking does not lead to alcohol abuse. In K. B. Balkin (Ed.), *Alcohol: Opposing viewpoints* (pp. 55–59). New York: Greenhaven Press.

Hughes, C. 1992. View from the pews: Hispanic and Anglo Catholics in a changing church. *Review of Religious Research* 33(4): 364–375.

Hurtado, A. 1995. Variations, combinations, and evolutions: Latino families in the United States. In R. E. Zambrano (Ed.), *Understanding Latino families: Scholarship, policy and practices* (pp. 42–61). Thousand Oaks, CA: Sage.

Hutson, H., D. Anglin, N. Kyriacou, J. Hart, and K. Spears. 1995. The epidemic of gang-related homicides in Los Angeles County. From 1979–1994. *Journal of America Medical Association* 274(13): 1031–1036.

Isasi-Díaz, A. M. 1993. *En la lucha*: In the struggle—A Hispanic woman's liberation theology. Minneapolis: Fortress Press.

Johnson, C. 1986. A personal training manual: The history of South Tucson. Unpublished manuscript. South Tucson Municipal Building, Arizona.

Johnson, G. 2004. Illegal drugs should be legalized. In T. L. Roleff (Ed.), *Opposing viewpoints: The war on drugs* (pp. 144–151). Farmington Hills, MI: Greenhaven Press.

Johnson, P. B., and H. L. Johnson. 1999. Cultural and familial influences that maintain the negative meaning of alcohol. In Alcohol and the family: Opportunities for prevention, Gayle M. Boyd (Ed.). *Journal of Studies on Alcohol.* Supplement. No. 13: 79–83.

Knipe, E. 1995. *Culture, society, and drugs: The social science approach to drug use.* Long Grove, IL: Waveland Press.

Kutsche, P. 1984. On the lack of machismo in Costa Rica and New Mexico. Paper presented at the American Anthropology Association meetings in Denver, CO.

Lashley, F. R. 1998. *Clinical genetics in nursing practice* (2nd ed.). New York: Springer.

Leon-Portillo, M. 2000. *Tonantzin Guadalupe: Pensamiento náhuatl y mensaje cristiano en el "Nican Mopohua."* (Mother-God Guadalupe: Nahuatl beliefs and Christian message in "Nican Mopohua," [narrative of the apparition of the Virgin of Guadalupe].) Mexico City: Fondo de Cultura Económica.

Lewis, O. 1961. *Children of Sanchez.* New York: Random House.

MacDonald, G., and M. R. Leary. 2005. Why does social exclusion hurt: The relationship between social and physical pain. *Psychological Bulletin* 131(2): 202–223.

Marin, G., and B. Marin. 1991. *Research with Hispanic populations.* Newbury Park, CA: Sage.

Markides, K. S., and J. Coreil. 1986. The health of Hispanics in the Southwestern United States: An epidemiological paradox. *Public Health Reports* 101(3): 253–270.

Martinez, O. T. 1994. *Border people: Life and society in the U.S.–Mexico borderlands.* Tucson: University of Arizona Press.

Menchaca, M. 2001. *Recovering history, constructing race: The Indian, Black and White roots of Mexican Americans.* Austin: University of Texas.

Mirande, A. 1997. *Hombres y machos: Masculinity and Latino culture.* Boulder, CO: Westview Press.

Montiel, M. 1975. The social science myth of the Mexican American. In O. Romano (Ed.), *Voice readings from El Grito* (pp. 54–64). Berkeley, CA: Quinto Sol.

Moore, J. W., and J. M. Hagedorn. 1996. What happens to girls in gangs? In C. R. Huff (Ed.), *Gangs in America* (pp. 205–218). Thousand Oaks, CA: Sage.

Morris, D. 1967. *The naked ape.* New York. New York: McGraw-Hill.

National Institutes of Health (NIH). 2004. Drinking at an early age leads to alcohol abuse. In Karen Balkin (Ed.), *Alcohol: Opposing viewpoints* (pp. 52–54). San Diego: Greenhaven Press.

O'Day, P., and R. Venecia. 1999. Cazuelas: An ethnographic study of drug trafficking in a small Mexican border town. *Journal of Contemporary Criminal Justice* 15(4): 421–443.

Peele, S., and R. DeGrandpre. 2004. The genetic influence on alcoholism is exaggerated. In Karen F. Balkin (Ed.), *Alcohol: Opposing viewpoints* (pp. 70–80). New York: Greenhaven Press.

Poppa, T. 1990. *Drug lord: The life and death of a Mexican kingpin.* New York: Pharos.

Ramos, S. 1962. *Profile of man and culture in Mexico.* Translated by Peter G. Earle. Austin: University of Texas Press.

Rodriguez, J. 1994. *Our Lady of Guadalupe: Faith and empowerment among Mexican American Women.* Mahwah, NJ: Paulis Press.

Romano, O. 1973. The anthropology and sociology of the Mexican American. The distortion of Mexican-American history. In O. Romano (Ed.), *Voices: Readings from El Grito* (pp. 43–56). Berkeley, CA: Quinto Sol.

Santos-Ortiz, M. C., J. L. Lao-Melendez, and A. Torres-Sanchez. 1998. Sex workers and the elderly male client. In J. E. Elias et al. (Eds.), *Prostitution: On whores, hustlers, and johns* (pp. 208–220). Amherst, NY: Prometheus.

Scheper-Hughes, N., and Bourgois, P. (Eds). 2004. *Violence in war and peace: An anthology.* Cornwall, England: Blackwell.

Schelling, T. 1971. Dynamic models of segregation. *Journal of Mathematicology* 1: 143–186.

Schwarcz, V. 1997. The pane of sorrow: Public uses of personal grief in modern China. In A. Kleinman, V. Das, and M. Lock (Eds.), *Social Suffering.* Berkeley: University of California Press.

Schwarz, J. E. 2005. *Freedom Reclaimed: Rediscovering the American vision.* Baltimore: Johns Hopkins University Press.

Sharry, F. 2006. National immigration forum. *Time,* April 10: 41.

Sheridan, T. E. 1995. *Arizona: A history.* Tucson: University of Arizona Press.

Singer, M. 2006a. *Something dangerous: Emergent and changing illicit drug use and community health.* Long Grove, IL: Waveland Press.

Singer, M. 2006b What is the "drug user community"?: Implications for public health. *Human Organization* 65(1): 72–81.

Spicer, Edward H. 1962. *Cycles of conquest.* Tucson: University of Arizona Press.

Stares, P. B. 1996. *Global habit: The drug problem in a borderless world.* Washington, DC: Brookings Institute.

Stevens, E. 1973. Marianismo: The other face of machismo. In Ann Pescatell (Ed.), *Male and female in Latin America* (pp. 89–101). Pittsburgh: University of Pittsburgh Press.

Stuart, V. C., Jr. 1995. Health perception and health care behaviors of homeless men. Unpublished master's thesis, University of Arizona. Tucson, Arizona.

Talking points. 2003. Coalition to Abolish the Death Penalty. www.abolishdeathpenalty.org/TalkingPoints.htm (Accessed 3/1/07).

Thomas, C. R. 2001. Gangs and antisocial behavior in the adolescent: What's changed in the 21st century? Paper presented at the American Society for Adolescent Psychiatry, March 22–25, 2001.

Tucson Weekly. 2001. A political fighter. September 11.

U.S. Census. 1992: *Vital statistics.* Washington, DC: U.S. Government Printing.

U.S. Census. 2001. *Vital statistics.* Washington, DC: U.S. Government Printing.

Uniform Crime Report. 1996. Washington, DC: U.S. Government Printing Office.

Uniform Crime Report. 2004. Washington, DC: U.S. Government Printing Office.

Vélez-Ibáñez, C. G. 1996. *Border visions: Mexican cultures of the Southwest Untied States.* Tucson: University of Arizona Press.

Vélez-Ibáñez, C. G. 2004. Regions of refuge in the United States: Issues, problems, and concerns for the future of Mexican-origin populations in the United States. *Human Organization* 63(1): 1–20.

Vigil, J. D. 1988. *Barrio gangs: Street life and identity in Southern California.* Austin: University of Texas Press.

Vigil, J. D., and S. C. Yun. 1996. Southern California gangs. In C. R. Huff (Ed.), *Gangs in America* (pp. 139–156). Thousand Oaks, CA: Sage.

Yablonsky, L. 1997. *Gangster.* New York: New York University Press.